REMINISCENCES OF THE GREAT MUTINY 1857-59

REMINISCENCES OF THE GREAT MUTINY 1857-59

INCLUDING THE RELIEF, SIEGE, AND CAPTURE OF LUCKNOW, AND THE CAMPAIGNS IN ROHILCUND AND OUDE

BY

WILLIAM FORBES-MITCHELL
LATE SERGEANT, NINETY-THIRD SUTHERLAND HIGHLANDERS

GYAN

Published by

Gyan Publishing House
5, Ansari Road
Daryaganj, New Delhi-110002
Phone: 011-47034999, 9811692060
E-mail: books@gyanbooks.com

Distribution Network
gyanbooks.com
India, USA, Canada, UK, Australia, France

ISBN : 978-81-212-3952-3 (HB)
First Published, 1893

2nd Impression 2020

Printed at: Gyan Press, Delhi.

Reminiscences
of the
Great Mutiny
1857-59
Author: William Forbes-Mitchell

REMINISCENCES

OF THE

GREAT MUTINY

1857-59

INCLUDING THE RELIEF, SIEGE, AND CAPTURE OF LUCKNOW, AND THE CAMPAIGNS IN ROHILCUND AND OUDE

BY

WILLIAM FORBES-MITCHELL

LATE SERGEANT, NINETY-THIRD SUTHERLAND HIGHLANDERS

London

MACMILLAN AND CO.

AND NEW YORK

1893

To the

OFFICERS, NON-COMMISSIONED OFFICERS, AND MEN,

STILL LIVING,

OF THE OLD NINETY-THIRD SUTHERLAND HIGHLANDERS,

AND TO THE MEMORY OF

THOSE WHO FELL DURING THE MUTINY

OR HAVE SINCE PASSED AWAY,

These Reminiscences

ARE RESPECTFULLY AND AFFECTIONATELY DEDICATED

BY THEIR OLD SERVANT AND COMRADE,

WILLIAM FORBES-MITCHELL,
LATE NINETY-THIRD SUTHERLAND HIGHLANDERS.

CALCUTTA, *April*, 1893.

INTRODUCTION

THESE Reminiscences are submitted to the public in the trust that they will be welcomed alike by soldier and civilian. They are recorded by one who was himself an actor in the scenes which he describes, and who viewed them from a novel and most unusual position for a military historian—the ranks.

They have been carefully perused by an officer who was present at many of the operations mentioned; and considerable pains have been taken to verify, wherever possible, those incidents of which he was not personally cognisant.

The interest of Mr. Forbes-Mitchell's straightforward and soldierlike story is enhanced by the coincidence that he takes up the pen where Lady Inglis laid it down; and it is hoped that this volume may prove an acceptable continuation of her touching narrative of the Defence of Lucknow, and that, as a record of the Great Mutiny, it may furnish another thrilling chapter in that unparalleled story of suffering and of heroism,—of man's bravery and of woman's devotion.

CONTENTS

CHAPTER I

CHAPTER II

CHAPTER III

CHAPTER IV

CHAPTER V

CHAPTER VI

CHAPTER VII

CHAPTER VIII

CHAPTER IX

CHAPTER X

CHAPTER XI

CHAPTER XII

CHAPTER XIII

CHAPTER XIV

CHAPTER XV

APPENDIX A

APPENDIX B

APPENDIX C

APPENDIX D

CHAPTER I

THE NINETY-THIRD—SAIL FOR CHINA—COUNTER-ORDERED TO CALCUTTA—ARRIVAL IN INDIA

I CANNOT truthfully commence these reminiscences with the usual formula of the amateur author,—namely, by stating that, "At the solicitation of numerous friends, the writer was most reluctantly prevailed upon to publish his narrative," and so forth. No one has asked me to write my recollections of the past and my impressions of the present. I do so to please myself, because on revisiting the scenes of the Mutiny I have been forcibly impressed with the fact that, like so many memories, the soldiers and civilians who were personal actors in the great uprising are fast passing away.

> They live but in time-stricken men,
> Or else lie hushed in clay.

Having served in the old Ninety-Third Sutherland Highlanders, and been present at every action in which that famous regiment played a part from the actual relief of Lucknow in November, 1857, till the final operations in Oude ended in November, 1859, and being blessed with a fairly retentive memory, I feel tempted to put on record the recollections of the past and the impressions which my recent return to those scenes has revived.

In writing of the past I shall be careful to discriminate between what I saw myself and what I heard from other eye-witnesses, whether native or European; but when I come to write of the present I may be permitted to make my own comparisons and to draw my own conclusions from present facts, or appearances, as they have been impressed on my own observation; and when recording my recollections of the many engagements in which the Ninety-Third played a prominent part, I intend to skip much that has already been recorded in the pages of history, and to more particularly notice the action of individual soldiers, and other incidents which came under my own notice, which have not, to my knowledge, been recorded by any historian or author of the numerous narratives, personal or other, which have been written about the Indian Mutiny.

Before entering on my reminiscences I may mention that I never previously had an opportunity of revisiting any of the scenes of which I am about to write since I had been an actor in them. My readers will, therefore, understand that it was with strongly mixed feelings both of pleasure and sorrow, not unmingled with gratitude, that I started by the mail train from Howrah in August, 1892, to revisit Cawnpore and Lucknow for the first time, with the terrible scenes of 1857 and 1858 still vividly photographed, as it were, on my memory. In the course of thirty-five years of the life of even the most commonplace individual there are events which are never forgotten, and certain friends are lost who are never replaced; so much so, that in thinking of the past one is almost compelled to exclaim with Solomon, —"Vanity of vanities, all is vanity! One generation passeth away and another generation cometh," and the end of all is "vanity and vexation of spirit." But to the Christian, in grand contrast to the vanity and changeableness of this life, stands out like a rock the promise of the Eternal, the Self-existing, and Unchangeable Jehovah. "The Eternal God is thy refuge, and underneath are the everlasting arms!" But I am no *padre*, and must not commence to moralise or preach. What tempts me do so is the fact that there is a class of writers in the present day who not only deny the truth of many of the fondly-treasured recollections of the past, which have become part of our national history, but who would, if it were possible, refine even God Himself out of creation, and hand us all over to blind chance for our existence! But enough; I must hark back to 1857.

On the return of the Ninety-Third from the Crimea they were quartered at Dover, and in April, 1857, the regiment was detailed for the expedition forming for China under Lord Elgin, and all time-expired men and those unfit for foreign service were carefully weeded from the service companies and formed into a depôt. The ten service companies were recruited by volunteers from the other Highland regiments, the Forty-Second, Seventy-Second, Seventy-Ninth, and Ninety-Second, each giving a certain number of men, bringing the Ninety-Third up to a corps of eleven hundred bayonets. About the 20th of May the Ninety-Third left Dover for Portsmouth, where we were reviewed by the Queen accompanied by Sir Colin Campbell, who took final leave, as he then supposed, of the regiment which had stood with him in the "thin red line" of Balaklava against the terrible Cossacks. On the first of June three companies, of which mine formed one, embarked in a coasting steamer for Plymouth, where we joined the *Belleisle*, an old 84-gun two-decker, which had been converted into a transport for the China expedition. This detachment of the Ninety-Third was under the command of Colonel the Honourable Adrian Hope, and the captains of the three companies were Cornwall, Dawson, and Williams—my company being that of Captain E. S. F. G. Dawson, an officer of great experience, who had served in another regiment (I forget which) throughout the Kaffir war in the Cape, and was adjutant of the Ninety-Third at the Alma, where he had his horse shot under him. The remaining seven companies, forming headquarters under Colonel A. S. Leith-Hay, sailed from Portsmouth in the steam transport *Mauritius* about ten days after us.

Although an old wooden ship, the *Belleisle* was a very comfortable transport and a good sailer, and we sighted land at the Cape on the morning of the 9th of August, having called and posted mails at both Madeira and the

Cape de Verde Islands on our way. We were at anchor in Simon's Bay by the afternoon of the 9th of August, where we heard the first news of the Indian Mutiny, and that our destination was changed from China to Calcutta; and during the 10th and 11th all was bustle, tightening up rigging, taking in fuel for cooking, and refilling our empty water-tanks. On the evening of the 11th, just as it was becoming dark, a steamer came up the bay, and anchored quite close to the *Belleisle;* and on our bugler's sounding the regimental call, it turned out to be the *Mauritius* with headquarters on board. Most of our officers immediately went on board, and many of the men in the three companies were gratified by receiving letters from parents, sweethearts, and friends, which had reached Portsmouth after our detachment had left. On the forenoon of the 12th of August the *Belleisle* left Simon's Bay, making all sail day and night for Calcutta. The ship's crew numbered nine hundred men, being made up of drafts for the ships of the China squadron. Every yard of canvas that the masts or spars could carry was crowded on day and night; and we reached the pilot station at the Sandheads on the 19th of September, thirty-eight days from the Cape, where we learned that the *Mauritius*, with our headquarters, had just proceeded up the river.

Early on the 20th, the anniversary of the Alma, we got tug steamers and proceeded up the Hooghly, anchoring off the steps at Prinsep's *ghât*[1] on the afternoon of the 21st of September. Our progress up the river was

[1] A landing-place.

all excitement. We had two tug steamers, the *Belleisle* being considered too large for a single tug of the horse-power of those days; and the pilot and tug commanders all sent bundles of the latest Calcutta papers on board, from which we learned the first news of the sieges of Delhi and Lucknow, of the horrible massacre at Cawnpore, and of the gallant advance of the small force under Generals Havelock, Neill, and Outram for the relief of Lucknow. When passing Garden Reach, every balcony, verandah, and housetop was crowded with ladies and gentlemen waving their handkerchiefs and cheering us, all our men being in full Highland dress and the pipers playing on the poop. In passing the present No. 46 Garden Reach the flood-tide was still running up too strong for the *Belleisle* to come into harbour, and we anchored for about an hour just opposite No. 46. The house and steps of the *ghât* were crowded with ladies and gentlemen cheering us; and one of my comrades, a young man named Frank Henderson, said to me, "Forbes Mitchell, how would you like to be owner of a palace like that?" when I, on the spur of the moment, without any thought, replied, "I'll be master of that house and garden yet before I leave India." Poor Henderson replied: "I firmly believe you will, if you make up your mind for it; but as for myself, I feel that I shall either die or be killed in this war. I am convinced I shall never see the end of it. I have dreamed of my dead father every night since we sighted the pilot-brig, and I know my days are numbered. But as for you,—I have also dreamed of you, and I am sure you will go safely through the war, and live for many years, and become a prosperous man in India. Mark my words; I am convinced of it." We had a Church of England chaplain on the *Belleisle*, and service every morning, and Henderson and myself, with many others, formed part of the chaplain's Sunday and Wednesday evening prayer-meeting class. "Since ever we sighted the pilot-brig," Henderson went on to say, "and my dead father has commenced to appear to me in my dreams, I have felt every day at morning prayers that the words, 'That we may return in safety to enjoy the blessings of the land, with the fruits of our labours, and with a thankful remembrance of Thy mercies, to praise and glorify Thy holy name, through Jesus Christ our Lord,' had no reference to me, and I cannot join in them. But when the chaplain read the prayers this morning he looked straight at you when he pronounced that part of the prayer, and I felt that the blessing prayed for rests on you. Mark my words, and remember them when I am dead and buried." Strange to say, on the 16th of November Henderson was severely wounded at the taking of the Shâh Nujeef, died in the retreat from Lucknow on the evening of the 20th of November, and was buried on the banks of the Ganges, just opposite the bridge of boats at Cawnpore. The Rev. Mr. Henderson of St. Andrew's Church, Calcutta, who had accompanied the Seventy-Eighth Highlanders to Lucknow, attended as chaplain to our wounded after we relieved the Residency, and being of the same name, he took a particular interest in poor Henderson. However, to return to Garden Reach. Stranger still as it may appear, just thirty-two years after, I took possession of the house No. 46, where I have established the Bon Accord Rope Works. But enough of this; I am not writing my autobiography.

The arrival of the Ninety-Third caused quite a sensation in Calcutta, where but few Highland regiments had ever been seen before. To quote the words of an eye-witness writing from Calcutta to friends at home, and published in the Aberdeen *Herald*, describing a party of the Ninety-Third which was sent ashore to store the heavy baggage which had to be left in Calcutta, he stated :—"On hearing the Ninety-Third in the streets, Scotchmen who had long been exiled from home rose from their desks, rushed out, and stood at the doors of their offices, looking with feelings of pride at their stalwart countrymen, and listening with smiles of pleasure to the sounds of their own northern tongue, long unfamiliar to their ears. Many brought out tankards of cool beer, and invited the men as they passed along to drink, and the Highlanders required but little pressing, for the sun was hot, and, to use their own vernacular, the exercise made them *gey an drauthy*."

CHAPTER II

MARCH UP COUNTRY—FUTTEHPORE—CAWNPORE

By the 25th of September the whole of the Ninety-Third were once more together in Chinsurah, and on the 28th the first company, the grenadiers under Captain Middleton, started by rail for Râneegunge *en route* for Lucknow, and a company followed daily in regular rotation till the light company left Chinsurah on the 7th of October. From Râneegunge to Benares the old bullock-train was arranged with relays of bullocks from eight to ten miles apart, according to the nature of the road, and six men were told off to each cart to ride and march by relief. Thus we proceeded, making an average advance of from twenty-five to thirty miles daily, halting every day about ten o'clock for cooking, resuming our march about four o'clock, and so on through the night for coolness; the bullocks did not average more than two and a half miles per hour, and there was always considerable delay at the different stations, changing teams. In this way my company reached Benares on the 17th of October. From Benares we proceeded by detachments of two or three companies to Allahabad; the country between Benares and Allahabad, being overrun by different bands of mutineers, was too dangerous for small detachments of one company. My company reached Allahabad on the 19th of October. There we were supplied with the usual Indian field equipment of tents, etc. By this time the railway had been pushed on in the direction of Cawnpore to a place called Lohunga, about forty-eight miles from Allahabad, but no stations were built. On the 22nd of October my company, with three others, left Allahabad, packed into open trucks or waggons used by the railway contractors for the construction of the line. From Lohunga we commenced our daily marches on foot, with our tents on elephants, *en route* for Cawnpore.

By this time a considerable force had assembled at Allahabad, consisting of artillery from the Cape, Peel's Naval Brigade, detachments of the Fifth Fusiliers, the Fifty-Third, and Ninetieth Light Infantry. But the only complete regiment was the Ninety-Third Highlanders, over a thousand men, in splendid condition, armed with the Enfield rifle, and, what was of more importance, well drilled to the use of it.

After leaving Lohunga, the first place of note which we reached was Futtehpore, seventy-two miles from Allahabad. At Futtehpore I met some native Christians whom I had first seen in Allahabad, and who were, or had been, connected with mission work, and could speak English. They had returned from Allahabad to look after property which they had been obliged to abandon when they fled from Futtehpore on the outbreak of the Mutiny. These men all knew Dr. Duff, or had heard of him, and were most anxious to talk to Dr. Duff's countrymen, as they called the Highlanders. From one of them I heard of the brave defence made by a solitary Englishman who refused to leave his post, and as I have never seen this alluded to in any of the histories of the Mutiny, I shall relate it.

When the insurrection broke out, Mr. Robert Tucker was the judge of Futtehpore, and like his namesake of Salvation Army fame, he combined the missionary with the civil-servant, and used to preach to the natives, who listened to him with seeming respect, but with concealed hatred in their hearts. One of the most regular attendants at these Christian meetings in the judge's house was a Mahommedan named Hikmut Oollah Khân, the native head of the police in Futtehpore, and Mr. Tucker had unbounded confidence in the friendship of this man and in the loyalty of the police. On the first certain signs of disturbance in the station Mr. Tucker despatched all the Christians, native and European, to Allahabad, but refused to move himself. My informant told me that he had stayed with the brave judge till the last, and had made his escape to Allahabad after Mr. Tucker was killed; but I had no means of testing the truth of that statement. He further stated that Mr. Tucker had sent away all the Christians to Allahabad during the night, and next day about noon he sent for Hikmut Oollah Khân, who had neglected to make his usual morning report, with an intimation that the judge wished to see him and his loyal police to make arrangements for the protection of the Treasury and other Government property. The "loyal and friendly" Hikmut Oollah Khân sent back a reply that it was then too hot for him to come out, and that the judge *sâhib* need not trouble himself about the Treasury. Considering that the Government of the English was at an end, the police would take care of the Treasury for the Bâdshâh of Delhi, to whom it rightly belonged, and till the cool of the evening the judge *sâhib* might repeat his Kaffir prayers, when the "loyal and friendly" Hikmut Oollah Khân, with a detachment of his loyal police, would come and give his Kaffir soul a quick despatch to Jehunnum. Such was the loyalty of Mr. Tucker's trusted and pampered friend!

The message of Hikmut Oollah Khân opened the eyes of the too confiding judge, but he did not flinch from his duty. Mr. Tucker had been a mighty hunter in his day, and possessed a good assortment of offensive and defensive arms, such as rifles, fowling-pieces, and hog-spears. He carefully arranged his ammunition and loaded every rifle and fowling-piece which he had, strongly barricaded the doors and windows of his house, and then sat quietly down to read his Bible. At sunset he saw a large body of the police, with the green banner of Islâm and Hikmut Oollah Khân at their head, entering his compound. They advanced, and called on Mr. Tucker to surrender in the name of the Bâdshâh of Delhi, and if he wished his life to be spared, he could have it on condition that he accepted the religion of Mahommed. This he resolutely refused to do, and tried to reason with the police, to which they replied by a volley. Mr. Tucker returned the fire, and before the doors of his house could be forced he had killed sixteen and wounded many more, when he fell pierced by both spears and bullets. So died the brave and God-fearing Robert Tucker, the glory of the Bengal Civil Service, and thus ended the defence of Futtehpore by one solitary Englishman against hundreds of rebels.

When the detachment of which my company formed part, marched through Futtehpore, it was rumoured that the Banda and Dinapore mutineers, joined by large bodies of *budmâshes*,[1] numbering over ten thousand men, with three batteries of regular artillery, mustering eighteen guns, had crossed the Jumna, and were threatening our communications with Allahabad. Owing to this report, No. 2, or Captain Cornwallis's company of the Ninety-Third, was left in the fort at Futtehpore to guard provisions, etc., as that post had been greatly strengthened by a party of sappers and was formed into a depôt for commissariat stores and ammunition, which were being pushed on by every available mode of conveyance from Allahabad. We left Futtehpore on the 25th of October, and arrived at Cawnpore on the morning of the 27th, having marched the forty-six miles in two days.

When we reached Cawnpore we found everything quiet, and Brigadier Wilson, of the Sixty-Fourth Regiment, in command. Wheeler's immortal entrenchment

[1] Bad characters, scoundrels.

was deserted, but a much stronger one had lately been built, or rather was still under construction on the right (the Cawnpore) bank of the Ganges, to protect the bridge of boats crossing into Oude. This place was constructed of strong and well-planned earthworks, and every available coolie in Cawnpore was at work, from daylight till dark, strengthening the place. Bastions and ramparts were being constructed of every conceivable material, besides the usual gabions and fascines. Bales of cotton were built into the ramparts, bags of every size and shape, soldiers' knapsacks, etc., were filled with earth; in brief, everything that could possibly hold a few spadefuls of earth, and could thereby assist in raising a defensive breastwork, had been appropriated for building the parapet-walls, and a ditch of considerable depth and width was being excavated. On my recent visit to Cawnpore I looked for this fort in vain. Eventually I learned from Colonel Baddeley that it was some time ago dismantled and converted into the Government Harness and Saddlery Factory, the ramparts having been levelled and the ditch filled in with earth.

The day before we reached Cawnpore, a strong column from Delhi had arrived under command of Sir Hope Grant, and was encamped on the plain near the spot where the railway station now stands. The detachment of the Ninety-Third did not pitch tents, but was accommodated in some buildings, on which the roofs were still left, near General Wheeler's entrenchment. My company occupied the *dâk* bungalow, which, on my revisit to Cawnpore, appeared to me to have given place to the present Victoria Hotel.

After a few hours' rest, we were allowed to go out in parties of ten or twelve to visit the horrid scene of the recent treachery and massacre. The first place my party reached was General Wheeler's so-called entrenchment, the ramparts of which at the highest places did not exceed four feet, and were so thin that at the top they could never have been bullet-proof! The entrenchment and the barracks inside of it were complete ruins, and the only wonder about it was how the small force could have held out so long. In the rooms of the building were still lying strewn about the remains of articles of women's and children's clothing, broken toys, torn pictures, books, pieces of music, etc. Among the books, I picked up a New Testament in Gaelic, but without any name on it. All the blank leaves had been torn out, and at the time I formed the opinion that they had been used for gun-waddings, because, close beside the Testament, there was a broken single-barrelled duck gun, which had evidently been smashed by a 9-pounder shot lying near. I annexed the Testament as a relic, and still have it. The Psalms and Paraphrases in Gaelic verses are complete, but the first chapter of Matthew and up to the middle of the seventh verse of the second chapter are wanting. The Testament must have belonged to some Scotch Highlander in the garrison. I have more than once thought of sending it home to the Highland Society as a relic of the Mutiny.

From the entrenchment we went to the Suttee Chowra *ghât*, where the doomed garrison were permitted to embark in the boats in which they were murdered, and traces of the treachery were still very plain, many skeletons, etc., lying about unburied among the bushes.

We then went to see the slaughter-house in which the unfortunate women and children had been barbarously murdered, and the well into which their mangled bodies were afterwards flung. Our guide was a native of the ordinary camp-follower class, who could speak intelligible barrack-room English. He told us that he had been born in a battery of European artillery, in which his forefathers had been shoeblacks for unknown generations, and his name, he stated, was "Peshawarie," because he had been born in Peshawur, when the English occupied it during the first advance to Caubul. His apparent age coincided with this statement. He claimed to have been in Sir Hugh Wheeler's entrenchment with the artillery all the time of the siege, and to have had a narrow escape of his life at the last. He told us a story which I have never seen mentioned elsewhere, that the Nânâ Sâhib, through a spy, tried to bribe the commissariat bakers who had remained with the English to put arsenic into the bread, which they refused to do, and that after the massacre of the English at the *ghât* the Nânâ had these bakers taken and put alive into their own ovens, and there cooked and thrown to the pigs. These bakers were Mahommedans. Of course, I had no means of testing the truth of this statement.[1] Our guide showed no desire to minimise the horrors of the massacre and the murders to which he said he had been an eye-witness. However, from the traces, still too apparent, the bare facts, without exaggeration, must have been horrible enough. But with reference to the women and children, from the cross-questions I put to our guide, I then formed the opinion, which I have never since altered, that most of the European women had been most barbarously murdered, but not dishonoured, with the exception of a few of the young and good-looking ones, who, our guide stated, were forcibly carried off to become Mahommedans. But I need not dwell on these points. These are the opinions I formed in October, 1857, three months after the massacre, and nothing which I have since learnt during my thirty-five years' residence in India has led me to alter them.

Most of the men of my company visited the slaughter-house and well, and what we there saw was enough to fill our hearts with feelings which I need not here dwell on; it was long before those feelings could be controlled. On the date of my visit a great part of the house had not been cleaned out; the floors of the rooms were still covered with congealed blood, littered with trampled, torn dresses of women and children, shoes, slippers, and locks of long hair, many of which had evidently been severed from the living scalps by sword-cuts. But among the traces

[1] This story was current in Upper India at the time.

of barbarous torture and cruelty which excited horror and a desire for revenge, one stood out prominently beyond all others. It was an iron hook fixed into the wall of one of the rooms in the house, about six feet from the floor. I could not possibly say for what purpose this hook had originally been fixed in the wall. I examined it carefully, and it appeared to have been an old fixture, which had been seized on as a diabolic and convenient instrument of torture by the inhuman wretches engaged in murdering the women and children. This hook was covered with dried blood, and from the marks on the whitewashed wall, it was evident that a little child had been hung on to it by the neck with its face to the wall, where the poor thing must have struggled for long, perhaps in the sight of its helpless mother, because the wall all round the hook on a level with it was covered with the hand-prints, and below the hook with the foot-prints, in blood, of a little child.

At the time of my visit the well was only about half-filled in, and the bodies of the victims only partially covered with earth. A gallows, with three or four ropes ready attached, stood facing the slaughter-house, half-way between it and the well; and during my stay three wretches were hanged, after having been flogged, and each made to clean about a square foot of the blood from the floor of the house. Our guide told us that these men had only been captured the day before, tried that morning, and found guilty as having assisted at the massacre.

During our visit a party of officers came to the slaughter-house, among whom was Dr. Munro, Surgeon of the Ninety-Third, now Surgeon-General Sir William Munro. When I saw him he was examining the hook covered with dried blood and the hand and foot-prints of the child on the wall, with the tears streaming down his cheeks. He was a most kind-hearted man, and I remember, when he came out of the house, that he cast a look of pity on the three wretches about to be hanged, and I overheard him say to another officer who was with him: "This is horrible and unchristian to look at; but I do hope those are the same wretches who tortured the little child on the hook inside that room." At this time there was no writing either in pencil or charcoal on the walls of the slaughter-house. I am positive on this point, because I looked for any writing. There was writing on the walls of the barracks inside General Wheeler's entrenchment, but not on the walls of the slaughter-house, though they were much splashed with blood and slashed with sword-cuts, where blows aimed at the victims had evidently been dodged and the swords had struck the walls. Such marks were most numerous in the corners of the rooms. The number of victims butchered in the house, counted and buried in the well by General Havelock's force, was one hundred and eighteen women and ninety-two children.

Up to the date of my visit, a brigade-order, issued by Brigadier-General J. G. S. Neill, First Madras Fusiliers, was still in force. This order bears date the

25th of July, 1857. I have not now an exact copy of it, but its purport was to this effect:—That, after trial and condemnation, all prisoners found guilty of having taken part in the murder of the European women and children, were to be taken into the slaughter-house by Major Bruce's *méhter*[1] police, and there made to crouch down, and with their mouths lick clean a square foot of the blood-soaked floor before being taken to the gallows and hanged. This order was carried out in my presence as regards the three wretches who were hanged that morning. The dried blood on the floor was first moistened with water, and the lash of the warder was applied till the wretches kneeled down and cleaned their square foot of flooring. This order remained in force till the arrival of Sir Colin Campbell in Cawnpore on the 3rd of November, 1857, when he promptly put a stop to it as unworthy of the English name and a Christian Government. General Neill has been much blamed for this order; but in condemning the action we must not overlook the provocation. The general saw more of the horrors of Cawnpore than I did; but what I saw, and the stories which were told by natives who claimed to have been eye-witnesses of the horrible scenes which they described, were enough to make the words *mercy* and *pardon* appear a mockery; and in passing judgment on him we must not forget the proclamations of the Nânâ Sâhib. These have often been published, and I will only give one extract bearing on the murder of the women and

[1] Sweeper, scavenger; one of the lowest castes.

children. The extract is as follows, and was part of a proclamation placarded all over Cawnpore: "To extinguish a fire and leave a spark, to kill a snake and preserve its young, is not the wisdom of men of sense."

However, let General Neill speak for himself. The following is a copy of one of his own letters, taken from Colonel White's *Reminiscences*. On page 135 he writes: "*The Well and Slaughter-house, Cawnpore.*—My object was to inflict a fearful punishment for a revolting, cowardly, and barbarous deed, and to strike terror into the rebels. The first I caught was a *subadar* or native officer, a high-caste Brahmin, who tried to resist my order of the 25th of July 1857, to clean the very blood which he had helped to shed; but I made the provost-marshall do his duty, and a few lashes compelled the miscreant to accomplish his work. When done he was taken out and immediately hanged, and buried in a ditch by the roadside. No one who has witnessed the scenes of murder, mutilation, and massacre can ever listen to the word 'mercy' as applicable to these fiends."

As already said, before condemning General Neill's order we must give due weight to the terrible provocation, the horrible scenes he saw, and the still more horrible stories he heard related by natives who either had or pretended to have been eye-witnesses of the facts they described. Even after the lapse of thirty-five years such horrors cannot be calmly contemplated; they can only be hinted at here. Such stories were common in camp, and believed not only by the soldiers in the ranks, but by officers of position; and in judging General Neill's order we must give due weight to the passionate nature of the man, and recollect that General Havelock, his senior, must have approved of the order, or he would have cancelled it.

But enough of massacre and revenge for the present; I shall return to General Neill's order when I describe my revisit to Cawnpore. In the meantime I should much like to know whether the late Major A. H. S. Neill, who commanded the Central India Horse, and was shot on parade by Sowar Mazar Ali, at Augur, Central India, on the 14th of March, 1887, was a son of General Neill of Mutiny fame. Mazar Ali was sentenced to death by Sir Lepel Griffin, as Governor-General's agent; but I did not see a full account of the trial, and I ask for the above information to corroborate a statement made to me, on my late visit to the scenes of the Mutiny, by a native who admitted that he had been an armourer in the rebel force at Cawnpore, but had joined the English after the defeat of the Gwalior Contingent in December, 1857.[1]

General Hope Grant's brigade and part of the Ninety-Third Highlanders crossed the bridge of boats at Cawnpore, and entered Oude on the 30th of October, with a convoy of provisions and ammunition *en route* to Lucknow. My company, with three others, remained in Cawnpore three days longer, and crossed into Oude on the 2nd of November, encamping a short distance from the bridge of boats.

[1] See Appendix A.

On the morning of the 3rd a salute was fired from the mud fort on the Cawnpore side, from which we learned, to the great delight of the Ninety-Third, that Sir Colin Campbell had come up from Calcutta. Shortly after the salute some of our officers joined us from the Cawnpore side, and gave us the news, which had been brought by the Commander-in-Chief, that a few days before three companies of the Fifty-Third and Captain Cornwallis's company, No. 2, of the Ninety-Third, which had been left at Futtehpore, with part of the Naval Brigade under Captain William Peel, had formed a force of about five hundred men under the command of Colonel Powell of the Fifty-Third, marched out from Futtehpore to a place called Khujwah, and attacked and beaten the Banda and Dinapore mutineers, numbering over ten thousand, who had been threatening our communications with Allahabad. The victory for some time had been doubtful, as the mutineers were a well-equipped force, strongly posted and numbering more than twenty to one of the attacking force, possessing moreover, three well-drilled batteries of artillery, comprising eighteen guns. Colonel Powell was killed early in the action, and the command then devolved on Captain Peel of the Naval Brigade. Although hard pressed at first, the force eventually gained a complete and glorious victory, totally routing the rebels, capturing most of their guns, and driving the remnant of them across the Jumna, whence they had come. The company of the Ninety-Third lost heavily, having one officer wounded and sixteen men killed or wounded. The officer, Lieutenant Cunyngham (now

Sir R. K. A. Dick-Cunyngham of Prestonfield, Edinburgh), was reported to have lost a leg, which caused general sorrow and regret throughout the regiment, as he was a most promising young officer and very popular with the men. During the day when more correct and fuller reports came in, we were all very glad to hear that, although severely wounded, the lieutenant had not lost a limb, and that the surgeons considered they would not only be able to save his leg, but that he might be fit to return to duty in a few months, which he eventually did, and was present at the siege of Lucknow.

During the afternoon of the 3rd of November more stores of provisions and ammunition crossed the river with some of Peel's 24-pounder guns, and on the morning of the 4th, long before daylight, we were on the march for Lucknow, under command of Colonel Leith-Hay, leaving Cawnpore and its horrors behind us, but neither forgotten nor disregarded. Every man in the regiment was determined to risk his life to save the women and children in the Residency of Lucknow from a similar fate. None were inclined to pay any heed to the French maxim that *les représailles sont toujours inutiles,* nor inclined to ponder and moralise on the lesson and warning given by the horrible catastrophe which had overtaken our people at Cawnpore. Many too were inclined to blame the Commander-in-Chief for having cancelled the brigade order of General Neill.

Before concluding this chapter I wish my readers to

note that I merely describe facts as they appeared to me in 1857. Nothing is further from my intention than to revive the old race-hatreds. The real causes of the Mutiny and its horrors have yet to be written. I merely mention facts to show the incentive the troops had to make light of forced marches, under short rations and a double load of ammunition for want of other means of carriage, with an overwhelming enemy in front, and no means whatever of obtaining reinforcements or recovering from a defeat.

CHAPTER III

START FOR LUCKNOW—SIR COLIN—THE DILKOOSHÁ—MARTINIÈRE—SECUNDRABÂGH

WHEN proceeding on our march to Lucknow it was clear as noonday to the meanest capacity that we were now in an enemy's country. None of the villages along the route were inhabited, the only visible signs of life about them being a few mangy pariah dogs. The people had all fled on the first advance of Havelock, and had not returned; and it needed no great powers of observation to fully understand that the whole population of Oude was against us.

The deserted villages gave the country a miserable appearance. Not only were they forsaken, but we found, on reaching our first halting-ground, that the whole of the small bazaar of camp-followers, consisting of goatherds, bread, milk, and butter-sellers, etc., which had accompanied us from Allahabad, had returned to Cawnpore, none daring to accompany the force into Oude. This was most disappointing for young soldiers with good appetites and sound digestions, who depended on bazaar *chupatties*,[1] with a *chittack* [2] of butter and a pint

[1] Unleavened girdle-cakes. [2] Rather less than two ounces.

of goat's milk at the end of the march, to eke out the scanty commissariat allowance of rations. What made the privation the more keenly felt, was the custom of serving out at one time three days' biscuits, supposed to run four to the pound, but which, I fear, were often short weight. Speaking for myself, I did not control my appetite, but commenced to eat from my haversack on the march, the whole of my three days' biscuits usually disappearing before we reached the first halting-ground, and believe me, I ran no danger of a fit of indigestion. To demolish twelve ordinary-sized ship's biscuits, during a march of twenty to twenty-five miles, was no great tax on a young and healthy stomach.

I may here remark that my experience is that, after a forced march, it would be far more beneficial to the men if the general commanding were to serve out an extra ration of tea or coffee with a pound of bread or biscuit instead of extra grog. The latter was often issued during the forced marches of the Mutiny, but never an extra ration of food; and my experience is that a pint of good tea is far more refreshing than a dram of rum. Let me also note here most emphatically that regimental canteens and the fixed ration of rum in the field are the bane of the army. At the same time I am no teetotaller. In addition to the bazaar people, our cooks and *dhobies*[1] had also deserted. This was not such a serious matter for the Ninety-Third just fresh from the Crimea, as it was for the old Indian regiments. Men for cooking were at once told off for

[1] Laundry-men.

each of our tents; but the cooking-utensils had also gone with the cooks, or not come on; the rear-guard had seen nothing of them. There were, however, large copper water-cans attached to each tent, and these were soon brought into use for cooking, and plenty of earthen pots were to be found in the deserted houses of the villagers. Highlanders, and especially Highlanders who are old campaigners, are not lacking in resources where the preparation of food is concerned.

I will relate a rather amusing incident which happened to the men of the colour-sergeant's tent of my company,—Colour-Sergeant David Morton, a Fifeshire man, an old soldier of close on twenty years' service, one of the old "unlimited service" men, whose regimental number was 1100, if I remember rightly. A soldier's approximate service, I may here state, can almost always be told from his regimental number, as each man on enlisting takes the next consecutive number in the regiment, and as these numbers often range up to 8000 or even 10,000 before commencing again at No. 1, it is obvious that the earlier numbers indicate the oldest soldiers. The men in the Ninety-Third with numbers between 1000 and 2000 had been with the regiment in Canada before the Crimean war, so David Morton, it will be seen, was an old soldier; but he had never seen tobacco growing in the field, and in the search for fuel to cook a dinner, he had come across a small plot of luxuriant tobacco leaf. He came back with an armful of it for Duncan Mackenzie, who was the improvised cook for the men of his tent, and told us all that he had secured a rare treat for our soup, having fallen on a plot of "real Scotch curly kail!" The men were all hungry, and the tobacco leaves were soon chopped fine, washed, and put into the soup. But when that soup was cooked it was a "caution." I was the only non-smoker in the squad, and was the first to detect that instead of "real Scotch curly kail" we had got "death in the pot!" As before remarked we were all hungry, having marched over twenty miles since we had last tasted food. Although noticing that there was something wrong about the soup and the "curly kail," I had swallowed enough to act as a powerful emetic before I was aware of the full extent of the bitter taste. At first we feared it was a deadly poison, and so we were all much relieved when the *bheestie*, who picked up some of the rejected stalks, assured us that it was only green tobacco which had been cooked in the soup.

The desertion of our camp-followers was significant. An army in India is followed by another army whose general or commander-in-chief is the bazaar *kotwal*.[1] These people carry all their household goods and families with them, their only houses being their little tents. The elder men, at the time of which I write, could all talk of the victories of Lords Lake and Combermere, and the Caubul war of 1840-42, and the younger hands could tell us of the victories of Lords Gough and Hardinge in the Punjâb. The younger

[1] The native official in charge of the bazaar; he possesses certain magisterial powers.

generations took up the handicrafts of their fathers, as barbers, cobblers, cooks, shoeblacks, and so forth, a motley hive bred in camps but unwarlike, always in the rear of the army. Most of these camp-followers were low-caste Hindoos, very few of them were Mahommedans, except the *bheesties*. I may remark that the *bheesties* and the *dooly*-bearers (the latter were under the hospital guard) were the only camp-followers who did not desert us when we crossed into Oude.[1] The natives fully believed that our column was doomed to extermination; there is no doubt that they knew of the powerful force collecting in our rear, consisting of the Gwalior Contingent, which had never yet been beaten and was supposed to be invincible; also of the Central India mutineers who were gathering for a fresh attack on Cawnpore under the leadership of Nânâ Sâhib, Kooer Sing, Tântia Topee, and other commanders. But we learned all this afterwards, when this army retook Cawnpore in our rear, which story I will relate in its proper place. For the present, we must resume our advance into Oude.

Every hour's march brought us three miles nearer Lucknow, and before we made our first halt, we could distinctly hear the guns of the enemy bombarding the Residency. Foot-sore and tired as they were, the report of each salvo made the men step out with a firmer tread and a more determined resolve to overcome all difficulties, and to carry relief to the beleaguered garrison

[1] The *bheesties*, or water-carriers, have been noted for bravery and fidelity in every Indian campaign.

and the helpless women and children. I may mention that the cowardly treachery of the enemy, and their barbarous murders of women and children, had converted the war of the Mutiny into a *guerre à la mort*,—a war of the most cruel and exterminating form, in which no quarter was given on either side. Up to the final relief of Lucknow and the second capture of Cawnpore, and the total rout of the Gwalior Contingent on the 6th of December, 1857, it would have been impossible for the Europeans to have guarded their prisoners, and, for that reason, it was obvious that prisoners were not to be taken; while on the part of the rebels, wherever they met a Christian or a white man, he was at once slain without pity or remorse, and natives who attempted to assist or conceal a distressed European did so at the risk of their own lives and property. It was both horrible and demoralising for the army to be engaged in such a war. Looking back to those days, over my long experience of thirty-five years in India, I must admit that, with few exceptions, the European soldiers went through the terrible scenes of the Mutiny with great moderation, especially where women and children, or even unarmed men, came into their power.

On the 10th of November the total force that could be collected for the final relief of Lucknow was encamped on the plain about five miles in front of the Alumbâgh. The total strength was under five thousand of all arms, and the only really complete regiment was the Ninety-Third Highlanders. By this time the whole regiment, consisting of ten companies, had reached the front, numbering over a thousand men in the prime of manhood, about seven hundred of them having the Crimean medals on their breasts. By the afternoon of the 11th of November, the whole force had been told off into brigades. The Fifty-Third Shropshire Light Infantry, the Ninety-Third, and the Fourth Punjâb Infantry, just come down from Delhi with Sir Hope Grant, formed the fourth brigade, under Colonel the Honourable Adrian Hope of the Ninety-Third as brigadier. If I am not mistaken, the whole of our regiment were not present. I think there were only six or seven companies, and there was no field-officer, Captain Walton, late commandant of the Calcutta Volunteers, being the senior captain present.[1] Under these circumstances Colonel Gordon, of ours, was temporarily put in command of the Fifty-Third. The whole force was formed up in a line of columns on the afternoon of the 11th for the inspection of the Commander-in-Chief. The Ninety-Third formed the extreme left of the line in quarter-distance column, in full Highland costume, with feather bonnets and dark waving plumes, a solid mass of brawny-limbed men. I have never seen a more magnificent regiment than the Ninety-Third looked that day, and I was, and still am, proud to have formed one of its units.

The old Chief rode along the line, commencing from the right, halting and addressing a short speech to each corps as he came along. The eyes of the Ninety-Third were eagerly turned towards Sir Colin and his staff as

[1] Now Colonel Bendyshe Walton, C.I.E.

he advanced, the men remarking among themselves that none of the other corps had given him a single cheer, but had taken whatever he had said to them in solemn silence. At last he approached us; we were called to attention, and formed close column, so that every man might hear what was said. When Sir Colin rode up, he appeared to have a worn and haggard expression on his face, but he was received with such a cheer, or rather shout of welcome, as made the echoes ring from the Alumbâgh and the surrounding woods. His wrinkled brow at once became smooth, and his wearied-looking features broke into a smile, as he acknowledged the cheer by a hearty salute, and addressed us almost exactly as follows. I stood near him and heard every word. "Ninety-Third! when I took leave of you in Portsmouth, I never thought I should see you again. I expected the bugle, or maybe the bagpipes, to sound a call for me to go somewhere else long before you would be likely to return to our dearly-loved home. But another commander has decreed it otherwise, and here I am prepared to lead you through another campaign. And I must tell you, my lads, there is work of difficulty and danger before us,—harder work and greater dangers than any we encountered in the Crimea. But I trust to you to overcome the difficulties and to brave the dangers. The eyes of the people at home,—I may say the eyes of Europe and of the whole of Christendom are upon us, and we must relieve our countrymen, women, and children, now shut up in the Residency of Lucknow. The lives at stake are not merely those of soldiers, who might well be expected to cut themselves out, or to die sword in hand. We have to rescue helpless women and children from a fate worse than death. When you meet the enemy, you must remember that he is well armed and well provided with ammunition, and that he can play at long bowls as well as you can, especially from behind loopholed walls. So when we make an attack you must come to close quarters as quickly as possible; keep well together, and use the bayonet. Remember that the cowardly sepoys, who are eager to murder women and children, cannot look a European soldier in the face when it is accompanied with cold steel. Ninety-Third! you are my own lads, I rely on you to do the work!" A voice from the ranks called out: "Ay, ay, Sir Colin, ye ken us and we ken you; we'll bring the women and children out o' Lucknow or die wi' you in the attempt!" and the whole regiment burst into another ringing cheer, which was taken up by the whole line.

I may here mention the service rendered to the relieving force by Mr. Kavanagh, an enterprise of consummate daring which won for him a well-deserved Victoria Cross; only those who know the state of Lucknow at the time can fully appreciate the perils he encountered, or the value of the service he rendered. My own company, made up to one hundred men, with a troop of the Ninth Lancers and a company of the Fourth Punjâb Infantry, formed the advance piquet at which Mr. Kavanagh, who had made his way from the Residency through the heart of the enemy, disguised as a native scout, arrived. I will not give any account of his venturesome march. He has already told his own story, and I need not repeat it. I only allude to the value of the service rendered, and how it was appraised in the force at the time. Oude had only been annexed in 1856, and the Mutiny broke out in May, 1857. There had been no time to complete a survey of Lucknow and its surroundings, and consequently the Commander-in-Chief had no plan of the city, and there was no officer in the force, or, for that matter, no European outside the Residency, who knew the strong positions of the enemy or the intricacies of the streets. When Generals Havelock and Outram forced their way into the Residency, their advance was through miles of intricate and narrow lanes. The sequel is well known. The relieving force got into the Residency, but they had lost so many men in the attempt that they were unable to come out again in charge of the women and children, and so they were themselves besieged. In our force, among the ranks (I don't know what the plans of the Commander-in-Chief were), it was understood that we were to advance on the Residency by the same route as Generals Havelock and Outram had done, and that the streets were all duly prepared for giving us a warm reception. But after "Lucknow" Kavanagh, who thoroughly knew the ground, came out to act as a guide to the relieving force, the Commander-in-Chief was supposed to have altered the plan of his line of advance. Instead of forcing his way through loopholed and narrow lanes, he decided to avoid the city altogether, and advance through the Dilkooshá park and by the right bank of the Goomtee, having thus only six or seven posts to force, instead of running the gauntlet of miles of fortified streets. The strongest positions which we had to attack on this route were the Dilkooshá palace and park, the Martinière college, the Thirty-Second mess-house, the Secundrabâgh, the Shâh Nujeef, and the Moti Munzil. The force in the Residency would thus be able to assist and to distract the enemy by advancing from their side to meet us at the Chutter Munzil and other positions. This was what was believed in the camp to be the intentions of the Commander-in-Chief, and the supposed change of route was attributed to the arrival of Mr. Kavanagh; and whatever history may say, I believe this is the correct statement of the position. It will thus be seen and understood by any one having a plan of Lucknow before him,—and there is no want of plans now—that the services rendered by Mr. Kavanagh were of the greatest value to the country and to the relieving force, and were by no means overpaid. I mention this because on my recent visit to Lucknow I met some gentlemen at the Royal Hotel who appeared to think lightly of Mr. Kavanagh's gallant deed, and that fact has made me, as a soldier of the relieving force, put on record my impressions of the great value of the service he rendered at a most critical juncture in the fortunes of the country.[1]

By the afternoon of the 12th of November the total

[1] Kavanagh was a European clerk in one of the newly-instituted Government offices.

force under command of Sir Colin Campbell for the final relief of Lucknow numbered only four thousand five hundred and fifty men of all arms and thirty-two guns—the heaviest being 24-pounders—and two 8-inch howitzers, manned by the Naval Brigade under Captain William Peel of glorious memory. I have read some accounts that mentioned 68-pounders, but this is a mistake; the 68-pounders had to be left at Allahabad when we started, for want of cattle to drag them. There are four 68-pounders now in the Residency grounds at Lucknow, which, during my recent visit, the guide pointed out to me as the guns which breached the walls of the Secundrabâgh,[1] and finally relieved the Residency; but this is an error. The 68-pounders did not reach Lucknow till the 2nd of March, 1858. I am positive on this point, because I myself assisted to drag the guns into position in the assault on the Secundrabâgh, and I was on guard on the guns in Allahabad when the 68-pounders had to be sent into the fort for want of bullocks, and I next saw them when they crossed the river at Cawnpore and joined the ordnance park at Oonâo in February, 1858. They were first used on the works in defence of the Martinière, fired from the Dilkooshá park, and were advanced as the outworks were carried till they breached the defences around the Begum's palace on the 11th of March. This is a small matter; I only wish to point out that the four 68-pounders now in the Residency grounds are

[1] *Bâgh* means a garden, usually surrounded by high walls.

not the guns which relieved the garrison in November, 1857.

On the 13th of November a strong force, of which the Ninety-Third formed the infantry, was sent to attack the mud fort of Jellâlabâd, lying between the Alumbâgh and the Dilkooshá, on the right of Sir Colin Campbell's advance. As soon as the artillery opened fire on the fort the enemy retired, and the force advanced and covered the engineers until they had completed arrangements for blowing in the main gate and breaching the ramparts so that it would be impossible for Jellâlabâd to be occupied in our rear. This was finished before dark, and the force returned to camp in front of the Alumbâgh, where we rested fully accoutred.

We commenced our advance on the Dilkooshá park and palace by daybreak next morning, the 14th. The fourth brigade, composed of the Fifty-Third, Ninety-Third, and Fourth Punjâb regiments, with a strong force of artillery, reached the walls of the Dilkooshá park as the sun was rising. Here we halted till a breach was made in the wall, sufficiently wide to allow the Ninety-Third to march through in double column of companies and to form line inside on the two centre companies.

While we were halted my company and No. 8, Captain Williams' company, were in a field of beautiful carrots, which the men were pulling up and eating raw. I remember as if it were only yesterday a young lad not turned twenty, Kenneth Mackenzie by name, of No. 8 company, making a remark that these might be the last carrots many of us would eat, and with that he asked the colour-sergeant of the company, who belonged to the same place as himself, to write to his mother should anything happen to him. The colour-sergeant of course promised to do so, telling young Mackenzie not to let such gloomy thoughts enter his mind. Immediately after this the order was passed for the regiment to advance by double column of companies from the centre, and to form line on the two centre companies inside the park. The enclosure swarmed with deer, both black buck and spotted, but there were no signs of the enemy, and a staff-officer of the artillery galloped to the front to reconnoitre. This officer was none other than our present Commander-in-Chief, then Lieutenant Roberts, Deputy Assistant Quartermaster-General of Artillery, who had joined our force at Cawnpore, and had been associated with the Ninety-Third in several skirmishes which had taken place in the advance on Alumbâgh. He was at that time familiarly known among us as "Plucky wee Bobs." About half of the regiment had passed through the breach and were forming into line right and left on the two centre companies, when we noticed the staff-officer halt and wheel round to return, signalling for the artillery to advance, and immediately a masked battery of six guns opened fire on us from behind the Dilkooshá palace. The first round shot passed through our column, between the right of No. 7 company and the line, as the company was wheeling into line, but the second shot was better aimed and struck the charger of Lieutenant Roberts just behind the rider, apparently cutting the horse in two, both horse and rider falling in a confused heap amidst the dust where the shot struck after passing through the loins of the horse. Some of the men exclaimed, "Plucky wee Bobs is done for!"[1] The same shot, a 9-pounder, ricochetted at almost a right angle, and in its course struck poor young Kenneth Mackenzie on the side of his head, taking the skull clean off just level with his ears. He fell just in front of me, and I had to step over his body before a single drop of blood had had time to flow. The colour-sergeant of his company turned to me and said, "Poor lad! how can I tell his poor mother. What would she think if she were to see him now! He was her favourite laddie!" There was no leisure for moralising, however; we were completely within the range of the enemy's guns, and the next shot cut down seven or eight of the light company, and old Colonel Leith-Hay was calling out, "Keep steady, men; close up the ranks, and don't waver in face of a battery manned by cowardly Asiatics." The shots were now coming thick, bounding along the hard ground, and MacBean, the adjutant, was behind the line telling the men in an undertone, "Don't mind the colonel; open out and let them [the round-shot] through, keep plenty of room and watch the shot." By this time the staff-officer, whose horse only had been killed under him, had got clear of the carcase, and the Ninety-Third, seeing him on his feet again, gave him a rousing cheer. He was soon in the saddle of a spare horse, and the artillery

[1] See note at end of chapter.

dashed to the front under his direction, taking the guns of the enemy in flank. The sepoys bolted down the hill for shelter in the Martinière, while our little force took possession of the Dilkooshá palace. The Ninety-Third had lost ten men killed and wounded by the time we had driven the enemy and their guns through the long grass into the entrenchments in front of the Martinière. I may note here that there were very few trees on the Dilkooshá heights at this time, and between the heights and the city there was a bare plain, so that signals could be passed between us and the Residency. A semaphore was erected on the top of the palace as soon as it was taken, and messages, in accordance with a code of signals brought out by Kavanagh, were interchanged with the Residency. The 15th was a Sunday; the force did not advance till the afternoon, as it had been decided to wait for the rear-guard and provisions and the spare ammunition, etc., to close up. About two o'clock Peel's guns, covered by the Ninety-Third, advanced, and we drove the enemy from the Martinière and occupied it, the semaphore being then removed from the Dilkooshá to the Martinière.

The Ninety-Third held the Martinière and the grounds to the left of it, facing the city, till about two A.M. on Monday the 16th of November, when Captain Peel's battery discharged several rockets as a signal to the Residency that we were about to commence our march through the city. We were then formed up and served with some rations, which had been cooked in the rear, each man receiving what was supposed to be three lbs. of beef, boiled in salt so that it would keep, and the usual dozen of commissariat biscuits and a canteenful of tea cooked on the ground. Just before we started I saw Sir Colin drinking his tea, the same kind as that served out to the men, out of a Ninety-Third soldier's canteen. Writing of the relief of Lucknow, Lady Inglis in her lately-published journal states, under date the 18th of November, 1857, two days after the time of which I write: "Sir Colin Campbell is much liked; he is living now exactly as a private soldier, takes his rations and lies down wherever he can to rest. This the men like, and he is a fine soldier. A Commander-in-Chief just now has indeed no enviable position." That is true; the Commander-in-Chief had only a staff-sergeant's tent (when he *had* a tent), and all his baggage was carried by one camel in a pair of camel trunks, marked "His Excellency the Commander-in-Chief." I suppose this was *pour encourager les autres,* some of whom required six or seven camels and as many as four bullock-hackeries, if they could have got them, to carry their stuff.

After getting our three days' rations and tea, the Ninety-Third were formed up, and the roll was called to see that none, except those known to be wounded or sick, were missing. Sir Colin again addressed the men, telling us that there was heavy work before us, and that we must hold well together, and as much as possible keep in threes, and that as soon as we stormed a position we were to use the bayonet. The centre man of each group of three was to make the attack, and the other two to come to his assistance with their bayonets right and left. We were not to fire a single bullet after we got inside a position, unless we were certain of hitting our enemy, for fear of wounding our own men. To use the bayonet with effect we were ordered, as I say, to group in threes and mutually assist each other, for by such action we would soon bayonet the enemy down although they might be ten to one; which as a matter of fact they were. It was by strictly following this advice and keeping cool and mutually assisting each other that the bayonet was used with such terrible effect inside the Secundrabâgh. It was exactly as Sir Colin had foretold in his address in front of the Alumbâgh. He knew the sepoys well, that when brought to the point of the bayonet they could not look the Europeans in the face. For all that they fought like devils. In addition to their muskets, all the men in the Secundrabâgh were armed with swords from the King of Oude's magazines, and the native *tulwârs* were as sharp as razors. I have never seen another fact noticed, that when they had fired their muskets, they hurled them amongst us like javelins, bayonets first, and then drawing their *tulwârs*, rushed madly on to their destruction, slashing in blind fury with their swords and using them as one sees sticks used in the sham fights on the last night of the *Mohurrum*.[1] As they rushed on us shouting "*Deen! Deen!* (The Faith! the Faith!)" they actually threw themselves under the

[1] The great Mussulman carnival.

bayonets and slashed at our legs. It was owing to this fact that more than half of our wounded were injured by sword-cuts.

From the Martinière we slowly and silently commenced our advance across the canal, the front of the column being directed by Mr. Kavanagh and his native guide. Just as morning broke we had reached the outskirts of a village on the east side of the Secundrabâgh. Here a halt was made for the heavy guns to be brought to the front, three companies of the Ninety-Third with some more artillery being diverted to the left under command of Colonel Leith-Hay, to attack the old Thirty-Second barracks, a large building in the form of a cross strongly flanked with earthworks. The rest of the force advanced through the village by a narrow lane, from which the enemy was driven by us into the Secundrabâgh.

About the centre of the village another short halt was made. Here we saw a naked wretch, of a strong muscular build, with his head closely shaven except for the tuft on his crown, and his face all streaked in a hideous manner with white and red paint, his body smeared with ashes. He was sitting on a leopard's skin counting a rosary of beads. A young staff-officer, I think it was Captain A. O. Mayne, Deputy Assistant Quartermaster-General, was making his way to the front, when a man of my company, named James Wilson, pointed to this painted wretch saying, "I would like to try my bayonet on the hide of that painted scoundrel, who looks a murderer." Captain

Mayne replied: "Oh don't touch him; these fellows are harmless Hindoo *jogees*,[1] and won't hurt us. It is the Mahommedans that are to blame for the horrors of this Mutiny." The words had scarcely been uttered when the painted scoundrel stopped counting the beads, slipped his hand under the leopard skin, and as quick as lightning brought out a short, brass, bell-mouthed blunderbuss and fired the contents of it into Captain Mayne's chest at a distance of only a few feet. His action was as quick as it was unexpected, and Captain Mayne was unable to avoid the shot, or the men to prevent it. Immediately our men were upon the assassin; there was no means of escape for him, and he was quickly bayoneted. Since then I have never seen a painted Hindoo, but I involuntarily raise my hand to knock him down. From that hour I formed the opinion (which I have never had cause to alter since) that the pampered high-caste Hindoo sepoys had far more to do with the Mutiny and the cowardly murders of women and children, than the Mahommedans, although the latter still bear most of the blame.

Immediately after this incident we advanced through the village and came in front of the Secundrabâgh, when a murderous fire was opened on us from the loopholed wall and from the windows and flat roof of a two-storied building in the centre of the garden. I may note that this building has long since been demolished; no trace of it now remains except the small garden-house with the row of pillars where the

[1] Religious mendicants.

wounded and dead of the Ninety-Third were collected; the marble flooring has, however, been removed. Having got through the village, our men and the sailors manned the drag-ropes of the heavy guns, and these were run up to within one hundred yards, or even less, of the wall. As soon as the guns opened fire the Infantry Brigade was made to take shelter at the back of a low mud wall behind the guns, the men taking steady aim at every loophole from which we could see the musket-barrels of the enemy protruding. The Commander-in-Chief and his staff were close beside the guns, Sir Colin every now and again turning round when a man was hit, calling out, "Lie down, Ninety-Third, lie down! Every man of you is worth his weight in gold to England to-day!"

The first shots from our guns passed through the wall, piercing it as though it were a piece of cloth, and without knocking the surrounding brickwork away. Accounts differ, but my impression has always been that it was from half to three-quarters of an hour that the guns battered at the walls. During this time the men, both artillery and sailors, working the guns without any cover so close to the enemy's loopholes, were falling fast, over two guns' crews having been disabled or killed before the wall was breached. After holes had been pounded through the wall in many places large blocks of brick-and-mortar commenced to fall out, and then portions of the wall came down bodily, leaving wide gaps. Thereupon a sergeant of the Fifty-Third, who had served under Sir Colin Campbell in the Punjâb, presuming on old acquaintance, called out: "Sir Colin, your Excellency, let the infantry storm; let the two 'Thirds' at them [meaning the Fifty-Third and Ninety-Third], and we'll soon make short work of the murdering villains!" The sergeant who called to Sir Colin was a Welshman, and I recognised him thirty-five years afterwards as old Joe Lee, the present proprietor of the Railway Hotel in Cawnpore. He was always known as Dobbin in his regiment; and Sir Colin, who had a most wonderful memory for names and faces, turning to General Sir William Mansfield who had formerly served in the Fifty-Third, said, "Isn't that Sergeant Dobbin?" General Mansfield replied in the affirmative; and Sir Colin, turning to Lee, said, "Do you think the breach is wide enough, Dobbin?" Lee replied, "Part of us can get through and hold it till the pioneers widen it with their crowbars to allow the rest to get in." The word was then passed to the Fourth Punjâbis to prepare to lead the assault, and after a few more rounds were fired, the charge was ordered. The Punjâbis dashed over the mud wall shouting the war-cry of the Sikhs, "*Jai Khâlsa Jee!*"[1] led by their two European officers, who were both shot down before they had gone a few yards. This staggered the Sikhs, and they halted. As soon as Sir Colin saw them waver, he turned to Colonel Ewart, who was in command of the seven companies of the Ninety-Third (Colonel Leith-Hay being in command of the assault), and said: "Colonel Ewart, bring on the tartan—let my own lads at them." Before the com-

[1] "Victory to the *Khâlsa!*"

mand could be repeated or the buglers had time to sound the advance, the whole seven companies, like one man, leaped over the wall, with such a yell of pent-up rage as I had never heard before nor since. It was not a cheer, but a concentrated yell of rage and ferocity that made the echoes ring again; and it must have struck terror into the defenders, for they actually ceased firing, and we could see them through the breach rushing from the outside wall to take shelter in the two-storied building in the centre of the garden, the gate and doors of which they firmly barred. Here I must not omit to pay a tribute of respect to the memory of Pipe-Major John M'Leod, who, with seven pipers, the other three being with their companies attacking the barracks, struck up the Highland Charge, called by some *The Haughs of Cromdell*, and by others *On wi' the Tartan*—the famous charge of the great Montrose when he led his Highlanders so often to victory. When all was over, and Sir Colin complimented the pipe-major on the way he had played, John said, "I thought the boys would fecht better wi' the national music to cheer them."

The storming of the Secundrabâgh has been so often described that I need not dwell on the general action. Once inside, the Fifty-Third (who got in by a window or small door in the wall to the right of the hole by which we got through) and the Sikhs who followed us, joined the Ninety-Third, and keeping together the bayonet did the work. As I before remarked, I could write pages about the actions of individual men whose names will never be known to history. Although pressed for space, I must notice the behaviour of one or two. But I must leave this to another chapter; the present one has already become too long.

NOTE.

With regard to the incident mentioned on page 40 Captain W. T. Furse, A.D.C. to his Excellency, wrote to me as follows: "Dear Forbes-Mitchell—His Excellency has read your Mutiny Reminiscences with great interest, and thinks they are a very true description of the events of that time. He wishes me, however, to draw your attention to a mistake you have made in stating that 'the horse of Lieutenant Roberts was shot down under him.' But the Chief remembers that though he was in the position which you assign to him at that moment, it was not his horse that was shot, but the horse of a trooper of the squadron commanded by Lieut. J. Watson (now Sir John Watson, V.C., K.C.B.), who happened to be near Lord Roberts at the time."

Now I could not understand this, because I had entered in my note-book that Lieutenant Fred. Roberts, Deputy Assistant Quartermaster-General of Artillery, was the first man to enter the Dilkooshá park and ride to the front to reconnoitre, that the enemy opened fire on him at point-blank range from a masked battery of 9-pounder guns, and that his horse was shot under him near the Yellow Bungalow (the name by which we then knew the Dilkooshá palace) on the morning of the 14th of November, 1857. And I was confident that about half-a-dozen men with Captain Dalziel ran out from the light company of the Ninety-Third to go to the assistance of Lieutenant Roberts, when we all saw him get on his feet and remount what we believed was a spare horse. The men of the light company, seeing that their assistance was not required, returned to the line, and directly we saw Lieutenant Roberts in the saddle again, unhurt, the whole regiment, officers and men, gave him a hearty cheer. But here was the Commander-in-Chief, through his aide-de-camp, telling me that I was incorrect! I could not account for it till I obtained an interview with his Excellency, when he explained to me that after he went past the Ninety-Third through the breach in the wall of the Dilkooshá park, Lieutenant Watson sent a trooper after him, and that the trooper was close to him when the battery unmasked and opened fire on them, the guns having been laid for their horses; that the second shot struck the trooper's horse as described by me, the horse and rider falling together amidst the dust knocked up by the other round shot; and that he, as a matter of course, dismounted and assisted the trooper to get from under the dead horse, and as he remounted after performing this humane and dangerous service to the fallen trooper, the Ninety-Third set up their cheer as I described.

Now I must say the true facts of this incident rather add to the bravery of the action. The young lieutenant, who could thus coolly dismount and extricate a trooper from under a dead horse within point-blank range of a well-served battery of 9-pounder guns, was early qualifying for the distinguished position which he has since reached.

CHAPTER IV

THE NINETY-THIRD—ANECDOTES OF THE SECUNDRABÂGH —GENERAL EWART—THE SHÂH NUJEEF

In the first chapter of these reminiscences I mentioned that, before leaving Dover, the Ninety-Third obtained a number of volunteers from the other Highland regiments serving in England. Ours was the only Highland regiment told off for the China expedition, and it was currently whispered that Lord Elgin had specially asked for us to form his guard of honour at the court of China after he had administered a due castigation to the Chinese. Whether the report was true or not, the belief did the regiment no harm; it added to the *esprit de corps* which was already a prominent feeling in the regiment, and enabled the boys to boast to the girls in Portsmouth that they were "a cut above" the other corps of the army. In support of this, the fact is worthy of being put on record that although the regiment was not (as is usually the case) confined to barracks the night before embarking, but were allowed leave till midnight, still, when the time to leave the barracks came, there was not a single man absent nor a prisoner in the guard-room; and General Britain put it in garrison orders that he had never been able to say the same of any other corps during the time he had commanded the Portsmouth garrison. But the Ninety-Third were no ordinary regiment. They were then the most Scotch of all the Highland regiments; in brief, they were a military Highland parish, minister and elders complete. The elders were selected from among the men of all ranks,—two sergeants, two corporals, and two privates; and I believe it was the only regiment in the army which had a regular service of Communion plate; and in time of peace the Holy Communion, according to the Church of Scotland, was administered by the regimental chaplain twice a year. I hope the young second battalion of the Argyle and Sutherland Highlanders are like the old Ninety-Third in this respect. At the same time, I don't ask them ever to pray for the men who took away the numbers from our regiments; may their beards be defiled, is the only feeling I have for them. By taking away the old numbers a great deal was lost, and as far as I can see nothing has been gained except confusion and the utter effacement of all the old traditions of the army. The old numbers could easily have been retained along with the territorial designations. I hope at all events that the present regiment will never forget they are the descendants of the old Ninety-Third, the "Thin Red Line" which Sir Colin Campbell disdained to form four deep to meet the Russian cavalry on the morning of the memorable 25th of October, 1854:— "Steady, Ninety-Third, keep steady! Damn all that eagerness!" were Sir Colin's memorable words. But I am describing the relief of Lucknow, not the "Thin Red Line" of Balaclava.

Among the volunteers who came from the Seventy-Second was a man named James Wallace. He and six others from the same regiment joined my company. Wallace was not his real name, but he never took any one into his confidence, nor was he ever known to have any correspondence. He neither wrote nor received any letters, and he was usually so taciturn in his manner that he was known in the company as the Quaker, a name which had followed him from the Seventy-Second. He had evidently received a superior education, for if asked for any information by a more ignorant comrade, he would at once give it; or questioned as to the translation of a Latin or French quotation in a book, he would give it without the least hesitation. I have often seen him on the voyage out walking up and down the deck of the *Belleisle* during the watches of the night, repeating the famous poem of Lamartine, *Le Chien du Solitaire*, commencing:

> Hélas! rentrer tout seul dans sa maison déserte
> Sans voir à votre approche une fenêtre ouverte.

Taking him all in all Quaker Wallace was a strange enigma which no one could solve. When pressed to take promotion, for which his superior education well fitted him, he absolutely refused, always saying that he had come to the Ninety-Third for a certain purpose, and when that purpose was accomplished, he only wished to die

> With his back to the field, and his feet to the foe !
> And leaving in battle no blot on his name,
> Look proudly to Heaven from the death-bed of fame.

During the march to Lucknow it was a common thing to hear the men in my company say they would give a day's grog to see Quaker Wallace under fire; and the time had now come for their gratification.

There was another man in the company who had joined the regiment in Turkey before embarking for the Crimea. He was also a man of superior education, but in many respects the very antithesis of Wallace. He was both wild and reckless, and used often to receive money sent to him from some one, which he as regularly spent in drink. He went under the name of Hope, but that was also known to be an assumed name, and when the volunteers from the Seventy-Second joined the regiment in Dover, it was remarked that Wallace had the address of Hope, and had asked to be posted to the same company. Yet the two men never spoke to one another; on the contrary they evidently hated each other with a mortal hatred. If the history of these two men could be known it would without doubt form material for a most sensational novel.

Just about the time the men were tightening their belts and preparing for the dash on the breach of the Secundrabâgh, this man Hope commenced to curse and swear in such a manner that Captain Dawson, who commanded the company, checked him, telling him that oaths and foul language were no signs of bravery. Hope replied that he did not care a d—— what the captain thought; that he would defy death; that the bullet was not yet moulded that would kill him; and he commenced exposing himself above the mud wall behind which we were lying. The captain was just on the point of ordering a corporal and a file of men to take Hope to the rear-guard as drunk and riotous in presence of the enemy, when Pipe-Major John M'Leod, who was close to the captain, said: "Don't mind the puir lad, sir; he's not drunk, he is fey! [meaning doomed]. It's not himself that's speaking; he will never see the sun set." The words were barely out of the pipe-major's mouth when Hope sprang up on the top of the mud wall, and a bullet struck him on the right side, hitting the buckle of his purse belt, which diverted its course, and instead of going right through his body it cut him round the front of his belly below the waist-belt, making a deep wound, and his bowels burst out falling down to his knees. He sank down at once, gasping for breath, when a couple of bullets went through his chest and he died without a groan. John M'Leod turned and said to Captain Dawson, "I told you so, sir. The lad was fey! I am never deceived in a fey man! It was not himself who spoke when swearing in yon terrible manner." Just at this time Quaker Wallace, who had evidently been a witness of Hope's tragic end, worked his way along to where the dead man lay, and looking on the distorted features he solemnly said, "The fool hath said in his heart, there is no God. Vengeance is mine, I will repay, saith the Lord. *I came to the Ninety-Third to see that man die!*" All this happened only a few seconds before the assault was ordered, and attracted but little attention except from those who were immediate witnesses of the incident. The gunners were falling fast, and almost all eyes were turned on them and the breach. When the signal for the assault was given, Quaker Wallace went into the Secundrabâgh like one of the Furies, if there are male Furies, plainly seeking death but not meeting it, and quoting the 116th Psalm, Scotch version in metre, beginning at the first verse:

> I love the Lord, because my voice
> And prayers He did hear.
> I, while I live, will call on Him,
> Who bow'd to me His ear.

And thus he plunged into the Secundrabâgh quoting the next verse at every shot fired from his rifle and at each thrust given by his bayonet:

> I'll of salvation take the cup,
> On God's name will I call;
> I'll pay my vows now to the Lord
> Before His people all.

It was generally reported in the company that Quaker Wallace single-handed killed twenty men, and one wonders at this, remembering that he took no comrade with him and did not follow Sir Colin's rule of "fighting in threes," but whenever he saw an enemy he "went for" him! I may here remark that the case of Wallace proved that, in a fight like the Secundrabâgh where the enemy is met hand to hand and foot to foot, the way to escape death is to brave it. Of course Wallace might have been shot from a distance, and in that respect he only ran an even chance with the others; but wherever he rushed with his bayonet, the enemy did their utmost to give him a wide berth.

By the time the bayonet had done its work of retribution, the throats of our men were hoarse with shouting "Cawnpore! you bloody murderers!" The taste of the powder (those were the days when the muzzle-loading cartridges had to be bitten with the teeth) made men almost mad with thirst; and with the sun high over head, and being fresh from England, with our feather bonnets, red coats, and heavy kilts, we felt the heat intensely.

In the centre of the inner court of the Secundrabâgh there was a large *peepul* [1] tree with a very bushy top, round the foot of which were set a number of jars full of cool water. When the slaughter was almost over, many of our men went under the tree for the sake of its shade, and to quench their burning thirst with a draught of the cool water from the jars. A number however lay dead under this tree, both of the Fifty-Third and Ninety-Third, and the many bodies lying in that particular spot attracted the notice of Captain Dawson. After having carefully examined the wounds, he noticed that in every case the men had

[1] *Ficus Indica.*

evidently been shot from above. He thereupon stepped out from beneath the tree, and called to Quaker Wallace to look up if he could see any one in the top of the tree, because all the dead under it had apparently been shot from above. Wallace had his rifle loaded, and stepping back he carefully scanned the top of the tree. He almost immediately called out, "I see him, sir!" and cocking his rifle he repeated aloud,

> I'll pay my vows now to the Lord
> Before His people all.

He fired, and down fell a body dressed in a tight-fitting red jacket and tight-fitting rose-coloured silk trousers; and the breast of the jacket bursting open with the fall, showed that the wearer was a woman. She was armed with a pair of heavy old-pattern cavalry pistols, one of which was in her belt still loaded, and her pouch was still about half full of ammunition, while from her perch in the tree, which had been carefully prepared before the attack, she had killed more than half-a-dozen men. When Wallace saw that the person whom he shot was a woman, he burst into tears, exclaiming: "If I had known it was a woman, I would rather have died a thousand deaths than have harmed her."

I cannot now recall, although he belonged to my company, what became of Quaker Wallace, whether he lived to go through the rest of the Mutiny or not. I have long since lost my pocket company-roll, but I think Wallace took sick and was sent to Allahabad from Cawnpore, and was either invalided to England or died in the country.

By this time all opposition had ceased, and over two thousand of the enemy lay dead within the building and the centre court. The troops were withdrawn, and the muster-roll of the Ninety-Third was called just outside the gate, which is still standing, on the level spot between the gate and the mound where the European dead are buried.

When the roll was called it was found that the Ninety-Third had nine officers and ninety-nine men, in all one hundred and eight, killed and wounded. The roll of the Fifty-Third was called alongside of us, and Sir Colin Campbell rode up and addressing the men, spoke out in a clear voice: "Fifty-Third and Ninety-Third, you have bravely done your share of this morning's work, and Cawnpore is avenged!" Whereupon one of the Fifty-Third sang out, "Three cheers for the Commander-in-Chief, boys," which was heartily responded to.

All this time there was perfect silence around us, the enemy evidently not being aware of how the tide of victory had rolled inside the Secundrabâgh, for not a soul escaped from it to tell the tale. The silence was so great that we could hear the pipers of the Seventy-Eighth playing inside the Residency as a welcome to cheer us all. There were lately, by the way, some writers who denied that the Seventy-Eighth had their bagpipes and pipers with them at Lucknow. This is not true; they had their pipes and played them too! But we had barely saluted the Commander-in-Chief with a cheer when a perfect hail of round-shot assailed us both from the Târa Kothi on our left and the Shâh Nujeef on our right front. But I must leave the account of our storming the Shâh Nujeef for a separate chapter.

I may here remark that on revisiting Lucknow I did not see a single tablet or grave to show that any of the Ninety-Third are buried there. Surely Captains Dalzell and Lumsden and the men who lie in the mound to the east of the gate of the Secundrabâgh are deserving of some memorial! But it is the old, old story which was said to have been first written on the walls of Badajoz:

> When war is rife and danger nigh,
> God and the Soldier is all the cry;
> When war is over, and wrongs are righted,
> God is forgot and the Soldier slighted.

I am surprised that the officers of the Ninety-Third Regiment have never taken any steps to erect some monument to the memory of the brave men who fell in Lucknow at its relief, and at the siege in March, 1858. Neither is there a single tablet in the Memorial Church at Cawnpore in memory of the Ninety-Third, although almost every one of the other regiments have tablets somewhere in the church. If I were a millionaire I would myself erect a statue to Sir Colin Campbell on the spot where the muster-roll of the Ninety-Third was called on the east of the gate of the Secundrabâgh, with a life-sized figure of a private of the Fifty-Third and Ninety-Third, a sailor and a Sikh at each corner, with the names of every man who fell in the assault on the 16th of November, 1857; and as the Royal Artillery were also there, Sir Colin should be represented in the centre standing on a gun, with a royal artilleryman holding a port-fire ready.

Since commencing these reminiscences I met a gentleman in Calcutta who told me that he had a cousin in the Ninety-Third, General J. A. Ewart, who was with the regiment in the storming of the Secundrabâgh, and he asked me if I remembered General Ewart. This leads me to believe that it would not be out of place if I were to relate the following narrative. General Ewart, now Sir John Alexander Ewart, I am informed, is still alive, and some mention of the part played by him, so far as I saw it, will form an appropriate conclusion to the story of the taking of the Secundrabâgh. And should he ever read this narrative, I may inform him that it is written by one who was present when he was adopted into the Clan Forbes by our chief, the late Sir Charles Forbes, of Newe and Edinglassie, Strathdon, Aberdeenshire, and this fact alone will make the general receive my remarks with the feelings of a clansman as well as of my old commander.

The reminiscence of Secundrabâgh which is here reproduced was called forth, I should state, by a paragraph which appeared at the time in the columns of *The Calcutta Statesman* regarding General Ewart. The paragraph was as follows:

General Ewart, not having been employed since he gave over the command of the Allahabad division on the 30th of November, 1879, was placed on the retired list on the 30th ultimo [Nov. 1884]. General Ewart is one of the few, if not the only general, who refused a transfer from the Allahabad Command to a more favourite division. He has served for over forty-six years, but has only been employed once since giving over the command of the Seventy-Eighth Highlanders in 1864, and that was for two and a half years in this country. He commanded the Ninety-Third for about eighteen months before joining the Seventy-Eighth. He is in possession of the Crimean medal with four clasps, a novelty rather nowadays. He lost his left arm at the battle of Cawnpore.

I accordingly wrote to *The Statesman* desiring to correct a slight inaccuracy in the statement that "General Ewart commanded the Ninety-Third for about eighteen months before joining the Seventy-Eighth." This is not, I remarked, strictly correct; General Ewart never commanded the Ninety-Third in the sense implied. He joined the regiment as captain in 1848, exchanging from the old Thirty-Fifth Royal Sussex with Captain Buchanan of the Ninety-Third, and served in the regiment till he received the regimental rank of lieutenant-colonel on the death, at Fort Rooyah in April, 1858, of the Hon. Adrian Hope. Colonel Ewart was then in England on sick-leave, suffering from the loss of his arm and other wounds, and exchanged into the Seventy-Eighth with Colonel Stisted about the end of 1859, so that he never actually commanded the Ninety-Third for more than a few days at most. I will now give a few facts about him which may interest old soldiers at least.

During the whole of his service in the Ninety-Third,

both as captain and field-officer, Colonel Ewart was singularly devoted to duty, while careful, considerate, and attentive to the wants of his men in a way that made him more beloved by those under his command than any officer I ever met during my service in the army. To the best of my recollection, he was the only officer of the Ninety-Third who received the clasp for Inkerman. At that battle he was serving on the staff of Lord Raglan as Deputy-Assistant-Quartermaster-General, and as such was on duty on the morning of the battle, and I believe he was the first officer of the British army who perceived the Russian advance. He was visiting the outposts, as was his custom when on duty, in the early morning, and gave the alarm to Sir George Brown's division, and then carried the news of the attack to Lord Raglan. For his services at Inkerman he was promoted brevet lieutenant-colonel, and on the termination of the war, besides the Crimean medal with four clasps (Alma, Balaklava, Inkerman, and Sebastopol), he received the Cross of the Legion of Honour and the Sardinian Medal, with the motto *Al valore Militare*, and also the Turkish Order of the Medjidie.

Early in the attack on the Secundrabâgh three companies of the Ninety-Third were detached under Colonel Leith-Hay to clear the ground to the left and carry the barracks, and Colonel Ewart was left in command of the other seven companies. For some time we lay down sheltered by a low mud wall not more than one hundred and fifty to two hundred yards from the walls of the Secundrabâgh, to allow time for the heavy guns to breach the garden wall. During this time Colonel Ewart had dismounted and stood exposed on the bank, picking off the enemy on the top of the building with one of the men's rifles which he took, making the owner of the rifle lie down.

It was an anxious moment. The artillerymen were falling fast, but, after a few discharges, a hole,—it could not be called a breach—was made, and the order was given to the Fourth Punjâb Rifles to storm. They sprang out of cover, as I have already described, but before they were half-way across the intervening distance, their commanding officer fell mortally wounded, and I think two others of their European officers were severely wounded. This caused a slight halt of the Punjâbis. Sir Colin called to Colonel Ewart, "Ewart, bring on the tartan;" one of our buglers who was in attendance on Sir Colin, sounded the *advance*, and the whole of the Ninety-Third dashed from behind the bank. It has always been a disputed point who got through the hole first. I believe the first man in was Lance-Corporal Donnelly of the Ninety-Third, who was killed inside; then Subadar Gokul Sing, followed by Sergeant-Major Murray, of the Ninety-Third, also killed, and fourth, Captain Burroughs, severely wounded.

It was about this time I got through myself, pushed up by Colonel Ewart who immediately followed. My feet had scarcely touched the ground inside, when a sepoy fired point-blank at me from among the long grass a few yards distant. The bullet struck the thick brass clasp of my waist-belt, but with such force that it sent me spinning heels over head. The man who fired was cut down by Captain Cooper, of the Ninety-Third, who got through the hole abreast with myself. When struck I felt just as one feels when tripped up at a football match. Before I regained my feet, I heard Ewart say as he rushed past me, "Poor fellow, he is done for." I was but stunned, and regaining my feet and my breath too, which was completely knocked out of me, I rushed on to the inner court of the building, where I saw Ewart bare-headed, his feather bonnet having been shot off his head, engaged in fierce hand-to-hand fight with several of the enemy. I believe he shot down five or six of them with his revolver. By that time the whole of the Ninety-Third and the Sikhs had got in either through the wall or by the principal gate which had now been forced open; the Fifty-Third, led by Lieutenant-Colonel Gordon of the Ninety-Third, and Captain B. Walton (who was severely wounded), had got in by a window in the right angle of the garden wall which they forced open. The inner court was rapidly filled with dead, but two officers of the mutineers were fiercely defending a regimental colour inside a dark room. Ewart rushed on them to seize it, and although severely wounded in his sword-arm, he not only captured the colour, but killed both the officers who were defending it.

By this time opposition had almost ceased. A few only of the defenders of the Secundrabâgh were left alive, and those few were being hunted out of dark corners, some of them from below heaps of slain. Colonel Ewart, seeing that the fighting was over, started with his colour to present it to Sir Colin Campbell; but whether it was that the old Chief considered that it was *infra dig.* for a field-officer to expose himself to needless danger, or whether it was that he was angry at some other thing, I know not, but this much I remember: Colonel Ewart ran up to him where he sat on his gray charger outside the gate of the Secundrabâgh, and called out: "We are in possession of the bungalows, sir. I have killed the last two of the enemy with my own hand, and here is one of their colours." "D—n your colours, sir!" said Sir Colin. "It's not your place to be taking colours: go back to your regiment this instant, sir!" However, the officers of the staff who were with Sir Colin gave a cheer for Colonel Ewart, and one of them presented him with a cap to cover his head, which was still bare. He turned back, apparently very much upset at the reception given to him by the old Chief; but I afterwards heard that Sir Colin sent for him in the afternoon, apologised for his rudeness, and thanked him for his services. Before I conclude, I may remark that I have often thought over this incident, and the more I think of it, the more I am convinced that, from the wild and excited appearance of Colonel Ewart, who had been by that time more than an hour without his hat in the fierce rays of the sun, covered with blood and powder smoke, and his eyes still flashing with the excitement of the fight, giving him the appearance of a man under the influence of something more potent than "blue ribbon" tipple—I feel pretty sure, I say, that, when Sir Colin first saw him, he thought he was drunk. When he found out his mistake he was of course sorry for his rudeness.

After the capture of the Shâh Nujeef, a field officer was required to hold the barracks, which was one of the most important posts on our left advance, and although severely wounded, having several sabre-cuts and many bruises on his body, Colonel Ewart volunteered for the post of commandant of the force. This post he held until the night of the evacuation of the Residency and the retreat from Lucknow, for the purpose of relieving Cawnpore for the second time from the grasp of the Nânâ Sâhib and the Gwalior Contingent. It was at the retaking of Cawnpore that Colonel Ewart eventually had his arm carried off by a cannon-shot; and the last time I saw him was when I assisted to lift him into a *dooly* on the plain of Cawnpore on the 1st of December, 1857. But I must leave the retaking of Cawnpore to its proper place in these reminiscences, and resume my narrative of the capture of the Secundrabâgh.

I mentioned previously that the muster-rolls had scarcely been called outside the gateway, when the enemy evidently became aware that the place was no longer held for them by living men, and a terrible fire was opened on us from both our right and left, as well as from the Shâh Nujeef in our direct front.

Let me here mention, before I take leave of the Secundrabâgh, that I have often been told that the hole in the wall by which the Ninety-Third entered is still in existence. This I had heard from several sources, and on Sunday morning, the 21st of August, 1892, when revisiting Lucknow, I left the Royal Hotel with a guide who did not know that I had ever seen Lucknow before, and who assured me that the breach had been preserved just as it was left on the 16th of November, 1857, after the Ninety-Third had passed through it; and I had made up my mind to re-enter the Secundrabâgh once again by the same old hole. On reaching the gate I therefore made the *gharry* stop, and walked round the outside of the wall to the hole; but as soon as I arrived at the spot I saw that the gap pointed out to me as the one by which the Ninety-Third entered was a fraud, and I astonished the guide by refusing to pass through it. The hole now shown as the one by which we entered was made through the wall by an 18-pounder gun, which was brought from Cawnpore by Captain Blount's troop of Royal Horse-Artillery. This was about twenty yards to the left of the real hole, and was made to enable a few men to keep up a cross fire through it till the stormers could get footing inside the actual breach. This post was held by Sergeant James Morrison and several sharp-shooters from my company, who, by direction of Sir Colin, made a rush on this hole before the order was given for the Fourth Punjâb Infantry to storm. Any military man of the least experience seeing the hole and its size now, thirty-five years after the event, will know this to be a fact. The real breach was much bigger and could admit three men abreast, and, as near as I can judge, was about the centre of the road which now passes through the Secundrabâgh. The guide, I may say, admitted such to be the case when he found that I had seen the Secundrabâgh before his time. Although it was only a hole, and not what is correctly called a breach, in the wall, it was so wide, and the surrounding parts of the wall had been so shaken by round-shot, that the upper portion forming the arch must have fallen down within a few years after 1857, and this evidently formed a convenient breach in the wall through which the present road has been constructed.[1] The smaller hole meanwhile has been laid hold of by the guides as the identical passage by which the Secundrabâgh was stormed.

Having corrected the guide on this point, I will now give my recollections of the assault on the Shâh Nujeef, and the Kuddum Russool which stands on its right, advancing from the Secundrabâgh.

The Kuddum Russool was a strongly-built domed mosque not nearly so large as the Shâh Nujeef, but it had been surrounded by a strong wall and converted into a powder magazine by the English between the annexation of Lucknow and the outbreak of the Mutiny. I think this fact is mentioned by Mr.

[1] The author is quite right in this surmise; the road was made through the old breach in 1861.

Gubbins in his *Mutinies in Oude.* The Kuddum Russool was still used by the mutineers as a powder-magazine, but the powder had been conveyed from it into the tomb of the Shâh Nujeef, when the latter was converted into a post of defence to bar our advance on the Residency.

Before the order was given for the attack on the Shâh Nujeef, I may mention that the quartermaster-general's department had made an estimate of the number of the enemy slain in the Secundrabâgh from their appearance and from their parade-states of that morning. The mutineers, let me say, had still kept up their English discipline and parade-forms, and their parade-states and muster-rolls of the 16th of November were discovered among other documents in a room of the Secundrabâgh which had been their general's quarters and orderly-room. It was then found that four separate regiments had occupied the Secundrabâgh, numbering about two thousand five hundred men, and these had been augmented by a number of *budmâshes* from the city, bringing up the list of actual slain in the house and garden to about three thousand. Of these, over two thousand lay dead inside the rooms of the main building and the inner court. The colours, drums, etc., of the Seventy-First Native Infantry and the Eleventh Oude Irregular Infantry were captured. The mutineers fought under their English colours, and there were several Mahommedan standards of green silk captured besides the English colours. The Seventy-First Native Infantry was one of the crack corps of the

Company's army, and many of the men were wearing the Punjâb medals on their breasts. This regiment and the Eleventh Oude Irregulars were simply annihilated. On examining the bodies of the dead, over fifty men of the Seventy-First were found to have furloughs, or leave-certificates, signed by their former commanding officer in their pockets, showing that they had been on leave when their regiment mutinied and had rejoined their colours to fight against us. It is a curious fact that after the Mutiny was suppressed, many sepoys tendered these leave-certificates as proof that they had *not* taken part in the rebellion; and I believe all such got enrolled either in the police or in the new regiments that were being raised, and obtained their back pay. And doubtless if the Ninety-Third and Fifty-Third bayonets had not cancelled those of the Seventy First Native Infantry all those *loyal* men would afterwards have presented their leave-certificates, and have claimed pay for the time they were fighting against us!

When the number of the slain was reported to Sir Colin, he turned to Brigadier Hope, and said: "This morning's work will strike terror into the sepoys,—it will strike terror into them," and he repeated it several times. Then turning to us again he said: "Ninety-Third, you have bravely done your share of this morning's work, and Cawnpore is avenged! There is more hard work to be done; but unless as a last resource, I will not call on you to storm more positions to-day. Your duty will be to cover the guns after they are dragged into position. But, my boys, if need be, remember I depend on you to carry the next position in the same daring manner in which you carried the Secundrabâgh." With that some one from the ranks called out, "Will we get a medal for this, Sir Colin?" To which he replied: "Well, my lads, I can't say what Her Majesty's Government may do; but if you don't get a medal, all I can say is you have deserved one better than any troops I have ever seen under fire. I shall inform the Governor-General, and, through him, Her Majesty the Queen, that I have never seen troops behave better." The order was then given to man the drag-ropes of Peel's guns for the advance on the Shâh Nujeef, and obeyed with a cheer; and, as it turned out, the Ninety-Third had to storm that position also.

The advance on the Shâh Nujeef has been so often described that I will cut my recollections of it short. At the word of command Captain Middleton's battery of Royal Artillery dashed forward with loud cheers, the drivers waving their whips and the gunners their caps as they passed us and Peel's guns at the gallop. The 24-pounder guns meanwhile were dragged along by our men and the sailors in the teeth of a perfect hail of lead and iron from the enemy's batteries. In the middle of the march a poor sailor lad, just in front of me, had his leg carried clean off above the knee by a round-shot, and, although knocked head over heels by the force of the shot, he sat bolt upright on the grass, with the blood spouting from the stump of his limb like water from the hose of a fire-engine, and shouted, "Here goes a shilling a day, a shilling a day! Pitch into them, boys, pitch into them! Remember Cawnpore, Ninety-Third, remember Cawnpore! Go at them, my hearties!" and he fell back in a dead faint, and on we went. I afterwards heard that the poor fellow was dead before a doctor could reach the spot to bind up his limb.

I will conclude this chapter with an extract from Sir Colin's despatch on the advance on the Shâh Nujeef:

> The Ninety-Third and Captain Peel's guns rolled on in one irresistible wave, the men falling fast, but the column advanced till the heavy guns were within twenty yards of the walls of the Shâh Nujeef, where they were unlimbered and poured in round after round against the massive walls of the building, the withering fire of the Highlanders covering the Naval Brigade from great loss. But it was an action almost unexampled in war. Captain Peel behaved very much as if he had been laying the *Shannon* alongside an enemy's frigate.

But in this despatch Sir Colin does not mention that he was himself wounded by a bullet after it had passed through the head of a Ninety-Third grenadier.

CHAPTER V

PERSONAL ANECDOTES—CAPTURE OF THE SHÂH NUJEEF —A FEARFUL EXPERIENCE

I MUST now leave for a little the general struggle, and turn to the actions of individual men as they fell under my own observation,—actions which neither appear in despatches nor in history; and, by the way, I may remark that one of the best accounts extant of the taking of the Shâh Nujeef is that of Colonel Alison, in *Blackwood's Magazine* for October, 1858. Both the Alisons were severely wounded on that occasion,—Colonel Archibald Alison, Military Secretary, and his brother, Captain F. M. Alison, A.D.C. to Sir Colin Campbell. I will now relate a service rendered by Sergeant M. W. Findlay, of my company, which was never noticed nor rewarded. Sergeant Findlay, let me state, merely considered that he had done his duty, but that is no reason why I should not mention his name. I believe he is still in India, and a distinguished officer of the Râjpootâna-Mâlwa Railway Volunteers at Ajmere. However, after Captain Peel's guns were dragged into position, the Ninety-Third took up whatever shelter they could get on the right and left of the guns, and I, with several others, got behind the walls of an unroofed mud hut, through which we made loop-holes on the side next to the Shâh Nujeef, and were thus able to keep up a destructive fire on the enemy. Let me add here that the surgeons of the force were overwhelmed with work, and attending to the wounded in the thick of the fire. Some time after the attack had commenced we noticed Captain Alison and his horse in a heap together a few yards behind where we were in shelter. Sergeant Findlay rushed out, got the wounded officer clear of his dead horse under a perfect hail of bullets and round-shot, and carried him under the shelter of the walls where we were lying. He then ran off in search of a surgeon to bandage his wounds, which were bleeding very profusely; but the surgeons were all too busy, and Sir Colin was most strict on the point of wounds being attended to. Officers, no matter what their rank, had no precedence over the rank-and-file in this respect; in fact, Sir Colin often expressed the opinion that an officer could be far more easily replaced than a well-drilled private. However, there was no surgeon available; so Sergeant Findlay took his own bandage,—every soldier on going on active service is supplied with lint and a bandage to have them handy in case of wounds—set to work, stanched the bleeding, and bandaged up the wounds of Captain Alison in such a surgeon-like manner that, when Dr. Menzies of the Ninety-Third at length came to see him, he thought he had been attended to by a doctor. When he did discover that it was Sergeant

Findlay who had put on the bandages, he expressed his surprise, and said that in all probability this prompt action had saved Captain Alison's life, who otherwise might have been weakened by loss of blood beyond recovery before a doctor could have attended to him. Dr. Menzies there and then applied to Captain Dawson to get Sergeant Findlay into the field-hospital as an extra assistant to attend to the wounded. In closing this incident I may remark that I have known men get the Victoria Cross for incurring far less danger than Sergeant Findlay did in exposing himself to bring Captain Alison under shelter. The bullets were literally flying round him like hail; several passed through his clothes, and his feather bonnet was shot off his head. When he had finished putting on the bandages he coolly remarked: "I must go out and get my bonnet for fear I get sunstruck;" so out he went for his hat, and before he got back scores of bullets were fired at him from the walls of the Shâh Nujeef.

The next man I shall refer to was Sergeant Daniel White, one of the coolest and most fearless men in the regiment. Sergeant White was a man of superior education, an excellent vocalist and reciter, with a most retentive memory, and one of the best amateur actors in the Ninety-Third. Under fire he was just as cool and collected as if he had been enacting the part of Bailie Nicol Jarvie in *Rob Roy*.

In the force defending the Shâh Nujeef, in addition to the regular army, there was a large body of archers on the walls, armed with bows and arrows which they discharged with great force and precision, and on White raising his head above the wall an arrow was shot right into his feather bonnet. Inside of the wire cage of his bonnet, however, he had placed his forage cap, folded up, and instead of passing right through, the arrow stuck in the folds of the forage cap, and "Dan," as he was called, coolly pulled out the arrow, paraphrasing a quotation from Sir Walter Scott's *Legend of Montrose*, where Dugald Dalgetty and Ranald MacEagh made their escape from the castle of M'Callum More. Looking at the arrow, "My conscience!" said White, "bows and arrows! bows and arrows! Have we got Robin Hood and Little John back again? Bows and arrows! My conscience, the sight has not been seen in civilised war for nearly two hundred years. Bows and arrows! And why not weavers' beams as in the days of Goliath? Ah! that Daniel White should be able to tell in the Saut Market of Glasgow that he had seen men fight with bows and arrows in the days of Enfield rifles! Well, well, Jack Pandy, since bows and arrows are the words, here's at you!" and with that he raised his feather bonnet on the point of his bayonet above the top of the wall, and immediately another arrow pierced it through, while a dozen more whizzed past a little wide of the mark.

Just then one poor fellow of the Ninety-Third, named Penny, of No. 2 company, raising his head for an instant a little above the wall, got an arrow right through his brain, the shaft projecting more than a foot out at the back of his head. As the poor lad fell dead at our feet, Sergeant White remarked, "Boys, this is no joke; we must pay them off." We all loaded and capped, and pushing up our feather bonnets again, a whole shower of arrows went past or through them. Up we sprang and returned a well-aimed volley from our rifles at point-blank distance, and more than half-a-dozen of the enemy went down. But one unfortunate man of the regiment, named Montgomery, of No. 6 company, exposed himself a little too long to watch the effect of our volley, and before he could get down into shelter again an arrow was sent right through his heart, passing clean through his body and falling on the ground a few yards behind him. He leaped about six feet straight up in the air, and fell stone dead. White could not resist making another quotation, but this time it was from the old English ballad of *Chevy Chase*.

> He had a bow bent in his hand
> Made of a trusty tree,
> An arrow of a cloth-yard long
> Up to the head drew he.
>
> Against Sir Hugh Montgomerie
> So right his shaft he set,
> The grey goose wing that was thereon
> In his heart's blood was wet.

Readers who have never been under the excitement of a fight like this which I describe, may think that such coolness is an exaggeration. It is not so. Remember the men of whom I write had stood in the "Thin Red Line" of Balaclava without wavering, and had made up their minds to die where they stood, if need be; men who had been for days and nights under shot and shell in the trenches of Sebastopol. If familiarity breeds contempt, continual exposure to danger breeds coolness, and, I may say, selfishness too; where all are exposed to equal danger little sympathy is, for the time being at least, displayed for the unlucky ones "knocked on the head," to use the common expression in the ranks for those who are killed. Besides, Sergeant Daniel White was an exceptionally cool man, and looked on every incident with the eye of an actor.

By this time the sun was getting low, a heavy cloud of smoke hung over the field, and every flash of the guns and rifles could be clearly seen. The enemy in hundreds were visible on the ramparts, yelling like demons, brandishing their swords in one hand and burning torches in the other, shouting at us to "Come on!" But little impression had been made on the solid masonry walls. Brigadier Hope and his aide-de-camp were rolling on the ground together, the horses of both shot dead; and the same shell which had done this mischief exploded one of our ammunition waggons, killing and wounding several men. Altogether the position looked black and critical when Major Barnston and his battalion of detachments were ordered to storm. This battalion of detachments was a body made up of almost every corps in the service,—at least as far as the regiments forming the expedition to China were concerned—and men belonging to the different corps which had entered the Residency with Generals Havelock and Outram. It also comprised some men who had been left (through sickness or wounds) at Allahabad and Cawnpore, and some of the Ninetieth Regiment which had been intercepted at Singapore on their way to China, under Captain (now General Lord) Wolseley. However, although a made-up battalion, they advanced bravely to the breach, and I think their leader, Major Barnston, was killed, and the command devolved on Captain Wolseley. He made a most determined attempt to get into the place, but there were no scaling-ladders, and the wall was still almost twenty feet high. During the heavy cannonade the masonry had fallen down in flakes on the outside, but still leaving an inner wall standing almost perpendicular, and in attempting to climb up this the men were raked with a perfect hail of missiles—grenades and round-shot hurled from wall-pieces, arrows and brickbats, burning torches of rags and cotton saturated with oil—even boiling water was dashed on them! In the midst of the smoke the breach would have made a very good representation of Pandemonium. There were scores of men armed with great burning torches just like what one may see in the sham fights of the *Mohurrum*, only these men were in earnest, shouting "*Allah Akbar!*" "*Deen! Deen!*" and "*Jai Kâli mâ ki!*" [1]

The stormers were driven back, leaving many dead and wounded under the wall. At this juncture Sir Colin called on Brigadier Hope to form up the

[1] "God is great!" "Religion! Religion!" "Victory to Mother Kâli!" The first two are Mussulman war-cries; the last is Hindoo.

Ninety-Third for a final attempt. Sir Colin, again addressing us, said that he had not intended to call on us to storm more positions that day, but that the building in our front must be carried before dark, and the Ninety-Third must do it, and he would lead us himself, saying again: "Remember, men, the lives at stake inside the Residency are those of women and children, and they must be rescued." A reply burst from the ranks: "Ay, ay, Sir Colin! we stood by you at Balaklava, and will stand by you here; but you must not expose yourself so much as you are doing. We can be replaced, but you can't. You must remain behind; we can lead ourselves."

By that time the battalion of detachments had cleared the front, and the enemy were still yelling to us to "Come on," and piling up missiles to give us a warm reception. Captain Peel had meanwhile brought his infernal machine, known as a rocket battery, to the front, and sent a volley of rockets through the crowd on the ramparts around the breach. Just at that moment Sergeant John Paton of my company came running down the ravine that separated the Kuddum Russool from the Shâh Nujeef, completely out of breath through exertion, but just able to tell Brigadier Hope that he had gone up the ravine at the moment the battalion of detachments had been ordered to storm, and had discovered a breach in the north-east corner of the rampart next to the river Goomtee. It appears that our shot and shell had gone over the first breach, and had blown out the wall on the other side in this particular spot. Paton told how he had climbed up to the top of the ramparts without difficulty, and seen right inside the place as the whole defending force had been called forward to repulse the assault in front.

Captain Dawson and his company were at once called out, and while the others opened fire on the breach in front of them, we dashed down the ravine, Sergeant Paton showing the way. As soon as the enemy saw that the breach behind had been discovered, and that their well-defended position was no longer tenable, they fled like sheep through the back gate next to the Goomtee and another in the direction of the Motee Munzil.[1] If No. 7 company had got in behind them and cut off their retreat by the back gate, it would have been Secundrabâgh over again! As it was, by the time we got over the breach we were able to catch only about a score of the fugitives, who were promptly bayoneted; the rest fled pell-mell into the Goomtee, and it was then too dark to see to use the rifle with effect on the flying masses. However, by the great pools of blood inside, and the number of dead floating in the river, they had plainly suffered heavily, and the well-contested position of the Shâh Nujeef was ours.

By this time Sir Colin and those of his staff remaining alive or unwounded were inside the position, and the front gate thrown open. A hearty cheer was given for the Commander-in-Chief, as he called the officers round him to give instructions for the disposition of

[1] The Pearl Mosque.

the force for the night. As it was Captain Dawson and his company who had scaled the breach, to them was assigned the honour of holding the Shâh Nujeef, which was now one of the principal positions to protect the retreat from the Residency. And thus ended the terrible 16th of November, 1857.

In the taking of the Secundrabâgh all the subaltern officers of my company were wounded, namely, Lieutenants E. Welch and S. E. Wood, and Ensign F. R. M'Namara. The only officer therefore with the company in the Shâh Nujeef was Captain Dawson. Sergeant Findlay, as already mentioned, had been taken over as hospital-assistant, and another sergeant named Wood was either sick or wounded, I forget which, and Corporals M'Kenzie and Mitchell (a namesake of mine, belonging to Balmoral) were killed. It thus fell to my lot as the non-commissioned officer on duty to go round with Captain Dawson to post the sentries. Mr. Kavanagh, who was officiating as a volunteer staff-officer, accompanied us to point out the direction of the strongest positions of the enemy, and the likely points from which any attempts would be made to recapture our position during the night. During the absence of the captain the command of the company devolved on Colour-Sergeant David Morton, of "Tobacco Soup" fame, and he was instructed to see that none of the enemy were still lurking in the rooms surrounding the mosque of the Shâh Nujeef, while the captain was going round the ramparts placing the sentries for the protection of our position.

As soon as the sentries were posted on the ramparts and regular reliefs told off, arrangements were made among the sergeants and corporals to patrol at regular intervals from sentry to sentry to see that all were alert. This was the more necessary as the men were completely worn out and fatigued by long marches and heavy fighting, and in fact had not once had their belts off for a week previous, while all the time carrying double ammunition on half-empty stomachs. Every precaution had therefore to be taken that the sentries should not go to sleep, and it fell to me as the corporal on duty to patrol the first two hours of the night, from eight o'clock till ten. The remainder of the company bivouacked around the piled arms, which were arranged carefully loaded and capped with bayonets fixed, ready for instant action should an attack be made on our position. After the great heat of the day the nights by contrast felt bitterly cold. There was a stack of dry wood in the centre of the grounds from which the men kindled a large fire near the piled arms, and arranged themselves around it, rolled in their great-coats but fully accoutred, ready to stand to arms at the least alarm.

In writing these reminiscences it is far from my wish to make them an autobiography. My intention is rather to relate the actions of others than recount what I did myself; but an adventure happened to me in the Shâh Nujeef which gave me such a nervous fright that to this day I often dream of it. I have forgotten to state that when the force advanced from the Alumbâgh each man carried his greatcoat rolled into what was then known in our regiment as the "Crimean roll," with ends strapped together across the right shoulder just over the ammunition pouch-belt, so that it did not interfere with the free use of the rifle, but rather formed a protection across the chest. As it turned out many men owed their lives to the fact that bullets became spent in passing through the rolled greatcoats before reaching a vital part. Now it happened that in the heat of the fight in the Secundrabâgh my greatcoat was cut right through where the two ends were fastened together, by the stroke of a keen-edged *tulwâr* which was intended to cut me across the shoulder, and as it was very warm at the time from the heat of the mid-day sun combined with the excitement of the fight, I was rather glad than otherwise to be rid of the greatcoat; and when the fight was over, it did not occur to me to appropriate another one in its place from one of my dead comrades. But by ten o'clock at night there was a considerable difference in the temperature from ten in the morning, and when it came to my turn to be relieved from patrol duty and to lie down for a sleep, I felt the cold wet grass anything but comfortable, and missed my greatcoat to wrap round my knees; for the kilt is not the most suitable dress imaginable for a bivouac, without greatcoat or plaid, on a cold, dewy November night in Upper India; with a raw north wind the climate of Lucknow feels uncommonly cold at night in November, especially when contrasted with the heat of the day. I have already mentioned that the sun had set before we entered the Shâh Nujeef, the surrounding enclosure of which contained a number of small rooms round the inside of the walls, arranged after the manner of the ordinary Indian native travellers' *serais.* The Shâh Nujeef, it must be remembered, was the tomb of Ghâzee-ood-deen Hyder, the first king of Oude, and consequently a place of Mahommedan pilgrimage, and the small rooms round the four walls of the square were for the accommodation of pilgrims. These rooms had been turned into quarters by the enemy, and, in their hurry to escape, many of them had left their lamps burning, consisting of the ordinary *chirâgs*[1] placed in small niches in the walls, leaving also their evening meal of *chupâties* in small piles ready cooked, and the curry and *dhâl*[2] boiling on the fires. Many of the lamps were still burning when my turn of duty was over, and as I felt the want of a greatcoat badly, I asked the colour-sergeant of the company (the captain being fast asleep) for permission to go out of the gate to where our dead were collected near the Secundrabâgh to get another one. This Colour-Sergeant Morton refused, stating that before going to sleep the captain had given strict orders that except those on sentry no man was to leave his post on any pretence whatever. I had therefore to try to make the best of my position, but although dead tired and wearied out I felt too uncomfortable to go to sleep,

[1] Little clay saucers of oil, with a loosely twisted cotton wick.

[2] Small pulse.

and getting up it struck me that some of the sepoys in their hurried departure might have left their great-coats or blankets behind them. With this hope I went into one of the rooms where a lamp was burning, took it off its shelf, and shading the flame with my hand walked to the door of the great domed tomb, or mosque, which was only about twenty or thirty yards from where the arms were piled and the men lying round the still burning fire. I peered into the dark vault, not knowing that it was a king's tomb, but could see nothing, so I advanced slowly, holding the *chirâg* high over my head and looking cautiously around for fear of surprise from a concealed enemy, till I was near the centre of the great vault, where my progress was obstructed by a big black heap about four or five feet high, which felt to my feet as if I were walking among loose sand. I lowered the lamp to see what it was, and immediately discovered that I was standing up to the ankles in *loose gunpowder!* About forty cwt. of it lay in a great heap in front of my nose, while a glance to my left showed me a range of twenty to thirty barrels also full of powder, and on the right over a hundred 8-inch shells, all loaded with the fuses fixed, while spare fuses and slow matches and port-fires in profusion lay heaped beside the shells.

By this time my eyes had become accustomed to the darkness of the mosque, and I took in my position and my danger at a glance. Here I was up to my knees in powder,—in the very bowels of a magazine with a naked light! My hair literally stood on end; I felt the skin of my head lifting my feather bonnet off my scalp; my knees knocked together, and despite the chilly night air the cold perspiration burst out all over me and ran down my face and legs. I had neither cloth nor handkerchief in my pocket, and there was not a moment to be lost, as already the overhanging wick of the *chirág* was threatening to shed its smouldering red tip into the live magazine at my feet with consequences too frightful to contemplate. Quick as thought I put my left hand under the down-dropping flame, and clasped it with a grasp of determination; holding it firmly I slowly turned to the door, and walked out with my knees knocking one against the other! Fear had so overcome all other feeling that I am confident I never felt the least pain from grasping the burning wick till after I was outside the building and once again in the open air; but when I opened my hand I felt the smart acutely enough. I poured the oil out of the lamp into the burnt hand, and kneeling down thanked God for having saved myself and all the men lying around me from horrible destruction. I then got up and, staggering rather than walking to the place where Captain Dawson was sleeping, and shaking him by the shoulder till he awoke, I told him of my discovery and the fright I had got.

At first he either did not believe me, or did not comprehend the danger. "Bah! Corporal Mitchell," was all his answer, "you have woke up out of your sleep, and have got frightened at a shadow," for my heart was still thumping against my ribs worse than it was when I first discovered my danger, and my voice was trembling. I turned my smarting hand to the light of the fire and showed the captain how it was scorched; and then, feeling my pride hurt at being told I had got frightened at a shadow, I said: "Sir, you're not a Highlander or you would know the Gaelic proverb '*The heart of one who can look death in the face will not start at a shadow*,' and you, sir, can yourself bear witness that I have not shirked to look death in the face more than once since daylight this morning." He replied, "Pardon me, I did not mean that; but calm yourself and explain what it is that has frightened you." I then told him that I had gone into the mosque with a naked lamp burning, and had found it half full of loose gunpowder piled in a great heap on the floor and a large number of loaded shells. "Are you sure you're not dreaming from the excitement of this terrible day?" said the captain. With that I looked down to my feet and my gaiters, which were still covered with blood from the slaughter in the Secundrabâgh; the wet grass had softened it again, and on this the powder was sticking nearly an inch thick. I scraped some of it off, throwing it into the fire, and said, "There is positive proof for you that I'm not dreaming, nor my vision a shadow!" On that the captain became almost as alarmed as I was, and a sentry was posted near the door of the mosque to prevent any one from entering it. The sleeping men were aroused, and the fire smothered out with as great care as possible, using for the purpose several earthen *ghurrahs*, or jars of water, which the enemy had left under the trees near where we were lying.

When all was over, Colour-Sergeant Morton coolly proposed to the captain to place me under arrest for having left the pile of arms after he, the colour-sergeant, had refused to give me leave. To this proposal Captain Dawson replied: "If any one deserves to be put under arrest it is you yourself, Sergeant Morton, for not having explored the mosque and discovered the gunpowder while Corporal Mitchell and I were posting the sentries; and if this neglect comes to the notice of either Colonel Hay or the Commander-in-Chief, both you and I are likely to hear more about it; so the less you say about the matter the better!" This ended the discussion and my adventure, and at the time I was glad to hear nothing more about it, but I have sometimes since thought that if the part I acted in this crisis had come to the knowledge of either Colonel Hay or Sir Colin Campbell, my burnt hand would have brought me something more than a proposal to place me under arrest, and take my corporal's stripes from me! Be that as it may, I got a fright that I have never forgotten, and, as already mentioned, even to this day I often dream of it, and wake up with a sudden start, the cold perspiration in great beads on my face, as I think I see again the huge black heap of powder in front of me.

After a sentry had been posted on the mosque and the fire put out, a glass lantern was discovered in one of the rooms, and Captain Dawson and I, with an escort of three or four men, made the circuit of the walls, searching every room. I remember one of the escort was James Wilson, the same man who wished to bayonet the Hindoo *jogie* in the village who afterwards shot poor Captain Mayne as told in my fourth chapter. As Wilson was peering into one of the rooms, a concealed sepoy struck him over the head with his *tulwâr*, but the feather bonnet saved his scalp as it had saved many more that day, and Captain Dawson being armed with a pair of double-barrelled pistols, put a bullet through the sepoy before he had time to make another cut at Wilson. In the same room I found a good cotton quilt which I promptly annexed to replace my lost greatcoat.

After all was quiet, the men rolled off to sleep again, and wrapping round my legs my newly-acquired quilt, which was lined with silk and had evidently belonged to a rebel officer, I too lay down and tried to sleep. My nerves were however too much shaken, and the pain of my burnt hand kept me awake, so I lay and listened to the men sleeping around me; and what a night that was! Had I the descriptive powers of a Tennyson or a Scott I might draw a picture of it, but as it is I can only very faintly attempt to make my readers imagine what it was like. The horrible scenes through which the men had passed during the day had told with terrible effect on their nervous systems, and the struggles,—eye to eye, foot to foot, and steel to steel—with death in the Secundrabâgh, were fought over again by most of the men in their sleep, oaths and shouts of defiance often curiously intermingled with prayers. One man would be lying calmly sleeping and commence muttering something inaudible, and then break out into a fierce battle-cry of "Cawnpore, you bloody murderer!"; another would shout "Charge! give them the bayonet!"; and a third, "Keep together, boys, don't fire; forward, forward; if we are to die, let us die like men!" Then I would hear one muttering, "Oh, mother, forgive me, and I'll never leave you again!"; while his comrade would half rise up, wave his hand, and call, "There they are! Fire low, give them the bayonet! Remember Cawnpore!" And so it was throughout that memorable night inside the Shâh Nujeef; and I have no doubt but it was the same with the men holding the other posts. The pain of my burnt hand and the terrible fright I had got kept me awake, and I lay and listened till nearly daybreak; but at length completely worn out, I, too, dosed off into a disturbed slumber, and I suppose I must have behaved in much the same way as those I had been listening to, for I dreamed of blood and battle, and then my mind would wander to scenes on Dee and Don side, and to the Braemar and Lonach gathering, and from that the scene would suddenly change, and I was a little boy again, kneeling beside my mother, saying my evening-hymn. Verily that night convinced me that Campbell's *Soldier's Dream* is no mere fiction, but must have been written or dictated from actual experience by one who had passed through such another day of excitement and danger as that of the 16th of November, 1857.

My dreams were rudely broken into by the crash of a round-shot through the top of the tree under which I was lying, and I jumped up repeating aloud the seventh verse of the ninety-first Psalm, Scotch version:

> A thousand at thy side shall fall,
> On thy right hand shall lie
> Ten thousand dead ; yet unto thee
> It shall not once come nigh.

Captain Dawson and the sergeants of the company had been astir long before, and a party of ordnance-lascars from the ammunition park and several warrant-officers of the Ordnance-Department were busy removing the gunpowder from the tomb of the Shâh Nujeef. Over sixty *maunds*[1] of loose powder were filled into bags and carted out, besides twenty barrels of the ordinary size of powder-barrels, and more than one hundred and fifty loaded 8-inch shells. The work of removal was scarcely completed before the enemy commenced firing shell and red-hot round-shot from their batteries in the Bâdshâhibâgh across the Goomtee, aimed straight for the door of the tomb facing the river, showing that they believed the powder was still there, and that they hoped they might manage to blow us all up.

[1] Nearly five thousand lbs.

CHAPTER VI

BREAKFAST UNDER DIFFICULTIES — LONG SHOTS — THE LITTLE DRUMMER—EVACUATION OF THE RESIDENCY BY THE GARRISON

By this time several of the old campaigners had kindled a fire in one of the small rooms, through the roof of which one of our shells had fallen the day before, making a convenient chimney for the egress of the smoke. They had found a large copper pot which had been left by the sepoys, and had it on the fire filled with a stew of about a score or more of pigeons which bad been left shut up in a dovecot in a corner of the compound. There were also plenty of pumpkins and other vegetables in the rooms, and piles of *chupâtis* which had been cooked by the sepoys for their evening meal before they fled. Everything in fact was there for making a good breakfast for hungry men except salt, and there was no salt to be found in any of the rooms; but as luck favoured us, I had one of the old-fashioned round cylinder-shaped wooden match-boxes full of salt in my haversack, which was more than sufficient to season the stew. I had carried this salt from Cawnpore, and I did so by the advice of an old veteran who had served in the Ninety-Second

Gordon Highlanders all through the Peninsular war, and finally at Waterloo. When as a boy I had often listened to his stories and told him that I would also enlist for a soldier, he had given me this piece of practical advice, which I in my turn present to every young soldier and volunteer. It is this: "Always carry a box of salt in your haversack when on active service; because the commissariat department is usually in the rear, and as a rule when an army is pressed for food the men have often the chance of getting hold of a bullock or a sheep, or of fowls, etc., but it is more difficult to find salt, and even good food without salt is very unpalatable." I remembered the advice, and it proved of great service to myself and comrades in many instances during the Mutiny. As it was, thanks to my foresight the hungry men in the Shâh Nujeef made a good breakfast on the morning of the 17th of November, 1857. I may here say that my experience is that the soldiers who could best look after their stomachs were also those who could make the best use of the bayonet, and who were the least likely to fall behind in a forced march. If I had the command of an army in the field my rule would be: "Cut the grog, and give double grub when hard work has to be done!"

After making a good breakfast the men were told off in sections, and we discharged our rifles at the enemy across the Goomtee,[1] and then spunged them

[1] It may be necessary to remind civilians that the rifles of 1857 were muzzle-loading.

out, which they sorely needed, because they had not been cleaned from the day we advanced from the Alumbâgh. Our rifles had in fact got so foul with four days' heavy work that it was almost impossible to load them, and the recoil had become so great that the shoulders of many of the men were perfectly black with bruises. As soon as our rifles were cleaned, a number of the best shots in the company were selected to try and silence the fire from the battery in the Bâdshâhibâgh across the river, which was annoying us by endeavouring to pitch hot shot and shell into the tomb, and to shorten the distance they had brought their guns outside the gate on to the open ground. They evidently as yet did not understand the range of the Enfield rifle, as they now came within about a thousand to twelve hundred yards of the wall of the Shâh Nujeef next the river. Some twenty of the best shots in the company, with carefully cleaned and loaded rifles, watched till they saw a good number of the enemy near their guns, then, raising sights to the full height and carefully aiming high, they fired a volley by word of command slowly given—*one, two, fire!* and about half a dozen of the enemy were knocked over. They at once withdrew their guns inside the Bâdshâhibâgh and shut the gate, and did not molest us any more.

During the early part of the forenoon we had several men struck by rifle bullets fired from one of the minarets in the Motee Mahal, which was said to be occupied by one of the ex-King of Oude's eunuchs who was a first-rate marksman, and armed with an excellent rifle; from his elevated position in the minaret he could see right into the square of the Shâh Nujeef. We soon had several men wounded, and as there was no surgeon with us Captain Dawson sent me back to where the field-hospital was formed near the Secundrabâgh, to ask Dr. Munro if an assistant-surgeon could be spared for our post. But Dr. Munro told me to tell Captain Dawson that it was impossible to spare an assistant-surgeon or even an apothecary, because he had just been informed that the Mess-House and Motee Mahal were to be assaulted at two o'clock, and every medical officer would be required on the spot; but he would try and send a hospital-attendant with a supply of lint and bandages. By the time I got back the assault on the Mess-House had begun, and Sergeant Findlay, before mentioned, was sent with a *dooly* and a supply of bandages, lint, and dressing, to do the best he could for any of ours who might be wounded.

About half an hour after the assault on the Mess-House had commenced a large body of the enemy, numbering at least six or seven hundred men, whose retreat had evidently been cut off from the city, crossed from the Mess-House into the Motee Mahal in our front, and forming up under cover of some huts between the Shâh Munzil and Motee Mahal, they evidently made up their minds to try and retake the Shâh Nujeef. They debouched on the plain with a number of men in front carrying scaling-ladders, and Captain Dawson being on the alert ordered all the men to kneel down behind the loopholes with rifles sighted for five hundred yards, and wait for the word of command. It was now our turn to know what it felt like to be behind loopholed walls, and we calmly awaited the enemy, watching them forming up for a dash on our position. The silence was profound, when Sergeant Daniel White repeated aloud a passage from the third canto of Scott's *Bridal of Triermain:*

> Bewcastle now must keep the Hold,
>   Speir-Adam's steeds must bide in stall,
> Of Hartley-burn the bowmen bold
>   Must only shoot from battled wall;
> And Liddesdale may buckle spur,
>   And Teviot now may belt the brand,
> Taras and Ewes keep nightly stir,
>   And Eskdale foray Cumberland.
> Of wasted fields and plunder'd flocks
>   The Borderers bootless may complain;
> They lack the sword of brave De Vaux,
>   There comes no aid from Triermain.

Captain Dawson, who had been steadily watching the advance of the enemy and carefully calculating their distance, just then called "Attention, five hundred yards, ready—*one, two, fire!*" when over eighty rifles rang out, and almost as many of the enemy went down like ninepins on the plain! Their leader was in front, mounted on a finely-accoutred charger, and he and his horse were evidently both hit; he at once wheeled round and made for the Goomtee, but horse and man both fell before they got near the river. After the first volley every man loaded and fired independently, and the plain was soon strewn with dead and wounded.

The unfortunate assaulters were now between two fires, for the force that had attacked the Shâh Munzil and Motee Mahal commenced to send grape and canister into their rear, so the routed rebels threw away their arms and scaling-ladders, and all that were able to do so bolted pell-mell for the Goomtee. Only about a quarter of the original number, however, reached the opposite bank, for when they were in the river our men rushed to the corner nearest to them and kept peppering at every head above water. One tall fellow, I well remember, acted as cunningly as a jackal; whether struck or not he fell just as he got into shallow water on the opposite side, and lay without moving, with his legs in the water and his head on the land. He appeared to be stone dead, and every rifle was turned on those that were running across the plain for the gate of the Bâdshâhibâgh, while many others who were evidently severely wounded were fired on as our fellows said, "*in mercy to put them out of pain.*" I have previously remarked that the war of the Mutiny was a horrible, I may say a demoralising, war for civilised men to be engaged in. The inhuman murders and foul treachery of the Nânâ Sâhib and others put all feeling of humanity or mercy for the enemy out of the question, and our men thus early spoke of putting a wounded Jack Pandy *out of pain,* just as calmly as if he had been a wild beast; it was even considered an act of mercy. It is now horrible to recall it all, but what I state is true. The only excuse is that *we* did not begin this war of extermination; and no apologist for the mutineers can say that they were actuated by patriotism to throw off the yoke of the oppressor. The cold-blooded cruelty of the mutineers and their leaders from first to last branded them in fact as traitors to humanity and cowardly assassins of helpless women and children. But to return to the Pandy whom I left lying half-covered with water on the further bank of the Goomtee opposite the Shâh Nujeef. This particular man was ever after spoken of as the "jackal," because jackals and foxes have often been known to sham dead and wait for a chance of escape; and so it was with Jack Pandy. After he had lain apparently dead for about an hour, some one noticed that he had gradually dragged himself out of the water; till all at once he sprang to his feet, and ran like a deer in the direction of the gate of the Bâdshâhibâgh. He was still quite within easy range, and several rifles were levelled at him; but Sergeant Findlay, who was on the rampart, and was himself one of the best shots in the company, called out, "Don't fire, men; give the poor devil a chance!" Instead of a volley of bullets, the men's better feelings gained the day, and Jack Pandy was reprieved, with a cheer to speed him on his way. As soon as he heard it he realised his position, and like the Samaritan leper of old, he halted, turned round, and putting up both his hands with the palms together in front of his face, he salaamed profoundly, prostrating himself three times on the ground by way of thanks, and then *walked* slowly towards the Bâdshâhibâgh, while we on the ramparts waved our feather bonnets and clapped our hands to him in token of goodwill. I have often wondered if that particular Pandy ever after fought the English, or if he returned to his village to relate his exceptional experience of our clemency.

Just at this time we noticed a great commotion in front, and heard our fellows and even those in the Residency cheering like mad. The cause we shortly after learned; that the generals, Sir Colin Campbell, Havelock, and Outram had met. The Residency was relieved and the women and children were saved, although not yet out of danger, and every man in the force slept with a lighter heart that night. If the cost was heavy, the gain was great.

I may here mention that there is an entry in my note-book, dated 18th of November 1857: "That Lieutenant Fred. Roberts planted the Union Jack three times on the top of the Mess-House as a signal to the force in the Residency that the Mess-House was in our possession, and it was as often shot down." Some time ago there was, I remember, a dispute about who was entitled to the credit of this action. Now I did not see it myself, but I must have got the information from some of the men of the other companies who witnessed the deed, as it was known that I was keeping a rough diary of the leading events.

Such was the glorious issue of the 17th of November. The meeting of the Generals, Sir Colin Campbell, Outram, and Havelock, proved that Lucknow was relieved and the women and children were safe; but to accomplish this object our small force had lost no less than forty-five officers and four hundred and ninety-six men—more than a tenth of our whole number! The brunt of the loss fell on the Artillery and Naval Brigade, and on the Fifty-Third, the Ninety-Third, and the Fourth Punjâb Infantry. These losses were respectively as follows:

Artillery and Naval Brigade . .	105	Men
Fifty-Third Regiment . .	76	„
Ninety-Third Highlanders . .	108	„
Fourth Punjâb Infantry . . .	95	„
Total . .	384	

leaving one hundred and twelve to be divided among the other corps engaged.

In writing mostly from memory thirty-five years after the events described, many incidents, though not entirely forgotten, escape being noticed in their proper sequence, and that is the case with the following, which I must here relate before I enter on the evacuation of the Residency.

Immediately after the powder left by the enemy had been removed from the tomb of the Shâh Nujeef, and the sun had dispelled the fog which rested over the Goomtee and the city, it was deemed necessary to signal to the Residency to let them know our position, and for this purpose our adjutant, Lieutenant William M'Bean, Sergeant Hutchinson, and Drummer Ross, a boy of about twelve years of age but even small for his years, climbed to the top of the dome of the Shâh Nujeef by means of a rude rope-ladder which was fixed on it; thence with the regimental colour of the Ninety-Third and a feather bonnet on the tip of the staff they signalled to the Residency, and the little drummer sounded the regimental call on his bugle from the top of the dome. The signal was seen, and answered from the Residency by lowering their flag three times. But the enemy on the Bâdshâhibâgh also saw the signalling and the daring adventurers on the dome, and turned their guns on them, sending several round-shots quite close to them. Their object being gained, however, our men descended; but little Ross ran up the ladder again like a monkey, and holding on to the spire of the dome with his left hand he waved his feather bonnet and then sounded the regimental call a second time, which he followed by the call known as *The Cock of the North*, which he sounded as a blast of defiance to the enemy. When peremptorily ordered to come down by Lieutenant M'Bean, he did so, but not before the little monkey had tootled out—

> There's not a man beneath the moon,
> Nor lives in any land he,
> That hasn't heard the pleasant tune
> Of Yankee Doodle Dandy!
>
> In cooling drinks and clipper ships,
> The Yankee has the way shown,
> On land and sea 'tis he that whips
> Old Bull, and all creation.

When little Ross reached the parapet at the foot of the dome, he turned to Lieutenant M'Bean and said: "Ye ken, sir, I was born when the regiment was in Canada when my mother was on a visit to an aunt in the States, and I could not come down till I had sung *Yankee Doodle*, to make my American cousins envious when they hear of the deeds of the Ninety-Third. Won't the Yankees feel jealous when they hear that the littlest drummer-boy in the regiment sang *Yankee Doodle* under a hail of fire on the dome of the highest mosque in Lucknow!"

As mentioned in the last chapter, the Residency was relieved on the afternoon of the 17th of November, and the following day preparations were made for the evacuation of the position and the withdrawal of the women and children. To do this in safety however was no easy task, for the mutineers and rebels showed but small regard for the laws of chivalry; a man might pass an exposed position in comparative safety, but if a helpless woman or little child were seen, they were made the target for a hundred bullets. So far as we could see from the Shâh Nujeef, the line of retreat was pretty well sheltered till the refugees emerged from the Motee Mahal; but between that and the Shâh Nujeef there was a long stretch of plain, exposed to the fire of the enemy's artillery and sharp-shooters from the opposite side of the Goomtee. To protect this part of their route a flying sap was constructed: a battery of artillery and some of Peel's guns, with a covering force of infantry, were posted in the north-east corner of the Motee Mahal; and all the best shots in the Shâh Nujeef were placed on the north-west corner of the ramparts next to the Goomtee. These men were under command of Sergeant Findlay, who, although nominally our medical officer, stuck to his post on the ramparts, and being one of the best shots in the company was entrusted with the command of the sharp-shooters for the protection of the retreating women and children. From these two points,—the north-east corner of the Motee Mahal and the north-west of the Shâh Nujeef—the enemy on the north bank of the Goomtee were brought under a cross-fire, the accuracy of which made them keep a very respectful distance from the river, with the result that the women and children passed the exposed part of their route without a single casualty. I remember one remarkably good shot made by Sergeant Findlay. He unhorsed a rebel officer close to the east gate of the Bâdshâhibâgh, who came out with a force of infantry and a couple of guns to open fire on the line of retreat; but he was no sooner knocked over than the enemy retreated into the *bâgh*, and did not show themselves any more that day.

By midnight of the 22nd of November the Residency was entirely evacuated, and the enemy completely deceived as to the movements; and about two o'clock on the morning of the 23rd we withdrew from the Shâh Nujeef and became the rear-guard of the retreating column, making our way slowly past the Secundrabâgh, the stench from which, as can easily be imagined, was something frightful. I have seen it stated in print that the two thousand odd of the enemy killed in the

Secundrabâgh were dragged out and buried in deep trenches outside the enclosure. This is not correct. The European slain were removed and buried in a deep trench, where the mound is still visible, to the east of the gate, and the Punjâbees recovered their slain and cremated them near the bank of the Goomtee. But the rebel dead had to be left to rot where they lay, a prey to the vulture by day and the jackal by night, for from the smallness of the relieving force no other course was possible; in fact, it was with the greatest difficulty that men could be spared from the piquets,—for the whole force simply became a series of outlying piquets—to bury our own dead, let alone those of the enemy. And when we retired their friends did not take the trouble, as the skeletons were still whitening in the rooms of the buildings when the Ninety-Third returned to the siege of Lucknow in March, 1858. Their bones were doubtless buried after the fall of Lucknow, but that would be at least six months after their slaughter.

By daylight on the 23rd of November the whole of the women and children had arrived at the Dilkooshá, where tents were pitched for them, and the rear-guard had reached the Martinière. Here the rolls were called again to see if any were missing, when it was discovered that Sergeant Alexander Macpherson, of No. 2 company, who had formed one of Colonel Ewart's detachment in the barracks, was not present. Shortly afterwards he was seen making his way across the plain, and reported that he had been left asleep in the barracks, and, on waking up after daylight and finding himself alone, guessed what had happened, and knowing the direction in which the column was to retire, he at once followed. Fortunately the enemy had not even then discovered the evacuation of the Residency, for they were still firing into our old positions. Sergeant Macpherson was ever after this known in the regiment as "Sleepy Sandy."

There was also an officer, Captain Waterman, left asleep in the Residency. He, too, managed to join the rear-guard in safety; but he got such a fright that I afterwards saw it stated in one of the Calcutta papers that his mind was affected by the shock to his nervous system. Some time later an Irishman in the Ninety-Third gave a good reason why the fright did not turn the head of Sandy Macpherson. In those days before the railway it took much longer than now for the mails to get from Cawnpore to Calcutta, and for Calcutta papers to get back again; and some time,—about a month or six weeks—after the events above related, when the Calcutta papers got back to camp with the accounts of the relief of Lucknow, I and Sergeant Macpherson were on outlying piquet at Futtehghur (I think), and the captain of the piquet gave me a bundle of the newspapers to read out to the men. In these papers there was an account of Captain Waterman's being left behind in the Residency, in which it was stated that the shock had affected his intellect. When I read this out, the men made some remarks concerning the fright which it must have given Sandy Macpherson when he found himself alone in the barracks, and Sandy joining in the remarks, was inclined to boast that the fright had not upset *his* intellect, when an Irishman of the piquet, named Andrew M'Onville, usually called "Handy Andy" in the company, joining in the conversation, said: "Boys, if Sergeant Macpherson will give me permission, I will tell you a story that will show the reason why the fright did not upset his intellect." Permission was of course granted for the story, and Handy Andy proceeded with his illustration as follows, as nearly as I can remember it.

"You have all heard of Mr. Gough, the great American Temperance lecturer. Well, the year before I enlisted he came to Armagh, giving a course of temperance lectures, and all the public-house keepers and brewers were up in arms to raise as much opposition as possible against Mr. Gough and his principles, and in one of his lectures he laid great stress on the fact that he considered moderation the parent of drunkenness. A brewer's drayman thereupon went on the platform to disprove this assertion by actual facts from his own experience, and in his argument in favour of *moderate* drinking, he stated that for upwards of twenty years he had habitually consumed over a gallon of beer and about a pint of whisky daily, and solemnly asserted that he had never been the worse for liquor in his life. To which Mr. Gough replied: 'My friends, there is no rule without its exception, and our friend here is an exception to the general rule of moderate drinking; but I will tell you a story that I think exactly illustrates his case. Some years ago, when I was a boy, my father had two negro servants, named Uncle Sambo and Snowball. Near our house there was a branch of one of the large fresh-water lakes which swarmed with fish, and it was the duty of Snowball to go every morning to catch sufficient for the breakfast of the household. The way Snowball usually caught his fish was by making them drunk by feeding them with Indian corn-meal mixed with strong whisky and rolled into balls. When these whisky balls were thrown into the water the fish came and ate them readily, but after they had swallowed a few they became helplessly drunk, turning on their backs and allowing themselves to be caught, so that in a very short time Snowball would return with his basket full of fish. But as I said, there is no rule without an exception, and one morning proved that there is also an exception in the matter of fish becoming drunk. As usual Snowball went to the lake with an allowance of whisky balls, and spying a fine big fish with a large flat head, he dropped a ball in front of it, which it at once ate and then another, and another, and so on till all the whisky balls in Snowball's basket were in the stomach of this queer fish, and still it showed no signs of becoming drunk, but kept wagging its tail and looking for more whisky balls. On this Snowball returned home and called old Uncle Sambo to come and see this wonderful fish which had swallowed nearly a peck of whisky balls and still was not drunk. When old Uncle Sambo set eyes on the fish, he exclaimed, "O Snowball, Snowball! you foolish boy, you will never be able to make that fish drunk with your whisky balls. That fish could live in a barrel of whisky and not get drunk. That fish, my son, is called a mullet-head: it has got no brains." And that accounts,' said Mr. Gough, turning to the brewer's drayman, 'for our friend here being able for twenty years to drink a gallon of beer and a pint of whisky daily and never become drunk.' And so, my chums," said Handy Andy, "if you will apply the same reasoning to the cases of Sergeant Macpherson and Captain Waterman I think you will come to the correct conclusion why the fright did not upset the intellect of Sergeant Macpherson." We all joined in the laugh at Handy Andy's story, and none more heartily than the butt of it, Sandy Macpherson himself.

But enough of digression. Shortly after the roll was called at the Martinière, a most unfortunate accident took place. Corporal Cooper and four or five men went into one of the rooms of the Martinière in which there was a quantity of loose powder which had been left by the enemy, and somehow,—it was never known how—the powder got ignited and they were all blown up, their bodies completely charred and their eyes scorched out. The poor fellows all died in the greatest agony within an hour or so of the accident, and none of them ever spoke to say how it happened. The quantity of powder was not sufficient to shatter the house, but it blew the doors and windows out, and burnt the poor fellows as black as charcoal. This sad accident cast a gloom over the regiment, and made me again very mindful of and thankful for my own narrow escape, and that of my comrades in the Shâh Nujeef on that memorable night of the 16th of November.

Later in the day our sadness increased when it was found that Colour-Sergeant Alexander Knox, of No. 2 company, was missing. He had called the roll of his company at daylight, and had then gone to see a friend in the Seventy-Eighth Highlanders. He had stayed some time with his friend and left to return to his own regiment, but was never heard of again. Poor Knox had two brothers in the regiment, and he was the youngest of the three. He was a most deserving and popular non-commissioned officer, decorated with the French war medal and the Cross of the Legion of Honour for valour in the Crimea, and was about to be promoted sergeant-major of the regiment, *vice* Murray killed in the Secundrabâgh. His fate was never known.

About two o'clock in the afternoon, the regiment being all together again, the following general order was read to us, and although this is well-known history, still there must be many of the readers of these reminiscences who have not ready access to histories. I will therefore quote the general order in question for the information of young soldiers.

HEADQUARTERS, LA MARTINIÈRE, LUCKNOW,
23rd November, 1857.

1. The Commander-in-Chief has reason to be thankful to the force he conducted for the relief of the garrison of Lucknow.

2. Hastily assembled, fatigued by forced marches, but animated by a common feeling of determination to accomplish the duty before them, all ranks of this force have compensated for

their small number, in the execution of a most difficult duty, by unceasing exertions.

3. From the morning of the 16th till last night the whole force has been one outlying piquet, never out of fire, and covering an immense extent of ground, to permit the garrison to retire scatheless and in safety covered by the whole of the relieving force.

4. That ground was won by fighting as hard as it ever fell to the lot of the Commander-in-Chief to witness, it being necessary to bring up the same men over and over again to fresh attacks; and it is with the greatest gratification that his Excellency declares he never saw men behave better.

5. The storming of the Secundrabâgh and the Shâh Nujeef has never been surpassed in daring, and the success of it was most brilliant and complete.

6. The movement of retreat of last night, by which the final rescue of the garrison was effected, was a model of discipline and exactness. The consequence was that the enemy was completely deceived, and the force retired by a narrow, tortuous lane, the only line of retreat open, in the face of 50,000 enemies, without molestation.

7. The Commander-in-Chief offers his sincere thanks to Major-General Sir James Outram, G.C.B., for the happy manner in which he planned and carried out his arrangements for the evacuation of the Residency of Lucknow.

By order of his Excellency the Commander-in-Chief,

W. Mayhew, *Major*,
Deputy Adjutant-General of the Army.

Thus were achieved the relief and evacuation of the Residency of Lucknow.[1] The enemy did not discover that the Residency was deserted till noon on the 23rd, and about the time the above general order was being read to us they fired a salute of one hundred and one guns, but did not attempt to follow us or to cut off our

[1] It must always be recollected that this was the *second* relief of Lucknow. The first was effected by the force under Havelock and Outram on the 25th September, 1857, and was in fact more of a reinforcement than a relief.

retreat. That night we bivouacked in the Dilkooshá park, and retired on the Alumbâgh on the 25th, the day on which the brave and gallant Havelock died. But that is a well-known part of the history of the relief of Lucknow, and I will turn to other matters.

CHAPTER VII

BAGPIPES AT LUCKNOW—A BEWILDERED BÂBOO—THE FORCED MARCH TO CAWNPORE—OPIUM—WYNDHAM'S MISTAKE

SINCE commencing these reminiscences, and more particularly during my late visit to Lucknow and Cawnpore, I have been asked by several people about the truth of the story of the Scotch girl and the bagpipes at Lucknow, and in reply to all such inquiries I can only make the following answer.

About the time of the anniversary dinner in celebration of the relief of Lucknow, in September, 1891, some writers in the English papers went so far as to deny that the Seventy-Eighth Highlanders had their bagpipes with them at Lucknow, and in *The Calcutta Statesman* of the 18th of October, 1891, I wrote a letter contradicting this assertion, which with the permission of the editor I propose to republish in this chapter. But I may first mention that on my late visit to Lucknow a friend showed me a copy of the original edition of *A Personal Narrative of the Siege of Lucknow*, by L. E. R. Rees, one of the surviving defenders, which I had never before seen, and on page 224 the following statement is given regarding the entry of Havelock's force. After describing the prevailing excitement the writer goes on to say: "The shrill tones of the Highlanders' bagpipes now pierced our ears; not the most beautiful music was ever more welcome or more joy-bringing," and so on. Further on, on page 226: "The enemy found some of us dancing to the sounds of the Highlanders' pipes. The remembrance of that happy evening will never be effaced from my memory." While yet again, on page 237, he gives the story related by me below about the Highland piper putting some of the enemy's cavalry to flight by a blast from his pipes. So much in proof of the fact that the Seventy-Eighth Highlanders had their bagpipes with them, and played them too, at the first relief of Lucknow.

I must now devote a few remarks to the incident of Jessie Brown, which Grace Campbell has immortalised in the song known as *Jessie's Dream*. In the *Indian Empire*, by R. Montgomery Martin, vol. ii. page 470, after denying that this story had its origin in Lucknow, the author gives the following foot-note: "It was originally a little romance, written by a French governess at Jersey for the use of her pupils; which found its way into a Paris paper, thence to the *Jersey Times*, thence to the London *Times*, December 12th, 1857, and afterwards appeared in nearly all the journals of the United Kingdom." With regard to this remark, I am positive that I heard the story in Lucknow in November, 1857, at the same time as I heard the story about the piper frightening the enemy's *sowars* with his bagpipes; and it appears a rather far-fetched theory about a French governess inventing the story in Jersey. What was the name of this governess, and, above all, why go for its origin to such an out-of-the-way place as Jersey? I doubt very much if it was possible for the news of the relief of Lucknow to have reached Jersey, and for the said French governess to have composed and printed such a romance in time for its roundabout publication in *The Times* of the 12th of December, 1857. This version of the origin of *Jessie's Dream* therefore to my thinking carries its own refutation on the face of it, and I should much like to see the story in its original French form before I believe it.

Be that as it may, in the letters published in the home papers, and quoted in *The Calcutta Statesman* in October, 1891, one lady gave the positive statement of a certain Mrs. Gaffney, then living in London, who asserted that she was, if I remember rightly, in the same compartment of the Residency with Jessie Brown at the very time the latter said that she heard the bagpipes when dull English ears could detect nothing besides the accustomed roar of the cannon. Now, I knew Mrs. Gaffney very well. Her husband, Sergeant Gaffney, served with me in the Commissariat Department in Peshawur just after the Mutiny, and I was present as his best man when he married Mrs. Gaffney. I forget now what was the name of her first husband, but she was a widow when Sergeant Gaffney married her. I think her first husband was a sergeant of the Company's Artillery, who was either killed in the defence of the Residency or died shortly after. However, she became Mrs. Gaffney either in the end of 1860 or beginning of 1861, and I have often heard her relate the incident of Jessie Brown's hearing the bagpipes in the underground cellar, or *tykhána*, of the Residency, hours before any one would believe that a force was coming to their relief, when in the words of of J. B. S. Boyle, the garrison were repeating in dull despair the lines so descriptive of their state :

> No news from the outer world !
> Days, weeks, and months have sped ;
> Pent up within our battlements,
> We seem as living dead.
>
> No news from the outer world !
> Have British soldiers quailed
> Before the rebel mutineers ?—
> Has British valour failed ?

If the foregoing facts do not convince my readers of the truth of the origin of *Jessie's Dream* I cannot give them any more. I am positive on the point that the Seventy-Eighth Highlanders *had* their bagpipes and pipers with them in Lucknow, and that I first heard the story of *Jessie's Dream* on the 23rd of November, 1857, on the Dilkooshá heights before Lucknow. The following is my letter of the 18th of October, 1891, on the subject, addressed to the editor of *The Calcutta Statesman.*

SIR,—In an issue of the *Statesman* of last week there was a letter from Deputy-Inspector-General Joseph Jee, V.C., C.B., late of the Seventy-Eighth Highlanders (Ross-shire Buffs), re-copied from an English paper, contradicting a report that had been published to the effect that the bagpipes of the Seventy-Eighth had been left behind at Cawnpore when the regiment went with General Havelock to the first relief of Lucknow; and I write to support the assertion of Deputy-Inspector-General Jee that if any late pipe-major or piper of the old Seventy-Eighth has ever made such an assertion, he must be mad! I was not in the Seventy-Eighth myself, but in the Ninety-Third, the regiment which saved the "Saviours of India" (as the Seventy-Eighth were then called), and rescued them from the Residency, and I am positive that the Seventy-Eighth had their bagpipes and pipers too inside the Residency; for I well remember they struck up the same tunes as the pipers of the Ninety-Third, on the memorable 16th of November, 1857. I recollect the fact as if it were only yesterday. When the din of battle had ceased for a time, and the roll of the Ninety-Third was being called outside the Secundrabâgh to ascertain how many had fallen in that memorable combat, which Sir Colin Campbell said had "never been surpassed and rarely equalled," Pipe-Major John M'Leod called me aside to listen to the pipers of the Seventy-Eighth, inside the Residency, playing *On wi' the Tartan*, and I could hear the pipes quite distinctly, although, except for the practised *lug* of John M'Leod, I could not have told the tune. However, I don't suppose there are many now living fitter to give evidence on the subject than Doctor Jee; but I may mention another incident. The morning after the Residency was evacuated, I visited the bivouac of the Seventy-Eighth near Dilkooshá, to make inquiries about an old school chum who had enlisted in the regiment. I found him still alive, and he related to me how he had been one of the men who were with Dr. Jee collecting the wounded in the streets of Lucknow on the 26th of September, and how they had been cut off from the main body and besieged in a house the whole night, and Dr. Jee was the only officer with the party, and that he had been recommended for the Victoria Cross for his bravery in defending the place and saving a large number of the wounded. I may mention another incident which my friend told me, and which has not been so much noticed as the Jessie Brown story. It was told to me as a fact at the time, and it afterwards appeared in a Glasgow newspaper. It was as follows: When Dr. Jee's detachment and the wounded were fighting their way to the Residency, a wounded piper and three others who had fired their last round of ammunition were charged by half-a-dozen rebel *sowars*[1] in a side street, and the three men with rifles prepared to defend themselves with the bayonet; but as soon as the *sowars* were within about twenty paces of the party, the piper pointed the drones of his bagpipes straight at them and blew such a wild blast that they turned tail and fled like the wind, mistaking the bagpipes for some infernal machine! But enough of Lucknow. Let us turn to more ancient history. Who ever heard of a Highland regiment going into action without their bagpipes and pipers, unless the latter were all "kilt"? No officer who ever commanded Highlanders knew the worth of a good piper better than Colonel John Cameron, "the grandson of Lochiel, the valiant Fassifern." And is there a Highland soldier worthy of the name who has not heard of his famous favourite piper who was shot at Cameron's side when playing the charge, while crossing the Nive in face of the French? The historian of the Peninsula war relates: "When the Ninety-Second Highlanders were in the middle of the stream, Colonel Cameron's favourite piper was shot by his side. Stooping from his saddle, Fassifern tried to rescue the body of the man who had so often cheered the regiment to victory, but in vain: the lifeless corpse was swept away by the torrent. 'Alas!' cried the brave Cameron, dashing the tears from his eyes, 'I would rather have lost twenty grenadiers than you.'" Let us next turn to M'Donald's *Martial Music of Scotland*, and we read: "The bagpipes are sacred to Scotland and speak a language which Scotchmen only know, and inspire feelings which Scotchmen only feel. Need it be told to how many fields of danger and victory the warlike strains of the bagpipes have led? There is not a battlefield that is honourable to Britain where their war-blast has not sounded! When every other instrument has been silenced by the confusion and the carnage of the scene, the bagpipes have been borne into the thick of battle, and many a devoted piper has sounded at once encouragement to his clansmen and his own *coronach!*"

In the garb of old Gaul, with the fire of old Rome,
From the heath-covered mountains of Scotia we come;
Our loud-sounding pipe breathes the true martial strain,
And our hearts still the old Scottish valour retain.

---

[1] Native cavalry troopers.

We rested at the Alumbâgh on the 26th of November, but early on the 27th we understood something had gone wrong in our rear, because, as usual with Sir Colin when he contemplated a forced march, we were served out with three days' rations and double ammunition,—sixty rounds in our pouches and sixty in our haversacks; and by two o'clock in the afternoon the whole of the women and children, all the sick and wounded, in every conceivable kind of conveyance, were in full retreat towards Cawnpore. General Outram's Division being made up to four thousand men was left in the Alumbâgh to hold the enemy in check, and to show them that Lucknow was not abandoned, while three thousand fighting men, to guard over two thousand women and children, sick and wounded, commenced their march southwards. So far as I can remember the Third and Fifth Punjâb Infantry formed the infantry of the advance-guard; the Ninth Lancers and Horse Artillery supplied the flanking parties; while the rear guard, being the post of honour, was given to the Ninety-Third, a troop of the Ninth Lancers and Bourchier's light field-battery, No. 17 of the Honourable East India Company's artillery. We started from the Alumbâgh late in the afternoon, and reached Bunnee Bridge, seventeen miles from Lucknow, about 11 P.M. Here the regiment halted till daylight on the morning of the 28th of November, but the advance-guard with the women and children, sick and wounded, had been moving since 2 A.M.

As already mentioned, all the subaltern officers in

my company were wounded, and I was told off, with a guard of about twenty men, to see all the baggage-carts across Bunnee Bridge and on their way to Cawnpore. While I was on this duty an amusing incident happened. A commissariat cart, a common country hackery, loaded with biscuits, got upset, and its wheel broke just as we were moving it on to the road. The only person near it belonging to the Commissariat Department was a young *bâboo* named Hera Lâll Chatterjee, a boy of about seventeen or eighteen years of age, who defended his charge as long as he could, but he was soon put on one side, the biscuits-bags were ripped open, and the men commenced filling their haversacks from them. Just at this time, an escort of the Ninth Lancers, with some staff-officers, rode up from the rear. It was the Commander-in-Chief and his staff. Hera Lâll seeing him rushed up and called out: "O my Lord, you are my father and my mother! what shall I tell you! These wild Highlanders will not hear me, but are stealing commissariat biscuits like fine fun." Sir Colin pulled up, and asked the *bâboo* if there was no officer present; to which Hera Lâll replied, "No officer, sir, only one corporal, and he tell me, 'Shut up, or I'll shoot you, same like rebel mutineer!'" Hearing this I stepped out of the crowd and saluting Sir Colin, told him that all the officers of my company were wounded except Captain Dawson, who was in front; that I and a party of men had been left to see the last of the carts on to the road; that this cart had broken down, and as there was no other means of carrying the biscuits, the men had filled their haversacks with them rather than leave them on the ground. On hearing that, Hera Lâll again came to the front with clasped hands, saying: "O my Lord, if one cart of biscuits short, Major Fitzgerald not listen to me, but will order thirty lashes with provost-marshal's cat! What can a poor *bâboo* do with such wild Highlanders?" Sir Colin replied: "Yes, *bâboo,* I know these Highlanders are very wild fellows when hungry; let them have the biscuits;" and turning to one of the staff, he directed him to give a voucher to the *bâboo* that a cart loaded with biscuits had broken down and the contents had been divided among the rear-guard by order of the Commander-in-Chief. Sir Colin then turned to us and said: "Men, I give you the biscuits; divide them with your comrades in front; but you must promise me should a cart loaded with rum break down, you will not interfere with it." We all replied: "No, no, Sir Colin, if rum breaks down we'll not touch it." "All right," said Sir Colin, "remember I trust you," and looking round he said, "I know every one of you," and rode on. We very soon found room for the biscuits, until we got up to the rest of the company, when we honestly shared them. I may add that *bâboo* Hera Lâll Chatterjee is still living, and is the only native employé I know who served through the second relief of Lucknow. He now holds the post of cashier in the offices of Messrs. M'Neill and Co., of Clive Ghât Street, Calcutta, which doubtless he finds more congenial employment than defending commissariat stores from hungry wild Highlanders, with the prospect of the provost-marshal's cat as the only reward for doing his best to defend his charge.

About five miles farther on a general halt was made for a short rest and for all stragglers to come up. Sir Colin himself, being still with the column, ordered the Ninety-Third to form up, and, calling the officers to the front, he made the first announcement to the regiment that General Wyndham had been attacked by the Nânâ Sâhib and the Gwalior Contingent in Cawnpore; that his force had been obliged to retire within the fort at the head of the bridge of boats, and that we must reach Cawnpore that night, because, if the bridge of boats should be captured before we got there, we would be cut off in Oude with fifty thousand of our enemies in our rear, a well-equipped army of forty thousand men, with a powerful train of artillery numbering over forty siege guns, in our front, and with all the women and children, sick and wounded, to guard. "So, Ninety-Third," said the grand old Chief, "I don't ask you to undertake this forced march, in your present tired condition, without good reason. You must reach Cawnpore to-night at all costs." And, as usual, when he took the men into his confidence, he was answered from the ranks, "All right, Sir Colin, we'll do it." To which he replied, "Very well, Ninety-Third, remember I depend on you." And he and his staff and escort rode on.

By this time we could plainly hear the guns of the Gwalior Contingent bombarding General Wyndham's position in Cawnpore; and although terribly footsore and tired, not having had our clothes off, nor a change of socks, since the 10th of the month (now eighteen days) we trudged on our weary march, every mile making the roar of the guns in front more audible. I may remark here that there is nothing to rouse tired soldiers like a good cannonade in front; it is the best tonic out! Even the youngest soldier who has once been under fire, and can distinguish the sound of a shotted gun from blank, pricks up his ears at the sound and steps out with a firmer tread and a more erect bearing.

I shall never forget the misery of that march! However, we reached the sands on the banks of the Ganges, on the Oude side of the river opposite Cawnpore, just as the sun was setting, having covered the forty-seven miles under thirty hours. Of course the great hardship of the march was caused by our worn-out state after eighteen days' continual duty, without a change of clothes or our accoutrements off. And when we got in sight of Cawnpore, the first thing we saw was the enemy on the opposite side of the river from us, making bonfires of our spare kits and baggage which had been left at Cawnpore when we advanced for the relief of Lucknow! Tired as we were, we assisted to drag Peel's heavy guns into position on the banks of the river, whence the Blue-jackets opened fire on the left flank of the enemy, the bonfires of our spare baggage being a fine mark for them.

Just as the Nânâ Sâhib had got his first gun to bear on the bridge of boats, that gun was struck on the side by one of Peel's 24-pounders and upset, and an 8-inch shell from one of his howitzers bursting in the midst of a crowd of them, we could see them bolting helter-skelter. This put a stop to their game for the night, and we lay down and rested on the sands till daybreak next morning, the 29th of November.

I must mention here an experience of my own which I always recall to mind when I read some of the insane ravings of the Anti-Opium Society against the use of that drug. I was so completely tired out by that terrible march that after I had lain down for about half an hour I positively could not stand up, I was so stiff and worn out. Having been on duty as orderly corporal before leaving the Alumbâgh, I had been much longer on my feet than the rest of the men; in fact, I was tired out before we started on our march on the afternoon of the 27th, and now, after having covered forty-seven miles under thirty hours, my condition can be better imagined than described. After I became cold, I grew so stiff that I positively could not use my legs. Now Captain Dawson had a native servant, an old man named Hyder Khân, who had been an officers' servant all his life, and had been through many campaigns. I had made a friend of old Hyder before we left Chinsurah, and he did not forget me. Having ridden the greater part of the march on the camel carrying his master's baggage, Hyder was comparatively fresh when he got into camp, and about the time our canteen-sergeant got up and was calling for orderly-corporals to draw grog for the men, old Hyder came looking for me, and when he saw my tired state, he said, in his camp English: "Corporal *sâhib*, you

God-damn tired; don't drink grog. Old Hyder give you something damn much better than grog for tired mans." With that he went away, but shortly after returned, and gave me a small pill, which he told me was opium, and about half a pint of hot tea, which he had prepared for himself and his master. I swallowed the pill and drank the tea, and *in less than ten minutes* I felt myself so much refreshed as to be able to get up and draw the grog for the men of the company and to serve it out to them while the colour-sergeant called the roll. I then lay down, rolled up in my sepoy officer's quilt, which I had carried from the Shâh Nujeef, and had a sound refreshing sleep till next morning, and then got up so much restored that, except for the sores on my feet from broken blisters, I could have undertaken another forty-mile march. I always recall this experience when I read many of the ignorant arguments of the Anti-Opium Society, who would, if they had the power, compel the Government to deprive every hard-worked *coolie* of the only solace in his life of toil. I am certainly not an opium-eater, and the abuse of opium may be injurious, as is the abuse of anything; but I am so convinced in my own mind of the beneficial effects of the temperate use of the drug, that if I were the general of an army after a forced march like that of the retreat from Lucknow to the relief of Cawnpore, I would make the Medical Department give every man a pill of opium and half a pint of hot tea, instead of rum or liquor of any sort! I hate drunkenness as much as anybody, but I have no sympathy with what I may call the intemperate temperance of most of our teetotallers and the Anti-Opium Society. My experience has been as great and as varied as that of most Europeans in India, and that experience has led me to the conviction that the members of the Anti-Opium Society are either culpably ignorant of facts, or dishonest in the way they represent what they wish others to believe to be facts. Most of the assertions made about the Government connection with opium being a hindrance to mission-work and the spread of Christianity, are gross exaggerations not borne out by experience, and the opium slave and the opium den, as depicted in much of the literature on this subject, have no existence except in the distorted imagination of the writers. But I shall have some more observations to make on this score elsewhere, and some evidence to bring forward in support of them.[1]

Early on the morning of the 29th of November the Ninety-Third crossed the bridge of boats, and it was well that Sir Colin had returned so promptly from Lucknow to the relief of Cawnpore, for General Wyndham's troops were not only beaten and cowed,—they were utterly demoralised.

When the Commander-in-Chief left Cawnpore for Lucknow, General Wyndham, known as the "Hero of the Redan," was left in command at Cawnpore with instructions to strengthen his position by every means, and to detain all detachments arriving from Calcutta after the 10th of November, because it was known that

[1] See Appendix D.

the Gwalior Contingent were in great force somewhere across the Jumna, and there was every probability that they would either attack Cawnpore, or cross into Oude to fall on the rear of the Commander-in-Chief's force to prevent the relief of Lucknow. But strict orders were given to General Wyndham that he was *on no account* to move out of Cawnpore, should the Gwalior Contingent advance on his position, but to act on the defensive, and to hold his entrenchments and guard the bridge of boats at all hazards. By that time the entrenchment or mud fort at the Cawnpore end of the bridge, where the Government Harness and Saddlery Factory now stands, had become a place of considerable strength under the able direction of Captain Mowbray Thomson, one of the four survivors of General Wheeler's force. Captain Thomson had over four thousand *coolies* daily employed on the defences from daybreak till dark, and he was a most energetic officer himself, so that by the time we passed through Cawnpore for the relief of Lucknow this position had become quite a strong fortification, especially when compared with the miserable apology for an entrenchment so gallantly defended by General Wheeler's small force and won from him by such black treachery. When we advanced for the relief of Lucknow, all our spare baggage, five hundred new tents, and a great quantity of clothing for the troops coming down from Delhi, were shut up in Cawnpore, with a large quantity of spare ammunition, harness, and saddlery; in brief, property to the value of over five *lakhs* of rupees was left stored in the church and in the houses which were still standing near the church between the town and the river, a short distance from the house in which the women and children were murdered. All this property, as already mentioned, fell into the hands of the Gwalior Contingent, and we returned just in time to see them making bonfires of what they could not use. Colonel Sir Robert Napier (afterwards Lord Napier of Magdala) lost all the records of his long service, and many valuable engineering papers which could never be replaced. As for us of the Ninety-Third, we lost all our spare kits, and were now without a chance of a change of underclothing or socks. Let all who may read this consider what it meant to us, who had not changed our clothes from the 10th of the month, and how, on the morning of the 29th, the sight of the enemy making bonfires of our kits, just as we were within reach of them, could hardly have been soothing to contemplate.

But to return to General Wyndham's force. By the 26th of November it numbered two thousand four hundred men, according to Colonel Adye's *Defence of Cawnpore;* and when he heard of the advance of the Nânâ Sâhib at the head of the Gwalior Contingent, Wyndham considered himself strong enough to disobey the orders of the Commander-in-Chief, and moved out of his entrenchment to give them battle, encountering their advance guard at Pândoo Nuddee about seven miles from Cawnpore. He at once attacked and drove it back through a village in its rear; but behind the village he found himself confronted by an army of over forty thousand men, twenty-five thousand of them being the famous Gwalior Contingent, the best disciplined troops in India, which had never been beaten and considered themselves invincible, and which, in addition to a siege train of thirty heavy guns, 24 and 32-pounders, had a well-appointed and well-drilled field-artillery. General Wyndham now saw his mistake, and gave the order for retreat. His small force retired in good order, and encamped on the plain outside Cawnpore on the Bithoor road for the night, to find itself out-flanked and almost surrounded by Tântia Topee and his Mahrattas on the morning of the 27th; and at the end of five hours' fighting a general retreat into the fort had again to be ordered.

The retiring force was overwhelmed by a murderous cannonade, and, being largely composed of young soldiers, a panic ensued. The men got out of hand, and fled for the fort with a loss of over three hundred,—mostly killed, because the wounded who fell into the hands of the enemy were cut to pieces,—and several guns. The Rev. Mr. Moore, Church of England Chaplain with General Wyndham's force, gave a very sad picture of the panic in which the men fled for the fort, and his description was borne out by what I saw myself when we passed through the fort on the morning of the 29th. Mr. Moore said: "The men got quite out of hand and fled pell-mell for the fort. An old Sikh *sirdâr* at the gate tried to stop them, and to form them up in some order, and when they pushed him aside and rushed past him, he lifted up his hands and said, 'You are not the brothers of the men who beat the Khâlsa army and conquered the Punjâb!'" Mr. Moore went on to say that, "The old Sikh followed the flying men through the Fort Gate, and patting some of them on the back said, 'Don't run, don't be afraid, there is nothing to hurt you!'" The fact is the men were mostly young soldiers, belonging to many different regiments, simply battalions of detachments. They were crushed by the heavy and well-served artillery of the enemy, and if the truth must be told, they had no confidence in their commander, who was a brave soldier, but no general; so when the men were once seized with panic, there was no stopping them. The only regiment, or rather part of a regiment, for they only numbered fourteen officers of all ranks and a hundred and sixty men, which behaved well, was the old Sixty-Fourth, and two companies of the Thirty-Fourth and Eighty-Second, making up a weak battalion of barely three hundred. This was led by brave old Brigadier Wilson, who held them in hand until he brought them forward to cover the retreat, which he did with a loss of seven officers killed and two wounded, eighteen men of the Sixty-Fourth killed and twenty-five wounded, with equally heavy proportions killed and wounded from the companies of the Thirty-Fourth and Eighty-Second. Brigadier Wilson first had his horse shot, and was then himself killed, while urging the men to maintain the honour of the regiment. The command then devolved on Major Stirling, one of the Sixty-Fourth, who was cut down in the act of spiking one of the enemy's guns, and Captain M'Crea of the same regiment was also cut down just as he had spiked his fourth gun. This charge, and these individual acts of bravery, retarded the advance of the enemy till some sort of order had been re-established inside the fort. The Sixty-Fourth were then driven back, and obliged to leave their dead.

This then was the state of matters when we reached Cawnpore from Lucknow. The whole of our spare baggage was captured: the city of Cawnpore and the whole of the river-side up to the house where the Nânâ had slaughtered the women and children were in the hands of the enemy; but they had not yet injured the bridge of boats, nor crossed the canal, and the road to Allahabad still remained open.

We marched through the fort, and took up ground near where the jute mill of Messrs. Beer Brothers and Co. and Joe Lee's hotel now stand. We crossed the bridge without any loss except one officer, who was slightly wounded by being struck on the shin by a spent bullet from a charge of grape. He was a long slender youth of about sixteen or seventeen years of age, whom the men had named "Jack Straw." He was knocked down just as we cleared the bridge of boats, among the blood of some camp-followers who had been killed by the bursting of a shell just in front of us. Sergeant Paton, of my company, picked him up, and put him into an empty *dooly* which was passing.

During the day a piquet of one sergeant, one corporal, and about twenty men, under command of Lieutenant Stirling, who was afterwards killed on the 5th of December, was sent out to bring in the body of Brigadier Wilson, and a man named Doran, of the Sixty-Fourth, who had gone up to Lucknow in the Volunteer Cavalry, and had there done good service and returned with our force, volunteered to go out with them to identify the brigadier's body, because there were many more killed near the same place, and their corpses having been stripped, they could not be identified by their uniform, and it would have been impossible to have brought in all without serious loss. The party reached the brigadier's body without apparently attracting the attention of the enemy; but just as two men, Rule of my regiment and Patrick Doran, were lifting it into the *dooly* they were seen, and the enemy opened fire on them. A bullet struck Doran and went right through his body from side to side, without touching any of the vital organs, just as he was bending down to lift the brigadier—a most extraordinary wound! If the bullet had deviated a hair's-breadth to either side, the wound must have been mortal, but Doran was able to walk back to the fort, and lived for many years after taking his discharge from the regiment.

During the time that this piquet was engaged the Blue-jackets of Peel's Brigade and our heavy artillery had taken up positions in front of the fort, and showed the gunners of the Gwalior Contingent that they were no longer confronted by raw inexperienced troops. By the afternoon of the 29th of November, the whole of the women and children and sick and wounded from Lucknow had crossed the Ganges, and encamped behind the Ninety-Third on the Allahabad road, and here I will leave them and close this chapter.

CHAPTER VIII

ANECDOTES—ACTION WITH THE GWALIOR CONTINGENT—ITS DEFEAT—PURSUIT OF THE NÂNÂ—BITHOOR—JOHN LANG AND JOTEE PERSHÂD

So far as I now remember, the 30th of November, 1857, passed without any movement on the part of the enemy, and the Commander-in-Chief, in his letter describing the state of affairs to the Governor-General, said, "I am obliged to submit to the hostile occupation of Cawnpore until the actual despatch of all my incumbrances towards Allahabad is effected." As stated in the last chapter, when our tents came up our camp was pitched (as near as I can now make out from the altered state of Cawnpore), about the spot where Joe Lee's hotel and the jute mill of Messrs. Beer Brothers and Co. now stand. St. Andrew's day and evening passed without molestation, except that strong piquets lined the canal and guarded our left and rear from surprise, and the men in camp slept accoutred, ready to turn out at the least alarm. But during the night, or early on the morning of the 1st of December, the enemy had quietly advanced some guns, unseen by our piquets, right up to the Cawnpore side of the canal, and suddenly opened fire on the Ninety-Third just as we were falling in for muster-parade, sending round-shot and shell right through our tents. One shrapnel shell burst right in the centre of Captain Cornwall's company severely wounding the captain, Colour-Sergeant M'Intyre, and five men, but not killing any one.

Captain Cornwall was the oldest officer in the regiment, even an older soldier than Colonel Leith-Hay who had then commanded it for over three years, and for long he had been named by the men "Old Daddy Cornwall." He was poor, and had been unable to purchase promotion, and in consequence was still a captain with over thirty-five years' service. The bursting of the shell right over his head stunned the old gentleman, and a bullet from it went through his shoulder, breaking his collar-bone and cutting a deep furrow down his back. The old man was rather stout and very short-sighted; the shock of the fall stunned him for some time, and before he regained his senses Dr. Munro had cut the bullet out of his back and bandaged up his wound as well as possible. Daddy came to himself just as the men were lifting him into a *dooly*. Seeing Dr. Munro standing by with the bullet in his hand, about to present it to him as a memento of Cawnpore, Daddy gasped out, "Munro, is my wound dangerous?" "No, Cornwall," was the answer, "not if you don't excite yourself into a fever; you will get over it all right." The next question put was, "Is the road clear to Allahabad?" To which Munro replied that it was, and that he hoped to have all the sick and wounded sent down country within a day or two. "Then by ——" said Daddy, with considerable emphasis, "I'm off." The poor old fellow had through long disappointment become like our soldiers in Flanders,—he sometimes swore; but considering how promotion had passed over him, that was perhaps excusable. All this occupied far less time than it takes to write it, and I may as well here finish the history of Daddy Cornwall before I leave him. He went home in the same vessel as a rich widow, whom he married on arrival in Dublin, his native place, the corporation of which presented him with a valuable sword and the freedom of the city. The death of Brigadier-General Hope in the following April gave Captain Cornwall his majority without purchase, and he returned to India in the end of 1859 to command the regiment for about nine months, retiring from the army in 1860, when we lay at Rawul Pindee.

But I must return to my story. Being shelled out of our tents, the regiment was advanced to the side of the canal under cover of the mud walls of what had formerly been the sepoy lines, in which we took shelter from the fire of the enemy. Later in the day Colonel Ewart lost his left arm by a round-shot striking him on the elbow just as he had dismounted from his charger on his return from visiting the piquets on the left and rear of our position, he being the field-officer for the day. This caused universal regret in the regiment, Ewart being the most popular officer in it.

By the evening of the 3rd of December the whole of the women and children, and as many of the wounded as could bear to be moved, were on their way to Allahabad; and during the 4th and 5th reinforcements reached Cawnpore from England, among them our old comrades of the Forty-Second whom we had left at Dover in May. We were right glad to see them, on the morning of the 5th December, marching in with bagpipes playing, which was the first intimation we had of another Highland regiment being near us. These reinforcements raised the force under Sir Colin Campbell to five thousand infantry, six hundred cavalry, and thirty-five guns.

Early on the morning of the 6th of December we struck our tents, which we loaded on elephants, and marched to a place of safety behind the fort on the river bank, where we formed up in rear of the unroofed barracks—the Forty-Second, Fifty-Third, Ninety-Third, and Fourth Punjâb Infantry, with Peel's Brigade and several batteries of artillery, among them Colonel Bourchier's light field-battery (No. 17 of the old Company's European artillery), a most daring lot of fellows, the Ninth Lancers, and one squadron of Hodson's Horse under command of Lieutenant Gough,[1] a worthy pupil of a famous master. This detachment of Hodson's Horse had come down with Sir Hope Grant from Delhi, and served at the final relief of Lucknow and the retreat to the succour of Cawnpore. The headquarters of the regiment under its famous commander had been left with Brigadier Showers.

As this force was formed up in columns, masked

[1] Now Lieutenant-General Sir Hugh Gough, V.C., K.C.B.

from the view of the enemy by the barracks on the plain of Cawnpore, the Commander-in-Chief rode up, and told us that he had just got a telegram informing him of the safe arrival of the women and children, sick and wounded, at Allahabad, and that now we were to give battle to the famous Gwalior Contingent, consisting of twenty-five thousand well-disciplined troops, with about ten thousand of the Nânâ Sâhib's Mahrattas and all the *budmâshes* of Cawnpore, Calpee, and Gwalior, under command of the Nânâ in person, who had proclaimed himself Peishwa and Chief of the Mahratta power, with Tântia Topee, Bâlâ Sâhib (the Nânâ's brother), and Râja Koor Sing, the Râjpoot Chief of Judgdespore, as divisional commanders, and with all the native officers of the Gwalior Contingent as brigade and regimental commanders. Sir Colin also warned us that there was a large quantity of rum in the enemy's camp, which we must carefully avoid, because it was reported to have been drugged. "But, Ninety-Third," he continued, "I trust you. The supernumerary rank will see that no man breaks the ranks, and I have ordered the rum to be destroyed as soon as the camp is taken."

The Chief then rode on to the other regiments and as soon as he had addressed a short speech to each, a signal was sent up from Peel's rocket battery, and General Wyndham opened the ball on his side with every gun at his disposal, attacking the enemy's left between the city and the river. Sir Colin himself led the advance, the Fifty-Third and Fourth Punjâb Infantry in skirmishing order, with the Ninety-Third in line, the cavalry on our left, and Peel's guns and the horse-artillery at intervals, with the Forty-Second in the second line for our support.

Directly we emerged from the shelter of the buildings which had masked our formation, the piquets fell back, the skirmishers advanced at the double, and the enemy opened a tremendous cannonade on us with round-shot, shell, and grape. But, nothing daunted, our skirmishers soon lined the canal, and our line advanced, with the pipers playing and the colours in front of the centre company, without the least wavering,—except now and then opening out to let through the round-shot which were falling in front, and rebounding along the hard ground—determined to show the Gwalior Contingent that they had different men to meet from those whom they had encountered under Wyndham a week before. By the time we reached the canal, Peel's Blue-jackets were calling out—"Damn these cow horses," meaning the gun-bullocks, "they're too slow! Come, you Ninety-Third, give us a hand with the drag-ropes as you did at Lucknow!" We were then well under the range of the enemy's guns, and the excitement was at its height. A company of the Ninety-Third slung their rifles, and dashed to the assistance of the Blue-jackets. The bullocks were cast adrift, and the native drivers were not slow in going to the rear. The drag-ropes were manned, and the 24-pounders wheeled abreast of the first line of skirmishers just as if they had been light field-pieces.

When we reached the bank the infantry paused for a moment to see if the canal could be forded or if we should have to cross by the bridge over which the light field-battery were passing at the gallop, and unlimbering and opening fire, as soon as they cleared the head of the bridge, to protect our advance. At this juncture the enemy opened on us with grape and canister shot, but they fired high and did us but little damage. As the peculiar *whish* (a sound when once heard never to be forgotten) of the grape was going over our heads, the Blue-jackets gave a ringing cheer for the "Red, white, and blue!" While the Ninety-Third, led off by Sergeant Daniel White, struck up *The Battle of the Alma,* a song composed in the Crimea by Corporal John Brown of the Grenadier Guards, and often sung round the camp-fires in front of Sebastopol. I here give the words, not for their literary merit, but to show the spirit of the men who could thus sing going into action in the teeth of the fire of thirty well-served, although not very correctly-aimed guns, to encounter a force of more than ten to one. Just as the Blue-jackets gave their hurrah for the "Red, white, and blue," Dan White struck up the song, and the whole line, including the skirmishers of the Fifty-Third and the sailors, joined in the stirring patriotic tune, which is a first-rate quick march:

> Come, all you gallant British hearts
> Who love the Red and Blue,[1]
> Come, drink a health to those brave lads
> Who made the Russians rue.

[1] "Red and Blue"—the Army and Navy. The tune is *The British Grenadiers.*

Fill up your glass and let it pass,
  Three cheers, and one cheer more,
For the fourteenth of September,
  Eighteen hundred and fifty-four.

We sailed from Kalimita Bay,
  And soon we made the coast,
Determined we would do our best
  In spite of brag and boast.
We sprang to land upon the strand,
  And slept on Russian shore,
On the fourteenth of September,
  Eighteen hundred and fifty-four.

We marched along until we came
  Upon the Alma's banks,
We halted just beneath their guns
  To breathe and close our ranks.
"Advance!" we heard, and at the word
  Right through the brook we bore,
On the twentieth of September,
  Eighteen hundred and fifty-four.

We scrambled through the clustering vines,
  Then came the battle's brunt;
Our officers, they cheered us on,
  Our colours waved in front;
And fighting well full many fell,
  Alas! to rise no more,
On the twentieth of September,
  Eighteen hundred and fifty-four.

The French were on the right that day,
  And flanked the Russian line,
While full upon their left they saw
  The British bayonets shine.
With hearty cheers we stunned their ears,
  Amidst the cannon's roar,
On the twentieth of September,
  Eighteen hundred and fifty-four.

A picnic party Menschikoff
 Had asked to see the fun;
The ladies came at twelve o'clock
 To see the battle won.
They found the day too hot to stay,
 The Prince felt rather sore,
On the twentieth of September,
 Eighteen hundred and fifty-four.

For when he called his carriage up,
 The French came up likewise;
And so he took French leave at once
 And left to them the prize.
The Chasseurs took his pocket-book,
 They even sacked his store,
On the twentieth of September,
 Eighteen hundred and fifty-four.

A letter to Old Nick they found,
 And this was what it said:
"To meet their bravest men, my liege,
 Your soldiers do not dread;
But devils they, not mortal men,"
 The Russian General swore,
"That drove us off the Alma's heights
 In September, fifty-four."

Long life to Royal Cambridge,
 To Peel and Camperdown,
And all the gallant British Tars
 Who shared the great renown,
Who stunned Russian ears with British cheers,
 Amidst the cannon's roar,
On the twentieth of September,
 Eighteen hundred and fifty-four.

Here's a health to noble Raglan,
 To Campbell and to Brown,
And all the gallant Frenchmen
 Who shared that day's renown.

Whilst we displayed the black cockade,
  They the tricolour bore;
The Russian crew wore gray and blue
  In September, fifty-four.

Come, let us drink a toast to-night,
  Our glasses take in hand,
And all around this festive board
  In solemn silence stand.
Before we part let each true heart
  Drink once to those no more,
Who fought their last fight on Alma's height
  In September, fifty-four!

Around our bivouac fires that night as *The Battle of the Alma* was sung again, Daniel White told us that when the Blue-jackets commenced cheering under the hail of grape-shot, he remembered that the Scots Greys and Ninety-Second Highlanders had charged at Waterloo singing *Bruce's Address at Bannockburn*, "Scots wha hae," and trying to think of something equally appropriate in which Peel's Brigade might join, he could not at the moment recall anything better than the old Crimean song aforesaid.

After clearing the canal and re-forming our ranks, we came under shelter of a range of brick kilns behind which stood the camp of the enemy, and behind the camp their infantry were drawn up in columns, not deployed in line. The rum against which Sir Colin had warned us was in front of the camp, casks standing on end with the heads knocked out for convenience; and there is no doubt but the enemy expected the Europeans would break their ranks when they saw the rum, and had formed up their columns to fall on us in the event of such a contingency. But the Ninety-Third marched right on past the rum barrels, and the supernumerary rank soon upset the casks, leaving the contents to soak into the dry ground.

As soon as we cleared the camp, our line of infantry was halted. Up to that time, except the skirmishers, we had not fired a shot, and we could not understand the reason of the halt till we saw the Ninth Lancers and the detachment of Hodson's Horse galloping round some fields of tall sugar-cane on the left, masking the light field-battery. When the enemy saw the tips of the lances (they evidently did not see the guns) they quickly formed squares of brigades. They were armed with the old musket, "Brown Bess," and did not open fire till the cavalry were within about three hundred yards. Just as they commenced to fire, we could hear Sir Hope Grant, in a voice as loud as a trumpet, give the command to the cavalry, "Squadrons, outwards!" while Bourchier gave the order to his gunners, "Action, front!" The cavalry wheeled as if they had been at a review on the Calcutta parade-ground; the guns, having previously been charged with grape, were swung round, unlimbered as quick as lightning within about two hundred and fifty yards of the squares, and round after round of grape was poured into the enemy with murderous effect, every charge going right through, leaving a lane of dead from four to five yards wide. By this time our line was advanced close up behind the battery, and we could see the mounted officers of the enemy, as soon as they caught sight of the guns, dash out of the squares and fly like lightning across the plain. Directly the squares were broken, our cavalry charged, while the infantry advanced at the double with the bayonet. The battle was won, and the famous Gwalior Contingent was a flying rabble, although the struggle was protracted in a series of hand-to-hand fights all over the plain, no quarter being given. Peel's guns were wheeled up, as already mentioned, as if they had been 6-pounders, and the left wing of the enemy taken in rear and their retreat on the Calpee road cut off. What escaped of their right wing fled along this road. The cavalry and horse-artillery led by Sir Colin Campbell in person, the whole of the Fifty-Third, the Fourth Punjâb Infantry, and two companies of the Ninety-Third, pursued the flying mass for fourteen miles. The rebels, being cut down by hundreds wherever they attempted to rally for a stand, at length threw away their arms and accoutrements to expedite their flight, for none were spared,—"neither the sick man in his weakness, nor the strong man in his strength," to quote the words of Colonel Alison. The evening closed with the total rout of the enemy, and the capture of his camp, the whole of his ordnance-park, containing a large quantity of ammunition and thirty-two guns of sizes, siege-train, and field-artillery, with a loss of only ninety-nine killed and wounded on our side.

As night fell, large bodies of the left wing of the enemy were seen retreating from the city between our piquets and the Ganges, but we were too weary and too few in number to intercept them, and they retired along

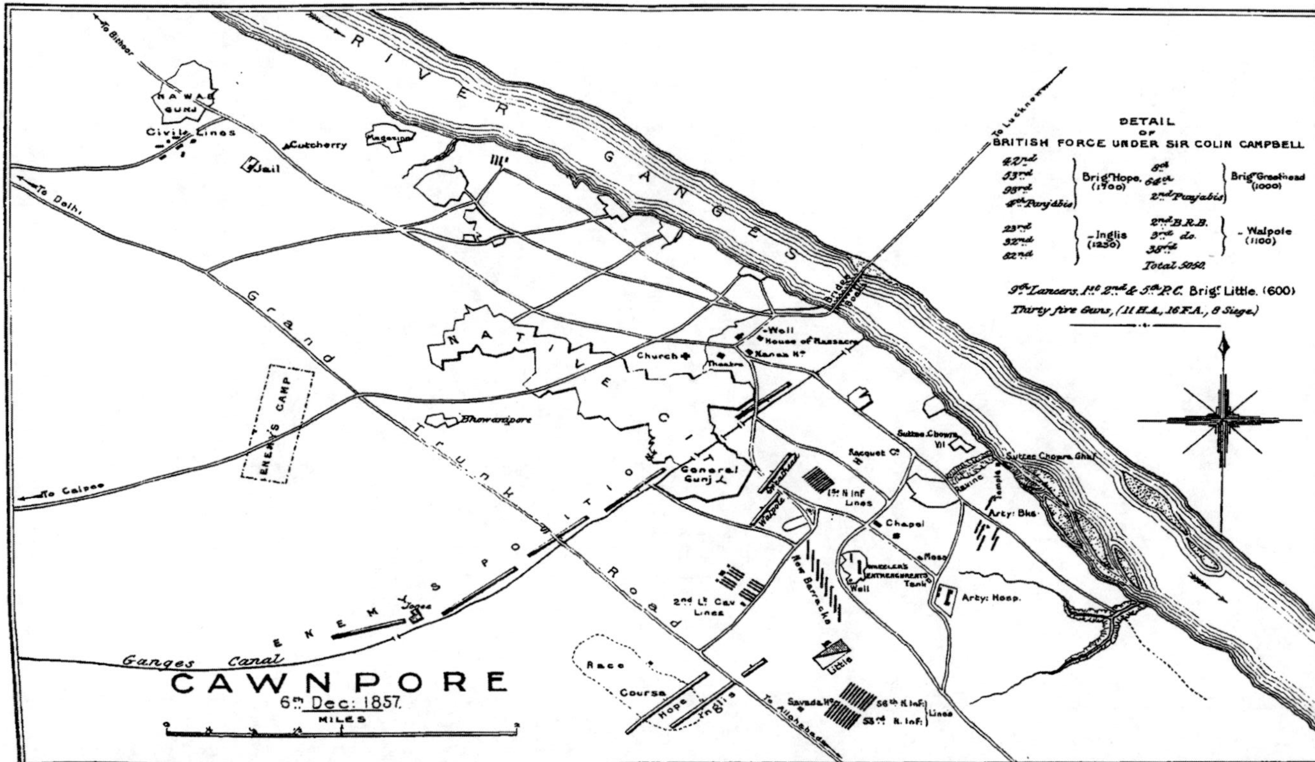

To face page 146

R. & R. Clark, Printers, Edinburgh.

the Bithoor road. About midnight the force which had followed the enemy along the Calpee road returned, bringing in a large number of ammunition-waggons and baggage-carts, the bullocks driven by our men, and those not engaged in driving sitting on the waggons or carts, too tired and footsore to walk. We rested hungry and exhausted, but a man of my company, named Bill Summers, captured a little pack-bullock loaded with two bales of stuff which turned out to be fine soft woollen socks of Loodiana manufacture, sufficient to give every man in the company three pairs,—a real godsend for us, since at that moment there was nothing we stood more in need of than socks; and as no commissariat had come up from the rear, we slaughtered the bullock and cut it into steaks, which we broiled on the tips of our ramrods around the bivouac fires. Thus we passed the night of the 6th of December, 1857.

Early on the morning of the 7th a force was sent into the city of Cawnpore, and patrolled it from end to end, east, west, north, and south. Not only did we meet no enemy, but many of the townspeople brought out food and water to our men, appearing very glad to see us.

During the afternoon our tents came up from the rear, and were pitched by the side of the Grand Trunk road, and the Forty-Second being put on duty that night, we of the Fifty-Third and Ninety-Third were allowed to take our accoutrements off for the first night's sleep without them since the 10th of November

—seven and twenty days! Our spare kits having all vanished with the enemy, as told in the last chapter, our quarter-master collected from the captured baggage all the underclothing and socks he could lay hands on. Thanks to Bill Summers and the little pack-bullock, my company got a change of socks; but there was more work before us before we got a bath or a change of shirts.

About noon on the 8th the Commander-in-Chief, accompanied by Sir Hope Grant and Brigadier Adrian Hope, had our brigade turned out, and as soon as Sir Colin rode in among us we knew there was work to be done. He called the officers to the front, and addressing them in the hearing of the men, told them that the Nânâ Sâhib had passed through Bithoor with a large number of men and seventeen guns, and that we must all prepare for another forced march to overtake him and capture these guns before he could either reach Futtehghur or cross into Oude with them. After stating that the camp would be struck as soon as we had got our dinners, the Commander-in-Chief and Sir Hope Grant held a short but animated conversation, which I have always thought was a pre-arranged matter between them for our encouragement. In the full hearing of the men, Sir Hope Grant turned to the Commander-in-Chief, and said, in rather a loud tone: "I'm afraid, your Excellency, this march will prove a wild-goose chase, because the infantry, in their present tired state, will never be able to keep up with the cavalry." On this, Sir Colin turned round in his saddle, and looking straight at us, replied in a tone equally loud, so as to be heard by all the men: "I tell you, General Grant, you are wrong. You don't know these men; these Highlanders will march your cavalry blind." And turning to the men, as if expecting to be corroborated by them, he was answered by over a dozen voices, "Ay, ay, Sir Colin, we'll show them what we can do!"

As soon as dinner was over we struck tents, loaded them on the elephants, and by two o'clock P.M. were on the march along the Grand Trunk road. By sunset we had covered fifteen miles from Cawnpore. Here we halted, lit fires, cooked tea, served out grog, and after a rest of three hours, to feed and water the horses as much as to rest the men, we were off again. By five A.M. on the 9th of December we had reached the thirtieth mile from the place where we started, and the scouts brought word to the general that we were ahead of the flying enemy. We then turned off the road to our right in the direction of the Ganges, and by eight o'clock came in sight of the enemy at Serai *ghât*, a ferry twenty-five miles above Cawnpore, preparing to embark the guns of which we were in pursuit.

Our cavalry and horse-artillery at once galloped to the front through ploughed fields, and opened fire on the boats. The enemy returned the fire, and some Mahratta cavalry made a dash at the guns, but their charge was met by the Ninth Lancers and the detachment of Hodson's Horse, and a number of them cut down. Seeing the infantry advancing in line, the enemy broke and fled for the boats, leaving all their fifteen guns, a large number of ordnance waggons loaded with ammunition, and a hundred carts filled with their baggage and the plunder of Cawnpore. Our horse-artillery and infantry advanced right up to the banks of the river and kept up a hot fire on the retreating boats, swamping a great number of them. The Nânâ Sâhib was among this lot; but the spies reported that his boat was the first to put off, and he gained the Oude side in safety, though some thousands of his Mahratta rebels must have been drowned or killed. This was some return we felt for his treachery at Suttee Chowrah *ghât* six months before. It was now our turn to be peppering the flying boats! There were a number of women and children left by the routed rebels among their baggage-carts; they evidently expected to be killed, but were escorted to a village in our rear, and left there. We showed them that we had come to war with men—not to butcher women! By the afternoon we had dragged the whole of the captured guns back from the river, and our tents coming up under the rear-guard, we encamped for the night, glad enough to get a rest.

On the morning of the 10th our quarter-master divided among us a lot of shirts and underclothing, mostly what the enemy had captured at Cawnpore, a great part of which we had now recovered; and we were allowed to go by wings to undress and have a bath in the sacred Ganges, and to change our underclothing, which we very much needed to do. The condition of our flannel shirts is best left undescribed, while our bodies round our waists, where held tight by our belts, were eaten to raw flesh. We sent our shirts afloat on the sacred waters of Mother Gunga, glad to be rid of them, and that night we slept in comfort. Even now, thirty-five years after, the recollection of the state of my own flannel when I took it off makes me shiver. This is not a pleasant subject, but I am writing these reminiscences for the information of our soldiers of to-day, and merely stating facts, to let them understand something of what the soldiers of the Mutiny had to go through.

Up to this time, the columns of the British had been mostly acting, as it were, on the defensive; but from the date of the defeat of the Gwalior Contingent, our star was in the ascendant, and the attitude of the country people showed that they understood which was the winning side. Provisions, such as butter, milk, eggs, and fruit, were brought into our camp by the villagers for sale the next morning, sparingly at first, but as soon as the people found that they were well received and honestly paid for their supplies, they came in by scores, and from that time there was no scarcity of provisions in our bazaars.

We halted at Serai *ghât* for the 11th and 12th December, and on the 13th marched back in triumph to Bithoor with our captured guns. The reason of our return to Bithoor was because spies had reported that the Nânâ Sâhib had concealed a large amount of treasure in a well there near the palace of the ex-

Peishwa of Poona. Rupees to the amount of thirty *lakhs*[1] were recovered, which had been packed in ammunition-boxes and sunk in a well; also a very large amount of gold and silver plate and other valuables, among other articles a silver howdah which had been the state howdah of the ex-Peishwa. Besides the rupees, the plate and other valuables recovered were said to be worth more than a million sterling, and it was circulated in the force that each private soldier would receive over a thousand rupees in prize-money. But we never got a *pie*![2] All we did get was hard work. The well was large. Four strong frames were erected on the top of it by the sappers, and large leathern buckets with strong iron frames, with ropes attached, were brought from Cawnpore; then a squad of twenty-five men was put on to each rope, and relieved every three hours, two buckets keeping the water down and two drawing up treasure. Thus we worked day and night from the 15th to the 26th of December, the Forty-Second, Fifty-Third, and Ninety-Third supplying the working-parties for pulling, and the Bengal Sappers furnishing the men to work in the well; these last, having to stand in the water all the time, were relieved every hour. It was no light work to keep the water down, so as to allow the sappers to sling the boxes containing the rupees; and to lift three million rupees, or thirty *lakhs*, out from a deep well required considerable labour. But the

[1] A *lakh* is 10,000, so that, at the exchange of the day, the amount of cash captured was £306,250. [2] One *pie* is half a farthing.

men, believing that the whole would be divided as prize-money, worked with a will. A paternal Government, however, ignored our general's assurance on this head, on the plea that we had merely recovered the treasure carried off by the Nânâ from Cawnpore. The plate and jewellery belonging to the ex-Peishwa were also claimed by the Government as State property, and the troops got—nothing! We had even to pay from our own pockets for the replacement of our kits which were taken by the Gwalior Contingent when they captured Wyndham's camp.

About this time *The Illustrated London News* reached India with a picture purporting to be that of the Nânâ Sâhib. I forget the date of the number which contained this picture; but I first saw it in Bithoor some time between the 15th and 25th December 1857. I will now give the history of that picture, and show how Ajoodia Pershâd, commonly known as Jotee Pershâd, the commissariat contractor, came to figure as the Nânâ Sâhib in the pages of *The Illustrated London News.* It is a well-known fact that there is no authentic portrait of the Nânâ in existence; it is even asserted that he was never painted by any artist, and photography had not extended to Upper India before 1857. I believe this is the first time that the history of the picture published as that of the Nânâ Sâhib by *The Illustrated London News* has been given. I learnt the facts which I am about to relate some years after the Mutiny, under a promise of secrecy so long as my informant, the late John Lang, barrister-at-law and editor and proprietor of *The Mofussilite,* should be alive. As both he and Ajoodia Pershâd have been many years dead, I commit no breach of confidence in now telling the story. The picture purporting to be that of the Nânâ having been published in 1857, it rightly forms a reminiscence of the Mutiny, although much of the following tale occurred several years earlier; but to make the history of the picture complete, the facts which led to it must be noticed.

There are but few Europeans now in India who remember the scandal connected with the trial of Ajoodia Pershâd, the commissariat contractor, for payment for the supplies and carriage of the army throughout the second Sikh war. When it came to a final settlement of his accounts with the Commissariat Department, Ajoodia Pershâd claimed three and a half *crores* of rupees (equal to three and a half millions sterling), in excess of what the auditor would pass as justly due to him; and the Commissariat Department, backed by the Government of India, not only repudiated the claim, but put Ajoodia Pershâd on his trial for falsification of accounts and attempting to defraud the Government. There being no high courts in those days, nor trial by jury, corrupt or otherwise, for natives in the Upper Provinces, an order of the Governor-General in Council was passed for the trial of Ajoodia Pershâd by special commission, with the judge-advocate-general as prosecutor. The trial was ordered to be held at Meerut, and the commission assembled there, commencing its sittings in the Artillery mess-house during the cold weather of 1851-52. There were no barristers or pleaders in India in those days—at least in the Mofussil, and but few in the presidency towns; but Ajoodia Pershâd, being a very wealthy man, sent an agent to England, and engaged the services of Mr. John Lang, barrister-at-law, to come out and defend him. John Lang left England in May, 1851, and came out round the Cape in one of Green's celebrated liners, the *Nile,* and he reached Meerut about December, when the trial commenced.

Everything went swimmingly with the prosecution till Mr. Lang began his cross-examination of the witnesses, he having reserved his privilege till he heard the whole case for the prosecution. Directly the cross-examination commenced, the weakness of the Government case became apparent. I need not now recall how the commissary-general, the deputy commissary-general, and their assistants were made to contradict each other, and to contradict themselves out of their own mouths. Mr. Lang, who appeared in court every day in his wig and gown, soon became a noted character in Meerut, and the night before he was to sum up the case for the defence, some officers in the Artillery mess asked him his opinion of the members of the commission. Not being a teetotaller, Mr. Lang may have been at the time somewhat under the influence of "John Exshaw," who was the ruling spirit in those days, and he replied that the whole batch, president and members, including the judge-advocate-general, were a parcel of "d—d *soors*."[1] Immediately several officers present offered to lay a bet of a thousand rupees with Mr. Lang that he was not game to tell them so to their faces in open court the following day. Lang accepted the bet, the stakes were deposited, and an umpire appointed to decide who should pocket the money. When the court re-assembled next morning, the excitement was intense. Mr. Lang opened his address by pulling the evidence for the prosecution to shreds, and warming to his work, he went at it somewhat as follows—I can only give the purport:—"Gentlemen of the commission forming this court, I now place the dead carcass of this shameful case before you in all its naked deformity, and the more we stir it up the more it stinks! The only stink in my long experience that I can compare it to is the experience gained in the saloon of the *Nile* on my passage out to India the day after a pig was slaughtered. We had a pig's cheek at the head of the table [indicating the president of the commission]; we had a roast leg of pork on the right [pointing to another member]; we had a boiled leg, also pork, on the left [indicating a third member]"; and so on he went till he had apportioned out the whole carcass of the supposed pig amongst the members of the commission. Then, turning to the judge-advocate-general, who was a little man dressed in an elaborately frilled shirt, and his assistant, who was tall and thin,

[1] Pigs.

pointing to each in turn, Mr. Lang proceeded,—"And for side-dishes we had chitterlings on one side, and sausages on the other. In brief, the whole saloon smelt of nothing but pork: and so it is, gentlemen, with this case. It is the Government of India who has ordered this trial. It is for the interest of that Government that my client should be convicted; therefore every member on this commission is a servant of Government. The officers representing the prosecution are servants of Government, and every witness for the prosecution is also a servant of Government. In brief, the whole case against my client is nothing but pork, and a disgrace to the Government of India, and to the Honourable East India Company, who have sanctioned this trial, and who put every obstacle in my way to prevent my coming out to defend my client. I repeat my assertion that the case is a disgrace to the Honourable Company and the Government of India, and to every servant of that Government who has had any finger in the manufacture of this pork-pie." And so Mr. Lang continued, showing how Ajoodia Pershâd had come forward to the assistance of the State in its hour of need, by supplying carriage for the materials of the army and rations for the troops, and so forth, till the judge-advocate-general declared that he felt ashamed to be connected with the case. The result was that Ajoodia Pershâd was acquitted on all counts, and decreed to be entitled to his claims in full, and the umpire decided that Mr. Lang had won the bet of a thousand rupees.

But my readers may ask—What has all this to do with the portrait of the Nânâ Sâhib? I am just coming to that. After his honourable acquittal, Ajoodia Pershâd was so grateful to Mr. Lang that he presented him with an honorarium of three *lakhs* of rupees, equal in those days to over £30,000, in addition to the fees on his brief; and Mr. Lang happening to say that he would very much like to have a portrait of his generous client, Ajoodia Pershâd presented him with one painted by a famous native artist of those days, and the portrait was enshrined in a jewelled frame worth another twenty-five thousand rupees. To the day of his death Mr. Lang used to carry this portrait with him wherever he went. When the Mutiny broke out he was in London, and the artists of *The Illustrated London News* were calling on every old Indian of position known to be in England, to try and get a portrait of the Nânâ. One of them was informed that Mr. Lang possessed a picture of an Indian prince —then, as now, all Indians were princes to the British public—which might be that of the arch-assassin of Cawnpore. The artist lost no time in calling on Mr. Lang to see the picture, and when he saw it he declared it was just the thing he wanted. Mr. Lang protested, pointing out that the picture no more resembled the Nânâ of Bithoor than it did her Gracious Majesty the Queen of England; that neither the dress nor the position of the person represented in the picture could pass in India for a Mahratta chief. The artist declared he did not care for people in India;

he required the picture for the people of England. So he carried it off to the engraver, and in the next issue of *The Illustrated London News* the picture of Ajoodia Pershâd, the commissariat contractor, appeared as that of the Nânâ Sâhib. When those in India who had known the Nânâ saw it, they declared it had no resemblance to him whatever, and those who had seen Ajoodia Pershâd declared that the Nânâ was very like Ajoodia Pershâd. But no one could understand how the Nânâ could ever have allowed himself to be painted in the dress of a Mârwâree banker. To the day of his death John Lang was in mortal fear lest Ajoodia Pershâd should ever come to hear how his picture had been allowed to figure as that of the arch-assassin of the Indian Mutiny.

So much for the Nânâ's picture. By Christmas Day, 1857, we had recovered all the gold and silver plate of the ex-Peishwa and the thirty *lakhs* of treasure from the well in Bithoor, and on the morning of the 27th we marched for the recapture of Futtehghur, which was held by a strong force under the Nawâb of Furruckabad. But I must leave the reoccupation of Futtehghur for another chapter.

NOTE

Jotee Pershâd was the native banker who, during the height of the Mutiny, victualled the Fort of Agra and saved the credit, if not the lives, of the members of the Government of the North-West Provinces.

CHAPTER IX

HODSON OF HODSON'S HORSE—ACTION AT THE KÂLEE NUDDEE—FUTTEHGHUR

As a further proof that the British star was now in the ascendant, before we had been many days in Bithoor each company had got its full complement of native establishment, such as cooks, water-carriers, washer-men, etc. We left Bithoor on the 27th of December *en route* for Futtehghur, and on the 28th we made a forced march of twenty-five miles, joining the Commander-in-Chief on the 29th. Early on the 30th we reached a place named Meerun-ke-serai, and our tents had barely been pitched when word went through the camp like wildfire that Hodson, of Hodson's Horse, and another officer[1] had arrived in camp with despatches from Brigadier Seaton to the Commander-in-Chief, having ridden from Mynpooree, about seventy miles from where we were.

We of the Ninety-Third were eager to see Hodson, having heard so much about him from the men of the Ninth Lancers. There was nothing, however daring or difficult, that Hodson was not believed capable of

[1] Lieutenant Macdowell, second in command of Hodson's Horse.

doing, and a ride of seventy miles more or less through a country swarming with enemies, where every European who ventured beyond the range of British guns literally carried his life in his hand, was not considered anything extraordinary for him. Personally, I was most anxious to see this famous fellow, but as yet there was no chance; Hodson was in the tent of the Commander-in-Chief, and no one knew when he might come out. However, the hours passed, and during the afternoon a man of my company rushed into the tent, calling, "Come, boys, and see Hodson! He and Sir Colin are in front of the camp; Sir Colin is showing him round, and the smile on the old Chief's face shows how he appreciates his companion." I hastened to the front of the camp, and was rewarded by having a good look at Hodson; and, as the man who had called us had said, I could see that he had made a favourable impression on Sir Colin. Little did I then think that in less than three short months I should see Hodson receive his death-wound, and that thirty-five years after I should be one of the few spared to give evidence to save his fair fame from undeserved slander. My memory always turns back to that afternoon at Meerunke-serai when I read any attack on the good name of Hodson of Hodson's Horse. And whatever prejudiced writers of the present day may say, the name of Hodson will be a name to conjure with among the Sikhs of the Punjâb for generations yet unborn.

On the 1st of January, 1858, our force reached the Kâlee Nuddee suspension bridge near Khoodâgunj, about fifteen miles from Futtehghur, just in time to prevent the total destruction of the bridge by the enemy, who had removed a good part of the planking from the roadway, and had commenced to cut the iron-work when we arrived. We halted on the Cawnpore side of the Kâlee Nuddee on New Year's Day, while the engineers, under cover of strong piquets, were busy replacing the planking of the roadway on the suspension bridge. Early on the morning of the 2nd of January the enemy from Futtehghur, under cover of a thick fog along the valley of the Kâlee Nuddee, came down in great force to dispute the passage of the river. The first intimation of their approach was a shell fired on our advance piquet; but our camp was close to the bridge, and the whole force was under arms in an instant. As soon as the fog lifted the enemy were seen to have occupied the village of Khoodâgunj in great force, and to have advanced one gun, a 24-pounder, planting it in the toll-house which commanded the passage of the bridge, so as to fire it out of the front window just as if from the porthole of a ship.

As soon as the position of the enemy was seen, the cavalry brigade of our force was detached to the left, under cover of the dense jungle along the river, to cross by a ford which was discovered about five miles up stream to our left, the intention of the movement being to get in behind the enemy and cut off his retreat to Futtehghur.

The Fifty-Third were pushed across the bridge to

reinforce the piquets, with orders not to advance, but to act on the defensive, so as to allow time for the cavalry to get behind the enemy. The right wing of the Ninety-Third was also detached with some horse-artillery guns to the right, to cross by another ford about three miles below the bridge, to attack the enemy on his left flank. The left wing was held in reserve with the remainder of the force behind the bridge, to be in readiness to reinforce the Fifty-Third in case of need.

By the time these dispositions were made, the enemy's gun from the toll-house had begun to do considerable damage. Peel's heavy guns were accordingly brought to bear on it, and, after a round or two to feel their distance, they were able to pitch an 8-inch shell right through the window, which burst under the gun, upsetting it, and killing or disabling most of the enemy in the house.

Immediately after this the Fifty-Third, being well in advance, noticed the enemy attempting to withdraw some of his heavy guns from the village, and disregarding the order of the Commander-in-Chief not to precipitate the attack, they charged these guns and captured two or three of them. This check caused the enemy's line to retire, and Sir Colin himself rode up to the Fifty-Third to bring to book the officer commanding them for prematurely commencing the action. This officer threw the blame on the men, stating that they had made the charge against his orders, and that the officers had been unable to keep them back. Sir Colin then turned on the men, threatening to send them to the rear, and to make them do fatigue-duty and baggage-guard for the rest of the campaign. On this an old Irishman from the ranks called out: "Shure, Sir Colin, you don't mean it! You'll never send us on fatigue-duty because we captured those guns that the Pandies were carrying off?" Hearing this, Sir Colin asked what guns he meant. "Shure, them's the guns," was the answer, "that Sergeant Dobbin [now Joe Lee of Cawnpore] and his section are dragging on to the road." Sir Colin seeing the guns, his stern countenance relaxed and broke into a smile, and he made some remark to the officer commanding that he did not know about the guns having been withdrawn before the regiment had made the rush on the enemy. On this the Irish spokesman from the ranks called out: "Three cheers for the Commander-in-Chief, boys! I told you he did not mean us to let the Pandies carry off those guns."

By this time our right wing and the horse-artillery had crossed the ford on our right and were well advanced on the enemy's left flank. But we of the main line, composed of the Eighth (the old "King's"—now called the Liverpool Regiment, I think), the Forty-Second, Fifty-Third, and left wing of the Ninety-Third under Adrian Hope, were allowed to advance slowly, just keeping them in sight. The enemy retired in an orderly manner for about three or four miles, when they formed up to make a stand, evidently thinking we were afraid to press them too closely. As soon as they faced round again, our line was halted only about seven hundred yards from them, and just then we could see our cavalry debouching on to the Grand Trunk road about a mile from where we were. My company was in the centre of the road, and I could see the tips of the lances of the Ninth wheeling into line for a charge right in the enemy's rear. He was completely out-generalled, and his retreat cut off.

The excitement was just then intense, as we dared not fire for fear of hitting our men in the rear. The Forty-First Native Infantry was the principal regiment of the enemy's line on the Grand Trunk road. Directly they saw the Lancers in their rear they formed square while the enemy's cavalry charged our men, but were met in fine style by Hodson's Horse and sent flying across the fields in all directions. The Ninth came down on the square of the Native Infantry, who stood their ground and opened fire. The Lancers charged well up to within about thirty yards, when the horses turned off right and left from the solid square. We were just preparing to charge it with the bayonet, when at that moment the squadrons were brought round again, just as a hawk takes a circle for a swoop on its prey, and we saw Sergeant-Major May, who was mounted on a powerful untrained horse, dash on the square and leap right into it, followed by the squadron on that side. The square being thus broken, the other troops of the Ninth rode into the flying mass, and in less than five minutes the Forty-First regiment of Native Infantry was wiped out of the ranks of the mutineers. The enemy's line of retreat became a total rout, and the plain for miles was strewn with corpses speared down by the Lancers or hewn down by the keen-edged sabres of Hodson's Horse.

Our infantry line now advanced, but there was nothing for us to do but collect the ammunition-carts and baggage of the enemy. Just about sunset we halted and saw the Lancers and Sikhs returning with the captured standards and every gun which the enemy had brought into the field in the morning. The infantry formed up along the side of the Grand Trunk road to cheer the cavalry as they returned. It was a sight never to be forgotten,—the infantry and sailors cheering the Lancers and Sikhs, and the latter returning our cheers and waving the captured standards and their lances and sabres over their heads! Sir Colin Campbell rode up, and lifting his hat, thanked the Ninth Lancers and Sikhs for their day's work. It was reported in the camp that Sir Hope Grant had recommended Sergeant-Major May for the Victoria Cross, but that May had modestly remonstrated against the honour, saying that every man in the Ninth was as much entitled to the Cross as he was, and that he was only able to break the square by the accident of being mounted on an untrained horse which charged into the square instead of turning off from it. This is of course hearsay, but I believe it is fact.

I may here remark that this charge of the Lancers forcibly impressed me with the absurdity of our cavalry-drill for the purpose of breaking an infantry square. On field-days in time of peace our cavalry were made to charge squares of infantry, and directly the horses came within thirty or forty yards the squadrons opened out right and left, galloping clear of the square under the blank fire of the infantry. The horses were thus drilled to turn off and gallop clear of the squares, instead of charging home right through the infantry. When it came to actual war the horses, not being reasoning animals, naturally acted just as on a field-day; instead of charging straight into the square, they galloped right past it, simply because they were drilled to do so. Of course, I do not propose that several battalions of infantry should be slaughtered every field-day for the purpose of training cavalry. But I would have the formation altered, and instead of having the infantry in solid squares, I would form them into quarter distance columns, with lanes between the companies wide enough for the cavalry to gallop through under the blank fire of the infantry. The horses would thus be trained to gallop straight on, and no square of infantry would be able to resist a charge of well-trained cavalry when it came to actual war. I am convinced, in my own mind, that this was the reason that the untrained remount ridden by Sergeant-Major May charged into the square of the Forty-First, and broke it, while the well-drilled horses galloped round the flanks in spite of their riders. But the square once being broken, the other horses followed as a matter of course. However, we are now in the age of breech-loaders and magazine rifles, and I fear the days of cavalry charging squares of infantry are over. But we are still a long way from the millennium, and the experience of the past may yet be turned to acccount for the wars of the future.

We reached Futtehghur on the morning of the 3rd of January to find it deserted, the enemy having got such a "drubbing" that it had struck terror into their reserves, which had bolted across the Ganges, leaving large quantities of Government property behind them, consisting of tents and all the ordnance stores of the Gun-carriage Agency. The enemy had also established a gun and shot and shell foundry here, and a powder-factory, all of which they had abandoned, leaving a number of brass guns in the lathes, half turned, with many more just cast, and large quantities of metal and material for the manufacture of both powder and shot.

During the afternoon of the day of our arrival the whole force was turned out, owing to a report that the Nawâb of Furruckabad was still in the town; and it was said that the civil officer with the force had sent a proclamation through the city that it would be given over to plunder if the Nawâb was not surrendered. Whether this was true or not, I cannot say. The district was no longer under martial law, as from the date of the defeat of the Gwalior Contingent the civil power had resumed authority on the right bank of the Ganges. But so far as the country was concerned, around Futtehghur at least, this merely meant that the hangmen's noose was to be substituted for rifle-bullet and bayonet. However, our force had scarcely been turned out to threaten the town of Furruckabad when the Nawâb was brought out, bound hand and foot, and carried by *coolies* on a common country *charpoy*.[1] I don't know what process of trial he underwent; but I fear he had neither jury nor counsel, and I know that he was first smeared over with pig's fat, flogged by sweepers, and then hanged. This was by the orders of the civil commissioner. Both Sir Colin Campbell and Sir William Peel were said to have protested against the barbarity, but this I don't know for certain.

We halted in Futtehghur till the 6th, on which date a brigade, composed of the Forty-Second, Ninety-Third, a regiment of Punjâb infantry, a battery of artillery, a squadron of the Ninth Lancers, and Hodson's Horse, marched to Pâlamhow in the Shumshabad district. This town had been a hot-bed of rebellion under the leadership of a former native collector of revenue, who had proclaimed himself Râja of the district, and all the bad characters in it had flocked to his standard. However, the place was occupied without opposition. We encamped outside the town, and the civil police, along with the commissioner, arrested great numbers, among them being the man who had proclaimed himself the Râja or Nawâb for the Emperor of Delhi. My company, with some of Hodson's Horse and two artillery guns, formed a guard for the civil commissioner in the *chowk* or principal square of the town. The commissioner held his court in what had formerly been the *kotwâlee* or police station. I cannot say what form of trial the prisoners underwent, or what evidence was recorded against them. I merely know that they were marched

[1] Bedstead.

up in batches, and shortly after marched back again to a large tree of the banian species, which stood in the centre of the square, and hanged thereon. This went on from about three o'clock in the afternoon till daylight the following morning, when it was reported that there was no more room on the tree, and by that time there were one hundred and thirty men hanging from its branches. A grim spectacle indeed!

Many charges of cruelty and want of pity have been made against the character of Hodson. This makes me here mention a fact that certainly does not tend to prove these charges. During the afternoon of the day of which I write, Hodson visited the squadron of his regiment forming the cavalry of the civil commissioner's guard. Just at the time of his visit the commissioner wanted a hangman, and asked if any man of the Ninety-Third would volunteer for the job, stating as an inducement that all valuables in the way of rings or money found on the persons of the condemned would become the property of the executioner. No one volunteering for the job, the commissioner asked Jack Brian, a big tall fellow who was the right-hand man of the company, if he would act as executioner. Jack Brian turned round with a look of disgust, saying: "Wha do ye tak' us for? We of the Ninety-Third enlisted to fight men with arms in their hands. I widna' become yer hangman for all the loot in India!" Captain Hodson was standing close by, and hearing the answer, said, "Well answered, my brave fellow. I wish to shake hands with you," which he did. Then turning to Captain Dawson,

Hodson said: "I'm sick of work of this kind. I'm glad I'm not on duty;" and he mounted his horse, and rode off. However, some *domes*[1] or sweeper-police were found to act as hangmen, and the trials and executions proceeded.

We returned to Futtehghur on the 12th of January and remained in camp there till the 26th, when another expedition was sent out in the same direction. But this time only the right wing of the Ninety-Third and a wing of the Forty-Second formed the infantry, so my company remained in camp. This second force met with more opposition than the first one. Lieutenant Macdowell, Hodson's second in command, and several troopers were killed, and Hodson himself and some of his men were badly wounded, Hodson having two severe cuts on his sword arm; while the infantry had several men killed who were blown up with gunpowder. This force returned on the 28th of January, and either on the 2nd or 3rd of February we left Futtehghur *en route* again for Lucknow *via* Cawnpore.

We reached Cawnpore by ordinary marches, crossed into Oude, and encamped at Oonâo till the whole of the siege-train was passed on to Lucknow.

[1] The lowest Hindoo caste.

CHAPTER X

THE STRANGE STORY OF JAMIE GREEN

WHEN we returned to Cawnpore, although we had been barely two months away, we found it much altered. Many of the burnt-down bungalows were being rebuilt, and the fort at the end of the bridge of boats had become quite a strong place. The well where the murdered women and children were buried was now completely filled up, and a wooden cross erected over it. I visited the slaughter-house again, and found the walls of the several rooms all scribbled over both in pencil and charcoal. This had been done since my first visit in October; I am positive on this point. The unfortunate women who were murdered in the house left no writing on the walls whatever. There was writing on the walls of the barrack-rooms of Wheeler's entrenchment, mostly notes that had been made during the siege, but none on the walls of the slaughter-house. As mentioned in my last chapter, we only halted one day in Cawnpore before crossing into Oude, and marching to Oonâo about the 10th of February, we encamped there as a guard for the siege-train and ordnance-park which was being pushed on to Lucknow.

While at Oonâo a strange thing happened, which I shall here set down. Men live such busy lives in India that many who may have heard the story at the time have possibly forgotten all about it, while to most of my home-staying readers it will be quite fresh.

Towards the end of February, 1858, the army for the siege of Lucknow was gradually being massed in front of the doomed city, and lay, like a huge boa-constrictor coiled and ready for its spring, all along the road from Cawnpore to the Alumbâgh. A strong division, consisting of the Forty-Second and Ninety-Third Highlanders, the Fifty-Third, the Ninth Lancers, Peel's Naval Brigade, the siege-train, and several batteries of field-artillery, with the Fourth Punjâb Infantry and other Punjâbee corps, lay at Oonâo under the command of General Sir Edward Lugard and Brigadier Adrian Hope. We had been encamped in that place for about ten days,—the monotony of our lives being only occasionally broken by the sound of distant cannonading in front—when we heard that General Outram's position at the Alumbâgh had been vigorously attacked by a force from Lucknow, sometimes led by the Moulvie, and at others by the Begum in person. Now and then somewhat duller sounds came from the rear, which, we understood, arose from the operations of Sir Robert Napier and his engineers, who were engaged in blowing up the temples of Siva and Kâlee overlooking the *ghâts* at Cawnpore; not, as some have asserted, out of revenge, but for military considerations connected with the safety of the bridge of boats across the Ganges.

During one of these days of comparative inaction, I was lying in my tent reading some home papers which had just arrived by the mail, when I heard a man passing through the camp, calling out, "Plum-cakes! plum-cakes! Very good plum-cakes! Taste and try before you buy!" The advent of a plum-cake *wallah* was an agreeable change from ration-beef and biscuit, and he was soon called into the tent, and his own maxim of "taste and try before you buy" freely put into practice. This plum-cake vendor was a very good-looking, light-coloured native in the prime of life, dressed in scrupulously clean white clothes, with dark, curly whiskers and mustachios, carefully trimmed after the fashion of the Mahommedan native officers of John Company's army. He had a well-developed forehead, a slightly aquiline nose, and intelligent eyes. Altogether his appearance was something quite different from that of the usual camp-follower. But his companion, or rather the man employed as *coolie* to carry his basket, was one of the most villainous-looking specimens of humanity I ever set eyes on. As was the custom in those days, seeing that he did not belong to our own bazaar, and being the non-commissioned officer in charge of the tent, I asked the plum-cake man if he was provided with a pass for visiting the camp? "Oh yes, Sergeant *sâhib*," he replied, "there's my pass all in order, not from the Brigade-Major, but from the Brigadier himself, the Honourable Adrian Hope. I'm Jamie Green, mess-*khânsama*[1] of the late (I forget the

[1] Butler.

regiment he mentioned), and I have just come to Oonâo with a letter of introduction to General Hope from Sherer *sâhib*, the magistrate and collector of Cawnpore. You will doubtless know General Hope's handwriting." And there it was, all in order, authorising the bearer, by name Jamie Green, etc. etc., to visit both the camp and outpost for the sale of his plum-cakes, in the handwriting of the brigadier, which was well known to all the non-commissioned officers of the Ninety-Third, Hope having been colonel of the regiment.

Next to his appearance what struck me as the most remarkable thing about Jamie Green was the purity and easy flow of his English, for he at once sat down beside me, and asked to see the newspapers, and seemed anxious to know what the English press said about the mutiny, and to talk of all subjects connected with the strength, etc., of the army, the preparations going forward for the siege of Lucknow, and how the newly-arrived regiments were likely to stand the hot weather. In course of conversation I made some remarks about the fluency of his English, and he accounted for it by stating that his father had been the mess-*khânsama* of a European regiment, and that he had been brought up to speak English from his childhood, that he had learned to read and write in the regimental school, and for many years had filled the post of mess-writer, keeping all the accounts of the mess in English. During this time the men in the tent had been freely trying the plum-cakes, and a squabble arose between one of them and Jamie Green's servant about payment.

When I made some remark about the villainous look of the latter Green replied: "Oh, never mind him; he is an Irishman, and his name is Micky. His mother belongs to the regimental bazaar of the Eighty-Seventh Royal Irish, and he lays claim to the whole regiment, including the sergeant-major's cook, for his father. He has just come down from the Punjâb with the Agra convoy, but the commanding officer dismissed him at Cawnpore, because he had a young wife of his own, and was jealous of the good looks of Micky. But," continued Jamie Green, "a joke is a joke, but to eat a man's plum-cakes and then refuse to pay for them must be a Highland joke!" On this every man in the tent, appreciating the good humour of Jamie Green, turned on the man who had refused payment, and he was obliged to fork out the amount demanded. Jamie Green and Micky passed on to another tent, after the former had borrowed a few of the latest of my newspapers. Thus ended my first interview with the plum-cake vendor.

The second one was more interesting, and with a sadder termination. On the evening of the day after the events just described, I was on duty as sergeant in charge of our camp rear-guard, and at sunset when the orderly-corporal came round with the evening grog, he told us the strange news that Jamie Green, the plum-cake *wallah*, had been discovered to be a spy from Lucknow, had been arrested, and was then undergoing examination at the brigade-major's tent; and that it being too late to hang him that night, he was to be made over to my guard for safe custody, and that men had been warned for extra sentry on the guard-tent. I need not say that I was very sorry to hear the information, for, although a spy is at all times detested in the army, and no mercy is ever shown to one, yet I had formed a strong regard for this man, and a high opinion of his abilities in the short conversation I had held with him the previous day; and during the interval I had been thinking over how a man of his appearance and undoubted education could hold so low a position as that of a common camp-follower. But now the news that he had been discovered to be a spy accounted for the anomaly.

It would be needless for me to describe the bitter feeling of all classes against the mutineers, or rebels, and for any one to be denounced as a spy simply added fuel to the flames of hatred. Asiatic campaigns have always been conducted in a more remorseless spirit than those between European nations, but the war of the Mutiny, as I have before remarked in these reminiscences, was far worse than the usual type of even Asiatic fighting. It was something horrible and downright brutalising for an English army to be engaged in such a struggle, in which no quarter was ever given or asked. It was a war of downright butchery. Wherever the rebels met a Christian or a white man he was killed without pity or remorse, and every native who had assisted any such to escape, or was known to have concealed them, was as remorselessly put to death wherever the rebels had the ascendant. And wherever a European in power, either civil or military, met a rebel in arms, or any native whatever on whom suspicion rested, his shrift was as short and his fate as sure. The farce of putting an accused native on his trial before any of the civil officers attached to the different army-columns, after the civil power commenced to reassert its authority, was simply a parody on justice and a protraction of cruelty. Under martial law, punishment, whether deserved or not, was stern but sharp. But the civilian officers attached to the different movable columns for the trial of rebels, as far as they came under my notice, were even more relentless. No doubt these men excused themselves by the consideration that they were engaged in suppressing rebellion and mutiny, and that the actors on the other side had perpetrated great crimes.[1] So far as the Commander-in-Chief was concerned, Sir Colin Campbell was utterly opposed to extreme measures, and deeply deplored the wholesale executions by the civil power. Although as a soldier he would have been the last man in the country to spare rebels caught with arms in their hands, or those whose guilt was well known (and I know for certain that he held the action of Major Hodson with regard to the Delhi princes to have been justifiable), I well remember how

[1] It must also be remembered that these officials knew much more of the terrible facts attending the Mutiny—of the wholesale murder (and even worse) of English women and the slaughter of English children—than the rank and file were permitted to hear; and that they were also, both from their station and their experience, far better able to decide the measures best calculated to crush the imminent danger threatening our dominion in India.

emphatically I once heard him express his disgust when, on the march back from Futtehghur to Cawnpore, he entered a mango-tope full of rotting corpses, where one of those special commissioners had passed through with a movable column a few days before.

But I must return to my story. I had barely heard the news that Green had been arrested as a spy, when he was brought to my guard by some of the provost-marshal's staff, and handed over to me with instructions to keep him safe till he should be called for next morning. He was accompanied by the man who had carried his basket, who had also been denounced as one of the butchers at Cawnpore in July, 1857. And here I may state that the appearance of this man certainly did tally with the description afterwards given of one of these butchers by Fitchett, an Eurasian drummer attached to the Sixth Native Infantry which mutinied at Cawnpore, who embraced the Mahommedan religion to save his life, and was enrolled in the rebel force, but afterwards made his escape and presented himself at Meerut for enlistment in the police levy raised in October, 1858. What I am relating took place in February, 1858, about eight months before the existence of Fitchett was known to the authorities. However, when it was discovered that Fitchett had been serving in one of the mutineers' regiments, he was called on to say what he knew about the Cawnpore massacre, and I remember his statement was considered the most consistent of any of the numerous narratives published about it. Fitchett alleged that the sepoys of the Sixth

Native Infantry and other regiments, including the Nânâ Sâhib's own guard, had refused to kill the European women and children in the *bibi-ghur*,[1] and that five men were then brought by a slave-girl or mistress of the Nânâ to do it. Of the five men employed, two were butchers and two were villagers, and the fifth man was "a stout *bilâitee*[2] with very hairy hands." Fitchett further described one of the butchers as a tall, ugly man, very dark, and very much disfigured by smallpox, all points that tallied exactly with the appearance of this *coolie*. I don't suppose that Fitchett could have known that a man answering to his description had been hanged, as being one of the actors in the Cawnpore tragedy, some eight months before, for I don't recollect ever having seen the matter which I am relating mentioned in any newspaper.

But to proceed with my own story. My prisoners had no sooner been made over to me, than several of the guard, as was usual in those days, proposed to bring some pork from the bazaar to break their castes, as a sort of preparation for their execution. This I at once denounced as a proceeding which I certainly would not tolerate so long as I held charge of the guard, and I warned the men that if any one attempted to molest the prisoners, I should at once strip them of their belts, and place them in arrest for disobedience of orders and conduct unworthy of a British soldier, and

[1] Lit. Lady-house.

[2] Foreigner. Among the sepoys the word usually signified an Afghan or Caubuli.

the better-disposed portion of the guard at once applauded my resolution. I shall never forget the look of gratitude which came over the face of the unfortunate man who had called himself Jamie Green, when he heard me give these orders. He at once said it was an act of kindness which he had never expected, and for which he was truly grateful; and he unhesitatingly pronounced his belief that Allah and his Prophet would requite my kindness by bringing me safely through the remainder of the war. I thanked my prisoner for his good wishes and his prayers, and made him the only return in my power, viz., to cause his hands to be unfastened to allow him to perform his evening's devotions, and permitted him as much freedom as I possibly could, consistent with safe custody. His fellow-prisoner merely received my kindness with a scowl of sullen hatred, and when reproved by his master, I understood him to say that he wished for no favour from infidel dogs; but he admitted that the sergeant *sâhib* deserved a Mussulman's gratitude for saving him from an application of pig's fat.

After allowing my prisoners to perform their evening devotions, and giving them such freedom as I could, I made up my mind to go without sleep that night, for it would have been a serious matter for me if either of these men had escaped. I also knew that by remaining on watch myself I could allow them more freedom, and I determined they should enjoy every privilege in my power for what would certainly be their last night on earth, since it was doubtful if they would be spared to see the sun rise. With this view, I sent for one of the Mahommedan shopkeepers from the regimental bazaar, and told him to prepare at my expense whatever food the prisoners would eat. To this the man replied that since I, a Christian, had shown so much kindness to a Mussulman in distress, the Mahommedan shopkeepers in the bazaar would certainly be untrue to their faith if they should allow me to spend a single *pie* from my own pocket.

After being supplied with a savoury meal from the bazaar, followed by a fragrant hookah, to both of which he did ample justice, Jamie Green settled himself on a rug which had been lent to him, and said "*Shook'r Khooda!* (Thanks be to God)," for having placed him under the charge of such a merciful *sâhib* for this the last night of his life! "Such," he continued, "has been my *kismut*, and doubtless Allah will reward you, Sergeant *sâhib*, in his own good time for your kindness to his oppressed and afflicted servant. You have asked me to give you some account of my life, and if it is really true that I am a spy. With regard to being a spy in the ordinary meaning of the term, I most emphatically deny the accusation. I am no spy; but I am an officer of the Begum's army, come out from Lucknow to gain reliable information of the strength of the army and siege-train being brought against us. I am the chief engineer of the army of Lucknow, and came out on a reconnoitring expedition, but Allah has not blessed my enterprise. I intended to have left on my return to Lucknow this evening, and if fate had been propitious, I would have reached it before sunrise to-morrow, for I had got all the information which was wanted; but I was tempted to visit Oonâo once more, being on the direct road to Lucknow, because I was anxious to see whether the siege-train and ammunition-park had commenced to move, and it was my misfortune to encounter that son of a defiled mother who denounced me as a spy. A contemptible wretch who, to save his own neck from the gallows (for he first sold the English), now wishes to divert attention from his former rascality by selling the lives of his own countrymen and co-religionists; but Allah is just, he will yet reap the reward of his treachery in the fires of Jehunnum.[1]

"You ask me," continued the man, "what my name is, and state that you intend to write an account of my misfortune to your friends in Scotland. Well, I have no objection. The people of England,—and by England I mean Scotland as well—are just, and some of them may pity the fate of this servant of Allah. I have friends both in London and in Edinburgh, for I have twice visited both places. My name is Mahomed Ali Khân. I belong to one of the best families of Rohilcund, and was educated in the Bareilly College, and took the senior place in all English subjects. From Bareilly College I passed to the Government Engineering College at Roorkee, and studied engineering

[1] This very man who denounced Jamie Green as a spy was actually hanged in Bareilly in the following May for having murdered his master in that station when the Mutiny first broke out.

for the Company's service, and passed out the senior student of my year, having gained many marks in excess of all the European pupils, both civil and military. But what was the result? I was nominated to the rank of *jemadar* of the Company's engineers, and sent to serve with a company on detached duty on the hill roads as a native commissioned officer, but actually subordinate to a European sergeant, a man who was my inferior in every way, except, perhaps, in mere brute strength, a man of little or no education, who would never have risen above the grade of a working-joiner in England. Like most ignorant men in authority, he exhibited all the faults of the Europeans which most irritate and disgust us, arrogance, insolence, and selfishness. Unless you learn the language of my countrymen, and mix with the better-educated people of this country, you will never understand nor estimate at its full extent the mischief which one such man does to your national reputation. One such example is enough to confirm all that your worst enemies can say about your national selfishness and arrogance, and makes the people treat your pretensions to liberality and sympathy as mere hypocrisy. I had not joined the Company's service from any desire for wealth, but from the hope of gaining honourable service; yet on the very threshold of that service I met with nothing but disgrace and dishonour, having to serve under a man whom I hated, yea, worse than hated, whom I despised. I wrote to my father, and requested his permission to resign, and he agreed with me that I, the descendant of princes, could not serve the Company under conditions such as I have described. I resigned the service and returned home, intending to offer my services to his late Majesty Nussir-ood-Deen, King of Oude; but just when I reached Lucknow I was informed that his Highness Jung Bahâdoor of Nepâl, who is now at Goruckpore with an army of Goorkhas coming to assist in the loot of Lucknow, was about to visit England, and required a secretary well acquainted with the English language. I at once applied for the post, and being well backed by recommendations both from native princes and English officials, I secured the appointment, and in the suite of the Mâharâja I landed in England for the first time, and, among other places, we visited Edinburgh, where your regiment, the Ninety-Third Highlanders, formed the guard of honour for the reception of his Highness. Little did I think when I saw a kilted regiment for the first time, that I should ever be a prisoner in their tents in the plains of Hindustan; but who can predict or avoid his fate?

"Well, I returned to India, and filled several posts at different native courts till 1854, when I was again asked to visit England in the suite of Azeemoolla Khân, whose name you must have often heard in connection with this mutiny and rebellion. On the death of the Peishwa, the Nânâ had appointed Azeemoolla Khân to be his agent. He, like myself, had received a good education in English, under Gunga Deen, head-master of the Government school at Cawnpore. Azeemoolla was confident that, if he could visit

England, he would be able to have the decrees of Lord Dalhousie against his master reversed, and when I joined him he was about to start for England, well supplied with money to engage the best lawyers, and also to bribe high officials, if necessary. But I need not give you any account of our mission. You already know that, so far as London drawing-rooms went, it proved a social success, but as far as gaining our end a political failure; and we left England after spending over £50,000, to return to India *via* Constantinople in 1855. From Constantinople we visited the Crimea, where we witnessed the assault and defeat of the English on the 18th of June, and were much struck by the wretched state of both armies in front of Sebastopol. Thence we returned to Constantinople, and there met certain real or pretended Russian agents, who made large promises of material support if Azeemoolla could stir up a rebellion in India. It was then that I and Azeemoolla formed the resolution of attempting to overthrow the Company's Government, and, *Shook'r Khooda!* we have succeeded in doing that; for from the newspapers which you lent me, I see that the Company's *ráj* has gone, and that their charter for robbery and confiscation will not be renewed. Although we have failed to wrest the country from the English, I hope we have done some good, and that our lives will not be sacrificed in vain; for I believe direct government under the English parliament will be more just than was that of the Company, and that there is yet a future before my oppressed and downtrodden countrymen, although I shall not live to see it.

"I do not speak, *sâhib,* to flatter you or to gain your favour. I have already gained that, and I know that you cannot help me any farther than you are doing, and that if you could, your sense of duty would not let you. I know I must die; but the unexpected kindness which you have shown to me has caused me to speak my mind. I came to this tent with hatred in my heart, and curses on my lips; but your kindness to me, unfortunate, has made me, for the second time since I left Lucknow, ashamed of the atrocities committed during this rebellion. The first time was at Cawnpore a few days ago, when Colonel Napier of the Engineers was directing the blowing up of the Hindoo temples on the Cawnpore *ghât,* and a deputation of Hindoo priests came to him to beg that the temples might not be destroyed. 'Now, listen to me,' said Colonel Napier in reply to them; 'you were all here when our women and children were murdered, and you also well know that we are not destroying these temples for vengeance, but for military considerations connected with the safety of the bridge of boats. But if any man among you can prove to me that he did a single act of kindness to any Christian man, woman, or child, nay, if he can even prove that he uttered one word of intercession for the life of any one of them, I pledge myself to spare the temple where he worships.' I was standing in the crowd close to Colonel Napier at the time, and I thought it was bravely spoken. There was no reply, and the cowardly Brahmins slunk away. Napier gave the signal and the temples leaped into the air; and I was so impressed with the justness of Napier's remarks that I too turned away, ashamed."

On this I asked him, "Were you in Cawnpore when the Mutiny broke out?" To which he replied: "No, thank God! I was in my home in Rohilcund; and my hands are unstained by the blood of any one, excepting those who have fallen in the field of battle. I knew that the storm was about to burst, and had gone to place my wife and children in safety, and I was in my village when I heard the news of the mutinies at Meerut and Bareilly. I immediately hastened to join the Bareilly brigade, and marched with them for Delhi. There I was appointed engineer-in-chief, and set about strengthening the defences by the aid of a party of the Company's engineers which had mutinied on the march from Roorkee to Meerut. I remained in Delhi till it was taken by the English in September. I then made my way to Lucknow with as many men as I could collect of the scattered forces. We first marched to Muttra, where we were obliged to halt till I threw a bridge of boats across the Jumna for the retreat of the army. We had still a force of over thirty thousand men under the command of Prince Feroz Shâh and General Bukht Khân. As soon as I reached Lucknow I was honoured with the post of chief-engineer. I was in Lucknow in November when your regiment assisted to relieve the Residency. I saw the horrible slaughter in the Secundrabâgh. I had directed the defences of that place the night before, and was looking on from the Shâh Nujeef when you assaulted it. I had posted over three thousand of the best troops in Lucknow in the Secundrabâgh, as it was the key to the position, and not a man escaped. I nearly fainted; my liver turned to water when I saw the green flag pulled down, and a Highland bonnet set up on the flag-staff which I had erected the night before. I knew then that all was over, and directed the guns of the Shâh Nujeef to open fire on the Secundrabâgh. Since then I have planned and superintended the construction of all the defensive works in and around Lucknow. You will see them when you return, and if the sepoys and artillerymen stand firmly behind them, many of the English army will lose the number of their mess, as you call it, before you again become masters of Lucknow."

I then asked him if it was true that the man he had called Micky on our first acquaintance had been one of the men employed by the Nânâ to butcher the women and children at Cawnpore in July? To this he replied: "I believe it is true, but I did not know this when I employed him; he was merely recommended to me as a man on whom I could depend. If I had known then that he was a murderer of women and children, I should have had nothing to do with him, for it is he who has brought bad luck on me; it is my *kismut,* and I must suffer. Your English proverb says, 'You cannot touch pitch and escape defilement,' and I must suffer; Allah is just. It is the conduct of wretches such as these that has brought the anger of Allah on our cause."

On this I asked him if he knew whether there was any truth in the report of the European women having been dishonoured before being murdered. "*Sâhib,*" he replied, "you are a stranger to this country or you would not ask such a question. Any one who knows anything of the customs of this country and the strict rules of caste, knows that all such stories are lies, invented to stir up race-hatred, as if we had not enough of that on both sides already. That the women and children were cruelly murdered I admit, but not one of them was dishonoured; and all the sentences written on the walls of the houses in Cawnpore, such as, 'We are at the mercy of savages, who have ravished young and old,' and such like, which have appeared in the Indian papers and been copied from them into the English ones, are malicious forgeries, and were written on the walls after the re-occupation of Cawnpore by General Outram's and Havelock's forces. Although I was not there myself, I have spoken with many who were there, and I know that what I tell you is true."

I then asked him if he could give me any idea of the reason that had led the Nânâ to order the commission of such a cold-blooded, cowardly crime. "Asiatics," he said, "are weak, and their promises are not to be relied on, but that springs more from indifference to obligations than from prearranged treachery. When they make promises, they intend to keep them; but when they find them inconvenient, they choose to forget them. And so it was, I believe, with the Nânâ

Sâhib. He intended to have spared the women and children, but they had an enemy in his *zenâna* in the person of a female fiend who had formerly been a slave-girl, and there were many about the Nânâ (Azeemoolla Khân for one) who wished to see him so irretrievably implicated in rebellion that there would be no possibility for him to draw back. So this woman was powerfully supported in her evil counsel, and obtained permission to have the English ladies killed; and after the sepoys of the Sixth Native Infantry and the Nânâ's own guard had refused to do the horrible work, this woman went and procured the wretches who did it. This information I have from General Tântia Topee, who quarrelled with the Nânâ on this same matter. What I tell you is true: the murder of the European women and children at Cawnpore was a woman's crime, for there is no fiend equal to a female fiend; but what cause she had for enmity against the unfortunate ladies I don't know—I never inquired."

Those of my readers who were in India at the time may remember that something about this slave-girl was said in all the native evidence collected at the time on the subject of the Cawnpore massacre.

I next asked Mahomed Ali Khân if he knew whether there was any truth in the stories about General Wheeler's daughter having shot four or five men with a revolver, and then leaped into the well at Cawnpore. "All these stories," was his answer, "are pure inventions with no foundation of truth. General Wheeler's daughter is still alive, and is now in Lucknow; she has become a Mussulmânee, and has married according to Mahommedan law the man who protected her; whether she may ever return to her own people I know not."

In such conversation I passed the night with my prisoner, and towards daybreak I permitted him to perform his ablutions and morning devotions, after which he once more thanked me, and prayed that Allah might reward me for my kindness to His oppressed servant. Once, and only once, did he show any weakness, in alluding to his wife and two boys in their far-away home in Rohilcund, when he remarked that they would never know the fate of their unfortunate father. But he at once checked himself, saying, "I have read French history as well as English; I must remember Danton, and show no weakness." He then produced a gold ring which was concealed among his hair, and asked me if I would accept it and keep it in remembrance of him, in token of his gratitude. It was, he said, the only thing he could give me, as everything of value had been taken from him when he was arrested. He went on to say that the ring in question was only a common one, not worth more than ten rupees, but that it had been given to him by a holy man in Constantinople as a talisman, though the charm had been broken when he had joined the unlucky man who was his fellow-prisoner. I accepted the ring, which he placed on my finger with a blessing and a prayer for my preservation, and he told me to look on it and remember Mahomed Khân when I was in front of the fortifications of Lucknow, and no evil would befall me. He had hardly finished speaking when a guard from the provost-marshal came with an order to take over the prisoners, and I handed this man over with a sincere feeling of pity for his fate.

Immediately after, I received orders that the division would march at sunrise for Lucknow, and that my party was to join the rear-guard, after the ammunition-park and siege-train had moved on. The sun was high in the heavens before we left the encamping-ground, and in passing under a tree on the side of the Cawnpore and Lucknow road, I looked up, and was horrified to see my late prisoner and his companion hanging stark and stiffened corpses! I could hardly repress a tear as I passed. But on the 11th of March, in the assault on the Begum's Kothee, I remembered Mahomed Ali Khân and looked on the ring. I am thankful to say that I went through the rest of the campaign without a scratch, and the thoughts of my kindness to this unfortunate man certainly did not inspire me with any desire to shirk danger. I still have the ring, the only piece of Mutiny plunder I ever possessed, and shall hand it down to my children together with the history of Mahomed Ali Khân.

CHAPTER XI

THE SIEGE OF LUCKNOW—SIR COLIN APPOINTED COLONEL OF THE NINETY-THIRD—ASSAULT ON THE MARTINIÈRE —A "RANK" JOKE.

AFTER leaving Oonâo our division under Sir Edward Lugard reached Buntera, six miles from the Alumbâgh, on the 27th of February, and halted there till the 2nd of March, when we marched to the Dilkooshá, encamping a short distance from the palace barely beyond reach of the enemy's guns, for they were able at times to throw round-shot into our camp. We then settled down for the siege and capture of Lucknow; but the work before us was considered tame and unimportant when compared with that of the relief of the previous November. Every soldier in the camp clearly recognised that the capture of the doomed city was simply a matter of time,—a few days more or less—and the task before us a mere matter of routine, nothing to be compared to the exciting exertions which we had to put forth for the relief of our countrywomen and their children.

At the time of the annexation of Oude Lucknow was estimated to contain from eight to nine hundred thousand inhabitants, or as many as Delhi and Benares

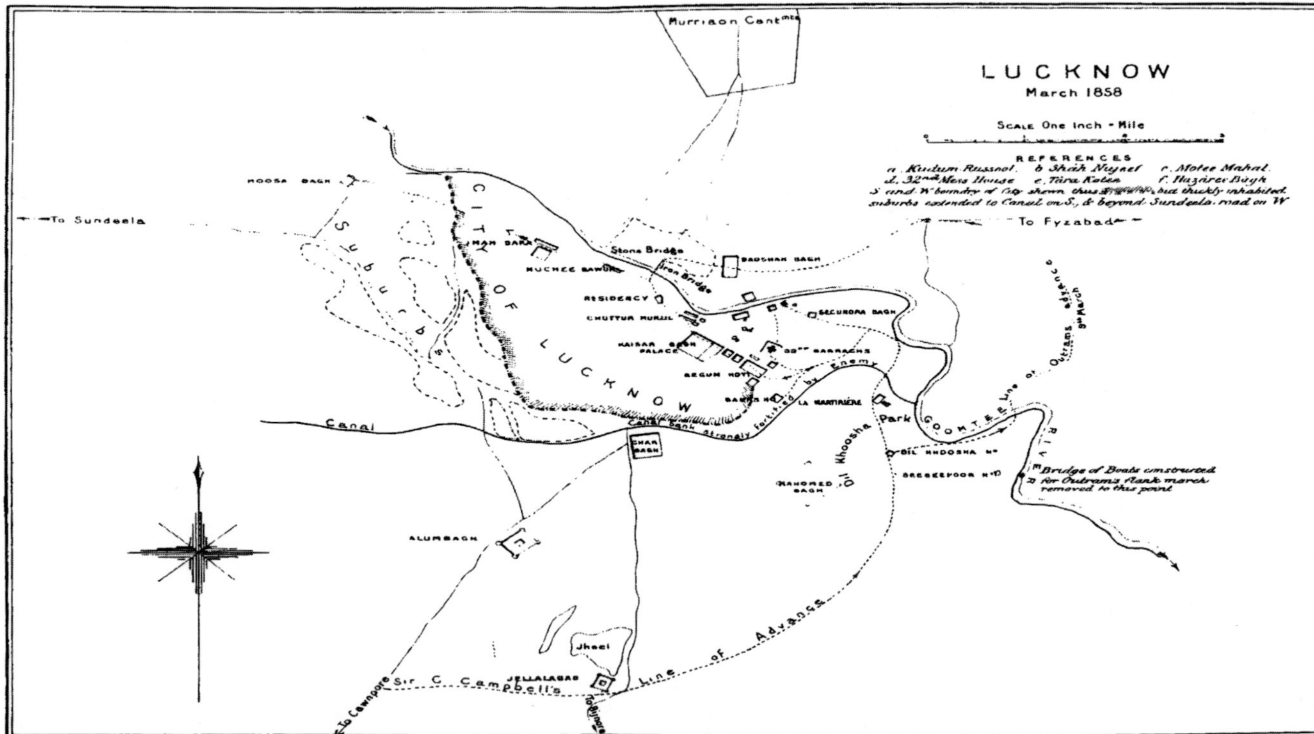

R & R Clark Printers Edinburgh

To face page 194

put together. The camp and bazaars of our force were full of reports of the great strength and determination of the enemy, and certainly all the chiefs of Oude, Mahommedan and Hindoo, had joined the standard of the Begum and had sworn to fight for their young king Brijis Kuddur. All Oude was therefore still against us, and we held only the ground covered by the British guns. Bazaar reports estimated the enemy's strength at from two hundred and fifty to three hundred thousand fighting men, with five hundred guns in position; but in the Commander-in-Chief's camp the strength of the enemy was computed at sixty thousand regulars, mutineers who had lately served the Company, and about seventy thousand irregulars, matchlock-men, armed police, dacoits, etc., making a total of one hundred and thirty thousand fighting men. To fight this large army, sheltered behind entrenchments and loophooled walls, the British force, even after being joined by Jung Bahâdoor's Goorkhas, mustered only about thirty-one thousand men of all arms, and one hundred and sixty-four guns.

From the heights of the Dilkooshá in the cool of the early morning, Lucknow, with its numerous domed mosques, minarets, and palaces, looked very picturesque. I don't think I ever saw a prettier scene than that presented on the morning of the 3rd of March, 1858, when the sun rose, and Captain Peel and his Bluejackets were getting their heavy guns, 68-pounders, into position. From the Dilkooshá, even without the aid of telescopes, we could see that the defences had been greatly strengthened since we retired from Lucknow in November, and I called to mind the warning of Jamie Green, that if the enemy stood to their guns like men behind those extensive earthworks, many of the British force would lose the number of their mess before we could take the city; and although the Indian papers which reached our camp affected to sneer at the Begum, Huzrut Mahal, and the legitimacy of her son Brijis Kuddur, whom the mutineers had proclaimed King of Oude, they had evidently the support of the whole country, for every chief and *zemindar* of any importance had joined them.

On the morning after we had pitched our camp in the Dilkooshá park, I went out with Sergeant Peter Gillespie, our deputy provost-marshal, to take a look round the bazaars, and just as we turned a corner on our way back to camp, we met some gentlemen in civilian dress, one of whom turned out to be Mr. Russell, the *Times*' correspondent, whom we never expected to have seen in India. "Save us, sir!" said Peter Gillespie. "Is that you, Maister Russell? I never did think of meeting you here, but I am right glad to see you, and so will all our boys be!" After a short chat and a few inquiries about the regiment, Mr. Russell asked when we expected to be in Lucknow, to which Peter Gillespie replied: "Well, I dinna ken, sir, but when Sir Colin likes to give the order, we'll just advance and take it." I may here mention that Sergeant Gillespie lived to go through the Mutiny, and the cholera epidemic in Peshawar in 1862, only to die of hydrophobia from the bite of a pet dog in Sialkote years after, when he was about to retire on his sergeant's pension. I mention this because Peter Gillespie was a well-known character in the old regiment; he had served on the staff of the provost-marshal throughout the Crimean war, and, so far as I now remember, Colonel Ewart and Sergeant Gillespie were the only two men in the regiment who gained the Crimean medal with the four clasps, for Alma, Balaklava, Inkerman, and Sebastopol.

On the 4th of March the Ninety-Third, a squadron of the Ninth Lancers, and a battery of artillery, were marched to the banks of the Goomtee opposite Beebeepore House, to form a guard for the engineers engaged in throwing a pontoon bridge across the Goomtee. The weather was now very hot in the day-time, and as we were well beyond the range of the enemy's guns, we were allowed to undress by companies and bathe in the river. As far as I can remember, we were two days on this duty. During the forenoon of the second day the Commander-in-Chief visited us, and the regiment fell in to receive him, because, he said, he had something of importance to communicate. When formed up, Sir Colin told us that he had just received despatches from home, and among them a letter from the Queen in which the Ninety-Third was specially mentioned. He then pulled the letter out of his pocket, and read the paragraph alluded to, which ran as follows, as nearly as I remembered to note it down after it was read: "The Queen wishes Sir Colin to convey the expression of her great admiration and gratitude to all European as well as native troops who have fought so nobly and so gallantly for the relief of Lucknow, amongst whom the Queen is rejoiced to see the Ninety-Third Highlanders." Colonel Leith-Hay at once called for three cheers for her Majesty the Queen, which were given with hearty good-will, followed by three more for the Commander-in-Chief. The colonel then requested Sir Colin to return the thanks of the officers, non-commissioned officers, and men of the regiment to her Majesty the Queen for her most gracious message, and for her special mention of the Ninety-Third, an honour which no one serving in the regiment would ever forget. To this Sir Colin replied that nothing would give him greater pleasure than to comply with this request; but he had still more news to communicate. He had also a letter from his Royal Highness the Duke of Cambridge to read to us, which he proceeded to do as follows: "One line in addition to my letter addressed to you this morning, to say that, in consequence of the Colonelcy of the Ninety-Third Highlanders having become vacant by the death of General Parkinson, I have recommended the Queen to remove you to the command of that distinguished and gallant corps, with which you have been so much associated, not alone at the present moment in India, but also during the whole of the campaign in the Crimea. I thought such an arrangement would be agreeable to yourself, and I know that it is the highest compliment that her Majesty could pay to the Ninety-Third Highlanders to see their dear old chief at their head." As soon as Sir Colin had read this letter, the whole regiment cheered till we were hoarse; and when Sir Colin's voice could again be heard, he called for the master-tailor to go to the head-quarters camp to take his measure to send home for a uniform of the regiment for him, feather bonnet and all complete; and about eighteen months afterwards Sir Colin visited us in Subâthoo, dressed in the regimental uniform then ordered.

Early on the 7th of March General Outram's division crossed the Goomtee by the bridge of boats, and we returned to our tents at the Dilkooshá. About mid-day we could see Outram's division, of which the Seventy-Ninth Cameron Highlanders formed one of the infantry corps, driving the enemy before them in beautiful style. We saw also the Queen's Bays, in their bright scarlet uniform and brass helmets, make a splendid charge, scattering the enemy like sheep, somewhere about the place where the buildings of the Upper India Paper Mills now stand. In this charge Major Percy Smith and several men galloped right through the enemy's lines, and were surrounded and killed. Spies reported that Major Smith's head was cut off, and, with his helmet, plume, and uniform, paraded through the streets of Lucknow as the head of the Commander-in-Chief. But the triumph of the enemy was short. On the 8th General Outram was firmly established on the north bank of the Goomtee, with a siege-train of twenty-two heavy guns, with which he completely turned and enfiladed the enemy's strong position.

On the 9th of March we were ordered to take our

dinners at twelve o'clock, and shortly after that hour our division, consisting of the Thirty-Eighth, Forty-Second, Fifty-Third, Ninetieth, Ninety-Third, and Fourth Punjâb Infantry, was under arms, screened by the Dilkooshá palace and the garden walls round it, and Peel's Blue-jackets were pouring shot and shell, with now and again a rocket, into the Martinière as fast as ever they could load. About two o'clock the order was given for the advance—the Forty-Second to lead and the Ninety-Third to support; but we no sooner emerged from the shelter of the palace and garden-walls than the orderly advance became a rushing torrent. Both regiments dashed down the slope abreast, and the earthworks, trenches, and rifle-pits in front of the Martinière were cleared, the enemy flying before us as fast as their legs could carry them. We pursued them right through the gardens, capturing their first line of works along the canal in front of Banks's bungalow and the Begum's palace. There we halted for the night, our heavy guns and mortar-batteries being advanced from the Dilkooshá; and I, with some men from my company, was sent on piquet to a line of unroofed huts in front of one of our mortar-batteries, for fear the enemy from the Begum's palace might make a rush on the mortars. This piquet was not relieved till the morning of the 11th, when I learned that my company had been sent back as camp-guards, the captains of companies having drawn lots for this service, as all were equally anxious to take part in the assault on the Begum's palace, and it was known the Ninety-Third were to form the storming-party. As soon as the works should be breached, I and the men who were with me on the advance-piquet were to be sent to join Captain M'Donald's company, instead of going back to our own in camp. After being relieved from piquet, our little party set about preparing some food. Our own company having gone back to camp, no rations had been drawn for us, and our haversacks were almost empty; so I will here relate a mild case of cannibalism. Of the men of my own company who were with me on this piquet one was Andrew M'Onvill,—Handy Andy, as he was called in the regiment—a good-hearted, jolly fellow, and as full of fun and practical jokes as his namesake, Lever's hero,—a thorough Paddy from Armagh, a soldier as true as the steel of a Damascus blade or a Scotch Andrea Ferrara. When last I heard of him, I may add, he was sergeant-major of a New Zealand militia regiment. Others were Sandy Proctor, soldier-servant to Dr. Munro, and George Patterson, the son of the carrier of Ballater in Aberdeenshire. I forget who the rest were, but we were joined by John M'Leod, the pipe-major, and one or two more. We got into an empty hut, well sheltered from the bullets of the enemy, and Handy Andy sallied out on a foraging expedition for something in the way of food. He had a friend in the Fifty-Third who was connected in some way with the quarter-master's department, and always well supplied with extra provender. The Fifty-Third were on our right, and there Handy Andy found his friend, and returned with a good big steak, cut from an artillery gun-bullock which had been killed by a round-shot; also some sheep's liver and a haversack full of biscuits, with plenty of pumpkin to make a good stew. There was no lack of cooking-pots in the huts around, and plenty of wood for fuel, so we kindled a fire, and very soon had an excellent stew in preparation. But the enemy pitched some shells into our position, and one burst close to a man named Tim Drury, a big stout fellow, killing him on the spot. I forget now which company he belonged to, but his body lay where he fell, just outside our hut, with one thigh nearly torn away. My readers must not for a moment think that such a picture in the foreground took away our appetites in the least. There is nothing like a campaign for making one callous and selfish, and developing the qualities of the wild beast in one's nature; and the thought which rises uppermost is—Well, it is his turn now, and it may be mine next, and there is no use in being down-hearted! Our steak had been broiled to a turn, and our stew almost cooked, when we noticed tiffin and breakfast combined arrive for the European officers of the Fourth Punjâb Regiment, and some others who were waiting sheltered by the walls of a roofless hut near where we were. Among them was a young fellow, Lieutenant Fitzgerald Cologan, attached to some native regiment, a great favourite with the Ninety-Third for his pluck. John M'Leod at once proposed that Handy Andy should go and offer him half of our broiled steak, and ask him for a couple of bottles of beer for our dinner, as it might be the last time we should have the chance of drinking his health. He and the other officers with him accepted the steak with thanks, and Andy returned, to our no small joy, with two quart bottles of Bass's beer. But, unfortunately he had attracted the attention of Charley F., the greatest glutton in the Ninety-Third, who was so well known for his greediness that no one would chum with him. Charley was a long-legged, humpbacked, cadaverous-faced, bald-headed fellow, who had joined the regiment as a volunteer from the Seventy-Second before we left Dover in the spring of 1857, and on account of his long legs and humpback, combined with the inordinate capacity of his stomach and an incurable habit of grumbling, he had been re-christened the "Camel," before we had proceeded many marches with that useful animal in India. Our mutual congratulations were barely over on the acquisition of the two bottles of beer, when, to our consternation, we saw the Camel dodging from cover to cover, as the enemy were keeping up a heavy fire on our position, and if any one exposed himself in the least, a shower of bullets was sent whistling round him. However, the Camel, with a due regard to the wholeness of his skin, steadily made way towards our hut. We all knew that if he were admitted to a share of our stew, very little would be left for ourselves. John M'Leod and I suggested that we should, at the risk of quarrelling with him, refuse to allow him any share, but Handy Andy said, "Leave him to me, and if a bullet doesn't knock him over as he comes round the next corner, I'll put him off asking for a share of the stew." By that time we had finished our beer. Well, the Camel took good care to dodge the bullets of Jack Pandy, and he no sooner reached a sheltered place in front of the hut, than Andy called out: "Come along, Charley, you are just in time; we got a slice of a nice steak from an artillery-bullock this morning, and because it was too small alone for a dinner for the four of us, we have just stewed it with a slice from Tim Drury, and bedad it's first-rate! Tim tastes for all the world like fresh pork"; and with that Andy picked out a piece of the sheep's liver on the prongs of his fork, and offered it to Charley as part of Tim Drury, at the same time requesting him not to mention the circumstance to any one. This was too much for the Camel's stomach. He plainly believed Andy, and turned away, as if he would be sick. However, he recovered himself, and replied: "No, thank you; hungry as I am, it shall never be in the power of any one to tell my auld mither in the Grass Market o' Edinboro' that her Charley had become a cannibal! But if you can spare me a drop of the beer I'll be thankful for it, for the sight of your stew has made me feel unco' queer." We expressed our sorrow that the beer was all drunk before we had seen Charley performing his oblique advance, and Andy again pressed him to partake of a little of the stew; but Charley refused to join, and sitting down in a sheltered spot in the corner of our roofless mud-hut, made wry faces at the relish evinced by the rest of us over our savoury stew. The Camel eventually discovered that he had been made a fool of, and he never forgave us for cheating him out of a share of the savoury mess.

CHAPTER XII

ASSAULT ON THE BEGUM'S KOTHEE—DEATH OF CAPTAIN M'DONALD—MAJOR HODSON WOUNDED—HIS DEATH

We had barely finished our meal when we noticed a stir among the staff-officers, and a consultation taking place between General Sir Edward Lugard, Brigadier Adrian Hope, and Colonel Napier. Suddenly the order was given to the Ninety-Third to fall in. This was quietly done, the officers taking their places, the men tightening their belts and pressing their bonnets firmly on their heads, loosening the ammunition in their pouches, and seeing that the springs of their bayonets held tight. Thus we stood for a few seconds, when Brigadier Hope passed the signal for the assault on the Begum's Kothee. Just before the signal was given two men from the Fifty-Third rushed up to us with a soda-water bottle full of grog. One of them was Lance-Corporal Robert Clary, who is at present, I believe, police-sergeant in the Municipal Market, Calcutta; the other was the friend of Andrew M'Onvill, who had supplied us with the steaks for our "cannibal feast." I may mention that Lance-Corporal Clary was the same man who led the party of the Fifty-Third to capture the guns at the Kâlee Nuddee bridge, and who called out: "Three cheers for the Commander-in-Chief, boys," when Sir Colin Campbell was threatening to send the regiment to the rear for breach of orders. Clary was a County Limerick boy of the right sort, such as filled the ranks of our Irish regiments of the old days. No Fenian nor Home Ruler; but ever ready to uphold the honour of the British Army by land or by sea, and to share the contents of his haversack or his glass of grog with a comrade; one of those whom Scott immortalises in *The Vision of Don Roderick.*

Hark! from yon stately ranks what laughter rings,
  Mingling wild mirth with war's stern minstrelsy,
His jest while each blithe comrade round him flings,
  And moves to death with military glee!
Boast, Erin, boast them! tameless, frank, and free,
  In kindness warm, and fierce in danger known,
Rough Nature's children, humorous as she.

When Captain M'Donald, whose company we had joined, saw the two Fifty-Third boys, he told them that they had better rejoin their own regiment. Clary replied, "Sure, Captain, you don't mean it;" and seeing Dr. Munro, our surgeon, busy giving directions to his assistants and arranging bandages, etc., in a *dooly*, Clary went on:—"We have been sent by Lieutenant Munro of our company to take care of his namesake your doctor, who never thinks of himself, but is sure to be in the thick of the fight, looking out for wounded men. You of the Ninety-Third don't appreciate his worth. There's not another doctor in the army to equal him or to replace him should he get knocked over in this scrimmage, and we of the Fifty-Third have come to take care of him." "If that is the case," said Captain M'Donald, "I'll allow you to remain; but you must take care that no harm befalls our doctor, for he is a great friend of mine." And with that Captain M'Donald stepped aside and plucked a rose from a bush close by, (we were then formed up in what had been a beautiful garden), and going up to Munro he gave him the flower saying, "Good-bye, old friend, keep this for my sake." I have often recalled this incident and wondered if poor Captain M'Donald had any presentiment that he would be killed! Although he had been a captain for some years, he was still almost a boy. He was a son of General Sir John M'Donald, K.C.B., of Dalchosnie, Perthshire, and was wounded in his right arm early in the day by a splinter from a shell, but he refused to go to the rear, and remained at the head of his company, led it through the breach, and was shot down just inside, two bullets striking him almost at once, one right in his throat just over the breast-bone, as he was waving his claymore and cheering on his company. After the fight was over I made my way to where the dead were collected and cut off a lock of his hair and sent it to a young lady, Miss M. E. Ainsworth, of Inverighty House, Forfar, who, I knew, was acquainted with Captain M'Donald's family. I intended the lock of hair for his mother, and I did not know if his brother officers would think of sending any memento of him. I don't know if ever the lock of hair reached his mother or not. When I went to do this I found Captain M'Donald's soldier-servant crying beside the lifeless body of his late master, wringing his hands and saying, "Oh! but it was a shame to kill him." And so it was! I never saw a more girlish-looking face than his was in death; his features were so regular, and looked strangely like those of a wax doll, which was, I think, partly the effect of the wound in the throat. But to return to the assault.

When Captain M'Donald fell the company was led by the senior lieutenant, and about twenty yards inside the breach in the outer rampart we were stopped by a ditch nearly eighteen feet wide and at least twelve to fourteen feet deep. It was easy enough to slide down to the bottom; the difficulty was to get up on the other side! However, there was no hesitation; the stormers dashed into the ditch, and running along to the right in search of some place where we could get up on the inside, we met part of the grenadier company headed by Lieutenant E. S. Wood, an active and daring young officer. I may here mention that there were two lieutenants of the name of Wood at this time in the Ninety-Third. One belonged to my company; his name was S. E. Wood and he was severely wounded at the relief of Lucknow and was, at the time of which I am writing, absent from the regiment. The one to whom I now refer was Lieutenant E. S. Wood of the grenadier company. When the two parties in the ditch met, both in search of a place to get out, Mr. Wood got on the shoulders of another grenadier and somehow scrambled up claymore in hand. He was certainly the first man inside the inner works of the Begum's palace, and when the enemy saw him emerge from the ditch they fled to barricade doors and windows to prevent us getting into the buildings. His action saved us, for the whole of us might have been shot like rats in the ditch if they had attacked Mr. Wood, instead of flying when they saw the tall grenadier claymore in hand. As soon as he saw the coast clear the lieutenant lay down on the top of the ditch, and was thus able to reach down and catch hold of the men's rifles by the bends of the bayonets; and with the aid of the men below pushing up behind, we were all soon pulled out of the ditch. When all were up, one of the men turned to Mr. Wood and said: "If any officer in the regiment deserves to get the Victoria Cross, sir, you do; for besides the risk you have run from the bullets of the enemy, it's more than a miracle that you're not shot by our own rifles; they're all on full-cock." And so it was! Seizing loaded rifles on full-cock by the muzzles, and pulling more than a score of men out of a deep ditch, was a dangerous thing to do; but no one thought of the danger, nor did any-one think of even easing the spring to half-cock, much less of firing his rifle off before being pulled up. However, Mr. Wood escaped, and after getting his captaincy he left the regiment and became Conservator of Forests in Oude. I may mention that Mr. Wood was a younger brother of Mr. H. W. I. Wood, for many years the well-known secretary to the Bengal Chamber of Commerce. He has just lately retired on his pension; I wonder if he ever recalls the danger he incurred from pulling his men out of the ditch of the Begum's palace by the muzzles of their loaded rifles on full-cock!

By the time we got out of the ditch we found every door and window of the palace buildings barricaded, and every loop-hole defended by an invisible enemy. But one barrier after another was forced, and men in small parties, headed by the officers, got possession of the inner square, where the enemy in large numbers stood ready for the struggle. But no thought of unequal numbers held us back. The command was given: "Keep well together, men, and use the bayonet; give them the Secundrabâgh and the sixteenth of November over again." I need not describe the fight. It raged for about two hours from court to court, and from room to room; the pipe-major, John M'Leod, playing the pipes inside as calmly as if he had been walking round the officers' mess-tent at a regimental festival. When all was over, General Sir Edward Lugard, who commanded the division, complimented the pipe-major on his coolness and bravery: "Ah, sir," said John, "I knew our boys would fight all the better when cheered by the bagpipes."

Within about two hours from the time the signal for the assault was given, over eight hundred and sixty of the enemy lay dead within the inner court, and no quarter was sought or given. By this time we were broken up in small parties in a series of separate fights, all over the different detached buildings of the palace. Captain M'Donald being dead, the men who had been on piquet with me joined a party under Lieutenant

Sergison, and while breaking in the door of a room, Mr. Sergison was shot dead at my side with several men. When we had partly broken in the door, I saw that there was a large number of the enemy inside the room, well armed with swords and spears, in addition to fire-arms of all sorts, and, not wishing to be either killed myself or have more of the men who were with me killed, I divided my party, placing some at each side of the door to shoot every man who showed himself, or attempted to rush out. I then sent two men back to the breach, where I knew Colonel Napier with his engineers were to be found, to get a few bags of gunpowder with slow-matches fixed, to light and pitch into the room. Instead of finding Napier, the two men sent by me found the redoubtable Major Hodson who had accompanied Napier as a volunteer in the storming of the palace. Hodson did not wait for the powder-bags, but, after showing the men where to go for them, came running up himself, sabre in hand. "Where are the rebels?" he said. I pointed to the door of the room, and Hodson, shouting "Come on!" was about to rush in. I implored him not to do so, saying, "It's certain death; wait for the powder; I've sent men for powder-bags." Hodson made a step forward, and I put out my hand to seize him by the shoulder to pull him out of the line of the doorway, when he fell back shot through the chest. He gasped out a few words, either "Oh, my wife!" or, "Oh, my mother!" —I cannot now rightly remember—but was immediately choked by blood. At the time I thought the bullet had passed through his lungs, but since then I have seen the memoir written by his brother, the Rev. George H. Hodson, Vicar of Enfield, in which it is stated that the bullet passed through his liver. However, I assisted to get him lifted into a *dooly* (by that time the bearers had got in and were collecting the wounded who were unable to walk), and I sent him back to where the surgeons were, fully expecting that he would be dead before anything could be done for him. It will thus be seen that the assertion that Major Hodson was looting when he was killed is untrue. No looting had been commenced, not even by Jung Bahâdoor's Goorkhas. That Major Hodson was killed through his own rashness cannot be denied; but for any one to say that he was looting is a cruel slander on one of the bravest of Englishmen.

Shortly after I had lifted poor Hodson into the *dooly* and sent him away in charge of his orderly, the two men who had gone for the powder came up with several bags, with slow-matches fixed in them. These we ignited, and then pitched the bags in through the door. Two or three bags very soon brought the enemy out, and they were bayoneted down without mercy. One of the men who were with me was, I think, Mr. Rule, who is now *sans* a leg, and employed by the G.I.P. Railway in Bombay, but was then a powerful young man of the light company. Rule rushed in among the rebels, using both bayonet and butt of his rifle, shouting, "Revenge for the death of Hodson!" and he killed more than half the men single-handed.

By this time we had been over two hours inside the breach, and almost all opposition had ceased. Lieutenant and Adjutant "Willie" MacBean, as he was known to the officers, and "Paddy" MacBean to the men, encountered a *havildâr*, a *nâik*, and nine sepoys at one gate, and killed the whole eleven, one after the other. The *havildâr* was the last; and by the time he got out through the narrow gate, several men came to the assistance of MacBean, but he called to them not to interfere, and the *havildâr* and he went at it with their swords. At length MacBean made a feint cut, but instead gave the point, and put his sword through the chest of his opponent. For this MacBean got the Victoria Cross, mainly, I believe, because Sir Edward Lugard, the general in command of the division, was looking down from the ramparts above and saw the whole affair. I don't think that MacBean himself thought he had done anything extraordinary. He was an Inverness-shire ploughman before he enlisted, and rose from the ranks to command the regiment, and died a major-general. There were still a number of old soldiers in the regiment who had been privates with MacBean when I enlisted, and many anecdotes were related about him. One of these was that when MacBean first joined, he walked with a rolling gait, and the drill-corporal was rather abusive with him when learning his drill. At last he became so offensive that another recruit proposed to MacBean, who was a very powerful man, that they should call the corporal behind the canteen in the barrack-yard and give him a good thrashing, to which proposal MacBean replied: "Toots, toots, man, that would never do. I am going to command this regiment before I leave it, and it would be an ill beginning to be brought before the colonel for thrashing the drill-corporal!" MacBean kept to his purpose, and *did* live to command the regiment, going through every rank from private to major-general. I have seen it stated that he was a drummer-boy in the regiment, but that is not correct. He was kept seven years lance-corporal, partly because promotion went slow in the Ninety-Third, but several were promoted over him because, at the time of the disruption in the Church of Scotland, MacBean joined the Free Kirk party. This fact may appear strange to military readers of the present day with our short service and territorial regiments; but in the times of which I am writing, as I have before mentioned, the Ninety-Third was constituted as much after the arrangements of a Highland parish as those of a regiment in the army; and, to use the words of old Colonel Sparks who commanded, MacBean was passed over four promotions because "He was a d—d Free Kirker."

But I must hark back to my story and to the Begum's palace on the evening of the 11th of March, 1858. By the time darkness set in all opposition had ceased, but there were still numbers of the mutineers hiding in the rooms. Our loss was small compared with that inflicted on the enemy. Our regiment had one captain, one lieutenant, and thirteen rank and file killed; Lieutenant Grimston, Ensign Hastie, and forty-five men wounded. Many of the wounded died afterwards; but eight hundred and sixty of the enemy lay dead in the centre court alone, and many hundreds more were killed in the different enclosures and buildings. That night we bivouacked in the courts of the palace, placing strong guards all round. When daylight broke on the morning of the 12th of March, the sights around were horrible. I have already mentioned that many sepoys had to be dislodged from the close rooms around the palace by exploding bags of gunpowder among them, and this set fire to their clothing and to whatever furniture there was in the rooms; and when day broke on the 12th, there were hundreds of bodies all round, some still burning and others half-burnt, and the stench was sickening. However, the Begum's palace was the key to the enemy's position. During the day large parties of camp-followers were brought in to drag out the dead of the enemy, and throw them into the ditch which had given us so much trouble to cross, and our batteries were advanced to bombard the Imâmbâra and Kaiserbâgh.

During the forenoon of the 12th, I remember seeing Mr. Russell of *The Times* going round making notes, and General Lugard telling him to take care and not to attempt to go into any dark room for fear of being "potted" by concealed Pandies. Many such were hunted out during the day, and as there was no quarter for them they fought desperately. We had one sergeant killed at this work and several men wounded. During the afternoon a divisional order by General Sir Edward Lugard was read to us, as follows:—

"Major-General Sir Edward Lugard begs to thank Brigadier the Honourable Adrian Hope, Colonel Leith-Hay, and the officers and men of the Ninety-Third who exclusively carried the position known as the Begum's Kothee. No words are sufficient to express the gallantry, devotion, and fearless intrepidity displayed by every officer and man in the regiment. The Major-General will not fail to bring their conduct prominently to the notice of his Excellency the Commander-in-Chief."

During the day Sir Colin himself visited the position, and told us that arrangements would be made for our relief the following day, and on Saturday, the 13th, we returned to camp and rested all the following Sunday. So far as I remember, the two men of the Fifty-Third, Lance-Corporal Clary and his comrade, remained with us till after the place was taken, and then returned to their own regiment when the fighting was over, reporting to Lieutenant Munro that they had gone to take care of his brother, Doctor Munro of the Ninety-Third.

There were many individual acts of bravery performed during the assault, and it is difficult to single them out. But before closing this chapter I may relate a rather laughable incident that happened to a man of my company named Johnny Ross. He was a little fellow, and there were two of the same name in the company, one tall and the other short, so they were named respectively John and Johnny. Before falling in for the assault on the Begum's palace, Johnny Ross and George Puller, with some others, had been playing cards in a sheltered corner, and in some way quarrelled over the game. When the signal was given for the "fall in," Puller and Ross were still arguing the point in dispute, and Puller told Ross to "shut up." Just at that very moment a spent bullet struck Ross in the mouth, knocking in four of his front teeth. Johnny thought it was Puller who had struck him, and at once returned the blow; when Puller quietly replied, "You d—d fool, it was not I who struck you; you've got a bullet in your mouth." And so it was: Johnny Ross put up his hand to his mouth, and spat out four front teeth and a leaden bullet. He at once apologised to Puller for having struck him, and added, "How will I manage to bite my cartridges the noo?" Those were the days of muzzle-loading cartridges, which had to be torn open with the teeth when loading.

We returned to our tents at the Dilkooshá on Saturday, the 13th, and the whole regiment formed a funeral party for our killed near the palace; but I could not find the place on my late visit to Lucknow, nor do I think any monument marks it. When going round the Dilkooshá heights I found no trace of the graves of the Ninety-Third, nor was there any one who could point them out to me. The guide took me to see the grave of Major Hodson. I found it in excellent preservation, with a wall round it, and an iron gate to it near the entrance to the Martinière College. This care had been taken of Hodson's last resting-place by his friend, Lord Napier of Magdala, and I cut a branch from the cypress-tree planted at his head, and posted half of it to the address of his brother in England.

NOTE

HODSON OF HODSON'S HORSE

Sir Colin Campbell wrote thus at the time of Major Hodson's death : "The whole army, which admired his talents, his bravery, and his military skill, deplores his loss. . . . I attended his funeral yesterday evening, in order to show what respect I could to the memory of one of the most brilliant officers under my command.—(Signed) C. CAMPBELL, Commander-in-Chief in East Indies."

The following tributes were also paid to Hodson's memory at the time. From a leading article in *The Times*: "The country will receive with lively regret the news that the gallant Major Hodson, who has given his name to an invincible and almost ubiquitous body of cavalry, was killed in the attack on Lucknow. Major Hodson has been from the very beginning of this war fighting everywhere and against any odds with all the spirit of a Paladin of old. His most remarkable exploit, the capture of the King of Delhi and his two sons, astonished the world by its courage and coolness. Hodson was indeed a man who, from his romantic daring and his knowledge of the Asiatic character, was able to beat the natives at their own weapons."

From *Blackwood's Magazine*: "Then fell one of the bravest in the Indian Army, an officer whose name has been brought too often before the public by those in high command to need my humble word of praise. There was not a man before Delhi who did not know Hodson ; always active, always cheery, it did one's heart good to look at his face when all felt how critical was our position."

CHAPTER XIII

JUNG BAHÂDOOR—GUNPOWDER—THE MOHURRUM AT LUCKNOW—LOOT

On the return of the regiment to camp at the Dilkooshá on the 13th of March I was glad to get back to my own company. The men were mortified because they had not shared in the honour of the assault on the Begum's palace; but as some compensation the company had formed the guard-of-honour for the reception of the Mâharâja Jung Bahâdoor, Commander-in-Chief of the Nepaulese Army, who had just reached Lucknow and been received in state by Sir Colin Campbell on the afternoon of the 11th, at the moment when the regiment was engaged in the assault on the palace. The *durbar* had at first proved a rather stiff ceremonial affair, but Jung Bahâdoor and his officers had hardly been presented and taken their seats, when a commotion was heard outside, and Captain Hope Johnstone, aide-de-camp to General Sir William Mansfield, covered with powder-smoke and the dust of battle, strode up the centre of the guard-of-honour with a message to the Commander-in-Chief from Mansfield, informing him that the Ninety-Third had taken the Begum's palace, the key of the enemy's position, with slight loss to themselves, but that they had killed over a thousand of the enemy. This announcement put an end to all ceremony on the part of Sir Colin, who jumped to his feet, rubbing his hands, and calling out, "I knew they would do it! I knew my boys of the Ninety-Third would do it!" Then telling Captain Metcalfe to interpret the news to the Mâharâja, and pointing to the guard-of-honour, Sir Colin said: "Tell him that these men are part of the regiment that has done this daring feat. Tell him also that they are *my* regiment; I'm their colonel!" The Mâharâja looked pleased, and replied that he remembered having seen the regiment when he visited England in 1852. As I have already said, the Ninety-Third had formed a guard-of-honour for him when in Edinburgh, and there were still many men in the regiment who remembered seeing Jung Bahâdoor. There was an oft-repeated story among the old soldiers that the Mâharâja was so pleased at the sight of them that he had proposed to buy the whole regiment, and was somewhat surprised to learn that British soldiers were volunteers and could not be sold, even to gratify the Mâharâja of Nepaul.

After returning to camp on the 13th of March, the regiment was allowed to rest till the 17th, but returned to the city on the morning of the 18th, taking up a position near the Imâmbâra and the Kaiserbâgh, both of which had been captured when we were in camp. We relieved the Forty-Second, and the sights that then met our eyes in the streets of Lucknow defy description. The city was in the hands of plunderers; Europeans and Sikhs, Goorkhas, and camp-followers of every class, aided by the scum of the native population. Every man in fact was doing what was right in his own eyes, and "Hell broke loose" is the only phrase in the English language that can give one who has never seen such a sight any idea of the scenes in and around the Imâmbâra, the Kaiserbâgh, and adjacent streets. The Sikhs and Goorkhas were by far the most proficient plunderers, because they instinctively knew where to look for the most valuable loot. The European soldiers did not understand the business, and articles that might have proved a fortune to many were readily parted with for a few rupees in cash and a bottle of grog. But the gratuitous destruction of valuable property that could not be carried off was appalling. Colour-Sergeant Graham, of Captain Burroughs' company, rescued from the fire a bundle of Government-of-India promissory notes to the value of over a *lakh* of rupees,[1] and Mr. Kavanagh, afterwards discovering the rightful owner, secured for Sergeant Graham a reward of five per cent on the amount. But with few exceptions the men of the Ninety-Third got very little. I could fill a volume on the plunder of Lucknow, and the sights which are still vividly impressed on my memory; but others have written at length on this theme, so I will leave it.

Before I proceed to other subjects, and to make my recollections as instructive as possible for young

[1] £10,000.

soldiers, I may mention some serious accidents that happened through the explosions of gunpowder left behind by the enemy. One most appalling accident occurred in the house of a nobleman named Ushruf-ood-dowlah, in which a large quantity of gunpowder had been left; this was accidentally exploded, killing two officers and forty men of the Engineers, and a great number of camp-followers, of whom no account was taken. The poor men who were not killed outright were so horribly scorched that they all died in the greatest agony within a few hours of the accident, and for days explosions with more or less loss of life occurred all over the city. From the deplorable accidents that happened, which reasonable care might have prevented, I could enumerate the loss of over a hundred men, and I cannot too strongly impress on young soldiers the caution required in entering places where there is the least chance of coming across concealed gunpowder. By the accident in the house of Ushruf-ood-dowlah, two of our most distinguished and promising Engineer officers,—Captains Brownlow and Clarke—lost their lives, with forty of the most valuable branch of the service. All through the Mutiny I never forgot my own experience in the Shâh Nujeef (as related in the fifth chapter of these reminiscences); and wherever I could prevent it, I never allowed men to go into unexplored rooms with lighted pipes, or to force open locked doors by the usual method of firing a loaded rifle into the lock. I think there ought to be a chapter of instructions on this head in every drill-book and soldiers' pocket-book. After the assault on a city like Lucknow some license and plundering is inevitable, and where discipline is relaxed accidents are sure to happen; but a judicious use of the provost-marshal's cat would soon restore discipline and order. Whatever opponents of the lash may say, my own firm opinion is that the provost-marshal's cat is the only general to restore order in times like those I am describing. I would have no courts-martial, drum-head or otherwise; but simply give the provost-marshal a strong guard of picked men and several sets of triangles, with full power to tie up every man, no matter what his rank, caught plundering, and give him from one to four dozen, not across the shoulders, but across the breech, as judicial floggings are administered in our jails; and if these were combined with roll-calls at short intervals, plundering, which is a most dangerous pastime, would soon be put down. In time of war soldiers ought to be taught to treat every house or room of an assaulted position as a powder-magazine until explored. I am surprised that cautions on this head have been so long overlooked.

As before stated, the Ninety-Third did not get much plunder, but in expelling the enemy from some mosques and other strong buildings near the Imâmbâra on the 21st of March, one company came across the tomb-model or royal *tázia*, and the Mohurrum paraphernalia which had been made at enormous expense for the celebration of the last Mohurrum in Lucknow in 1857. The royal family and court of Lucknow were *Sheeáhs*;

and to enable European readers to understand the value of the plunder to which I allude, before entering on the actual details, I will quote from the chapter on the celebration of the Mohurrum in Lucknow in *The Private Life of an Eastern King*, by William Knighton, a member of the household of his late Majesty Nussir-ood-Deen King of Oude, a book which, I believe, is now out of print. Few people seem to know the meaning of those symbols, the star and crescent or half-moon, on Mahommedan standards or banners and on the domes of mosques or tombs of deceased persons of importance, as also on the tomb-models, or *tâzias* used in the celebration of the Mohurrum. For the explanation of these symbols we must turn to the science of heraldry, which was well known in the sixth century A.D., when Mahommed established his religion. The star is meant to represent Mahommed himself, as the prophet of God, and the crescent represents the Mahommedan religion, which every sincere follower of the Prophet believes will eventually become a full moon and cover the whole earth.

The fanatical rites of the Mohurrum are celebrated on the anniversary of the death of two leaders of the faithful, near relatives of Mahommed himself, Hussun and Hoosein, and are observed by more than one-half the population of India as a period of deep humiliation and sorrow. The Mussulman faithful are divided into two sects, Sheeâhs and the Soonies, who feel towards each other much as fanatical Protestants and Roman Catholics mutually do. The Sheeâhs regard the deaths of Hussun and Hoosein as barbarous murders; the Soonies look on them as lawful executions of pretenders to supreme power by the reigning Caliph, the true head of the faithful. On the first day of the Mohurrum the vast population of Lucknow appears to be suddenly snatched away from all interests and employments in the affairs of this world; the streets are deserted; every one is shut up in his house, mourning with his family. On the second day the streets are crowded, but with people in mourning attire, parading the thoroughfares in funeral procession to the tomb-models set up here and there as tributes of respect to the memory of Hussun and Hoosein. These models, called *tâzias*, are representations of the mausoleum at Kerbela where the two chiefs are buried. The *tâzias* are placed in an *imâmbâra* belonging to a chief, or in the house of some wealthy Mussulman. The *tâzia* belonging to the king of Oude was made for his Majesty's father, and was composed of panels of green glass fixed in gold mouldings, and was regarded as peculiarly holy. [I only take extracts from the chapter on the Mohurrum from the work I have named. The *tâzia* belonging to the king accompanied him from Lucknow on the annexation of Oude.] It is on record at Lucknow that the celebration of the Mohurrum often cost a reigning Nawâb upwards of £300,000 or Rs. 3,000,000. In Lucknow, before the Mutiny, it was believed that they had the true metal crest of the banner of Hoosein, a relic regarded as peculiarly sacred, and enshrined in a building called the Doorgâh. The name of the charger which Hoosein rode when he was killed was Dhulldhull, represented in the procession of the Mohurrum by a spotless white Arab of elegant proportions. The trappings of Dhulldhull are all of solid gold, and a golden bow and quiver of arrows are fixed on the saddle.

These extracts from a history of Lucknow before the Mutiny will enable my readers to form some idea of the splendour of the Mohurrum of 1857, and the value of the *tâzia* and paraphernalia found, as I said, by a company of the Ninety-Third. I learned from native troopers that the golden *tâzia* belonging to the crown jewels of Lucknow having accompanied the king to Calcutta, a new one was made, for which the Mahommedan population of Lucknow subscribed *lakhs* of rupees, In the eleventh chapter of his *Defence of the Residency*, Mr. L. E. R. Rees states that the Mohurrum was celebrated with unusual splendour and fanaticism, commencing that year on the 25th of August, and that on the *kutal-ka-râth*, or night of slaughter, a certain Mr. Jones, with ten other Christians, deserted to the enemy by undoing a barricaded door when one of their own number was on sentry over it. But, instead of a favourable reception as they anticipated, the deserters received the fitting reward of their treachery from the insurgents; for they were all immediately killed as a sacrifice, and their blood sprinkled on the different *tâzias* throughout the city. To return to my own story; I was told by a native jeweller, who was in Lucknow in 1857, that the crescent and star alone of the new *tâzia* made for the young king, Brijis Kuddur, cost five *lakhs* of rupees. Be that as it may, it fell to a company of the Ninety-Third to assault the Doorgâh, where all this consecrated paraphernalia was stored, and there they found this golden *tâzia*, with all the gold-embroidered standards, saddle, and saddle-cloth, the gold quiver and arrows of Dhull-dhull. There was at the time I write, a certain lieutenant in the company whom I shall call Jamie Blank. He was known to be very poor, and it was reported in the regiment that he used to regularly remit half of his lieutenant's pay to support a widowed mother and a sister, and this fact made the men of the company consider Jamie Blank entitled to a share in the loot. So when the *tâzia* was discovered, not being very sure whether the diamonds in the crescent and star on the dome were real or imitation, they settled to cut off the whole dome, and give it to Jamie; which they did. I don't know where Jamie

Blank disposed of this particular piece of loot, but I was informed that it eventually found its way to London, and was sold for £80,000. The best part of the story is, however, to come. There was a certain newspaper correspondent in the camp (not Mr. Russell), who depended on his native servant to translate Hindoostânee names into English. When he heard that a company of the Ninety-Third had found a gold *tâzia* of great value, and that they had presented the senior lieutenant with the lid of it to enable him to deposit money to purchase his captaincy, the correspondent asked his Madrassi servant the English equivalent for *tâzia*. Samuel, perhaps not knowing the English word *tomb*, but knowing that the *tâzia* referred to a funeral, told his master that the English for *tâzia* was *coffin*; so it went the round of the English papers that among the plunder of Lucknow a certain company of the Ninety-Third had found a gold coffin, and that they had generously presented the senior lieutenant with the lid of it, which was studded with diamonds and other precious stones. So far as I am aware, this is the first time that the true explanation of Jamie Blank's golden coffin-lid has been given to the world.

As already mentioned, with the exception of the company which captured the golden *tâzia* and the Mohurrum paraphernalia, the Ninety-Third got very little loot; and by the time we returned to the city order was in some measure restored, prize-agents appointed, and guards placed at the different thoroughfares to intercept camp-followers and other plunderers on their way back to camp, who were thus made to disgorge their plunder, nominally for the public good or the benefit of the army. But it was shrewdly suspected by the troops that certain small caskets in battered cases, which contained the redemption of mortgaged estates in Scotland, England, and Ireland, and snug fishing and shooting-boxes in every game-haunted and salmon-frequented angle of the world, found their way inside the uniform-cases of even the prize-agents. I could myself name one deeply-encumbered estate which was cleared of mortgage to the tune of £180,000 within two years of the plunder of Lucknow. But to what good? I only wish I had to go through a similar campaign with the experience I have now. But that is all very fine thirty-five years after! "There is a tide in the affairs of men which taken at the flood"—my readers know the rest. I missed the flood, and the tide is not likely to turn my way again. Before we left Lucknow the plunder accumulated by the prize-agents was estimated at over £600,000 (according to *The Times* of 31st of May, 1858), and within a week it had reached a million and a quarter sterling. What became of it all? Each private soldier who served throughout the relief and capture of Lucknow got prize-money to the value of Rs. 17.8; but the thirty *lakhs* of treasure which were found in the well at Bithoor, leaving the plunder of the Nânâ Sâhib's palace out of the calculation, much more than covered that amount. Yet I could myself name over a dozen men who served throughout every engagement, two of whom gained the Victoria Cross, who have died in the almshouse of their native parishes, and several in the almshouse of the Calcutta District Charitable Society! But enough of moralising; I must get back to 1858.

Many camp-followers and others managed to evade the guards, and cavalry-patrols were put on duty along the different routes on both banks of the Goomtee and in the wider thoroughfares of Lucknow.

In my last chapter I gave it as my opinion that the provost-marshal's cat is the only general which can put a stop to plundering and restore order in times like those I describe, or rather I should say, *which I cannot* describe, because it is impossible to find words to depict the scenes which met one's eyes at every turn in the streets of Lucknow. In and around Huzrutgunge, the Imâmbâra, and Kaiserbâgh mad riot and chaos reigned, —sights fit only for the Inferno. I had heard the phrase "drunk with plunder"; I then saw it illustrated in real earnest. Soldiers mad with pillage and wild with excitement, followed by crowds of camp-followers too cowardly to go to the front, but as ravenous as the vultures which followed the army and preyed on the carcases of the slain. I have already said that many of the enemy had to be dislodged from close rooms by throwing in bags of gunpowder with slow matches fixed to them. When these exploded they set fire to clothing, cotton-padded quilts, and other furniture in the rooms; and the consequence was that in the inner apartments of the palaces there were hundreds of dead bodies half burnt; many wounded were burnt alive with the dead, and the stench from such rooms was horrible! Historians tell us that Charles the Ninth of France asserted that the smell of a dead enemy was always sweet. If he had experienced the streets of Lucknow in March, 1858, he might have had cause to modify his opinion.

CHAPTER XIV

AN UNGRATEFUL DUTY—CAPTAIN BURROUGHS—THE DILKOOSHÁ AGAIN—GENERAL WALPOLE AT ROOYAH —THE RÂMGUNGA.

AFTER the Mutiny some meddling philanthropists in England tried to get up an agitation about such stories as wounded sepoys being burnt alive; but owing to the nature of the war it was morally impossible to have prevented such accidents. As to cases of real wanton cruelty or outrage committed by European soldiers, none came under my own notice, and I may be permitted to relate here a story which goes far to disprove any accusations of the sort.

My company had been posted in a large building and garden near the Mint. Shortly after our arrival an order came for a non-commissioned officer and a guard of selected men to take charge of a house with a harem, or *zenâna*, of about eighty women who had been rescued from different harems about the Kaiserbâgh,—begums of rank and of no rank, dancing girls and household female slaves, some young and others of very doubtful age. Mr. MacBean, our adjutant, selected me for the duty, first because he said he knew I would not get drunk and thus overlook my sense of responsibility; and, secondly, because by that time I had picked up a considerable knowledge of colloquial Hindoostânee, and was thus able to understand natives who could not speak English, and to make myself understood by them. I got about a dozen old soldiers with me, several of whom had been named for the duty by Sir Colin Campbell himself, mostly married men of about twenty years' service. Owing to the vicissitudes of my chequered life I have lost my pocket roll-book, and do not now recollect the whole of the names of the men who formed this guard. However, John Ellis, whose wife had acted as laundress for Sir Colin in the Crimea, was one of them, and James Strachan, who was nick-named "the Bishop," was another; John M'Donald, the fourth of the name in my company, was a third; I cannot now name more of them. If any of that guard are alive now, they must be from three-score and ten to fourscore years of age, because they were then all old men, tried and true, and, as our adjutant said, Sir Colin had told him that no other corps except the Ninety-Third could be trusted to supply a guard for such a duty. MacBean, along with a staff or civil officer, accompanied the guard to the house, and was very particular in impressing on my attention the fact that the guard was on no pretence whatever to attempt to hold any communication with the begums, except through a shrivelled, parchment-faced, wicked-looking old woman (as I supposed), who, the staff-officer told me, could speak English, and who had been directed to report any shortcomings of the guard, should we not behave ourselves circumspectly. But I must say I had little to fear on that head, for I knew every one of my men could be trusted to be proof against the temptation of begums, gold, or grog, and as for myself, I was then a young non-commissioned officer with a very keen sense of my responsibility.

Shortly after we were installed in our position of trust, and the officers had left us, we discovered several pairs of bright eyes peeping out at us through the partly shattered venetians forming the doors and windows of the house; and the person whom I had taken for a shrivelled old woman came out and entered into conversation with me, at first in Hindoostânee, but afterwards in very good and grammatical English. I then discovered that what I had mistaken for a crack-voiced old woman, a second edition of "the mother of the maids," was no other than a confidential eunuch of the palace, who told me he had been over thirty years about the court of Lucknow, employed as a sort of private secretary under successive kings, as he was able to read and write English, and could translate the English newspapers, etc., and could also, judging from his villainous appearance, be trusted to strangle a refractory begum or cut the throat of any one prying too closely into court secrets. He was almost European in complexion, and appeared to me to be more than seventy years of age, but he may have been much younger. He also told me that most of his early life had been spent at the court of Constantinople, and that he had there learned English, and had found this of great use to him at the court of Lucknow, where he had not only kept up the knowledge, but had improved it by reading.

By this time one of the younger begums, or nautch girls (I don't know which), came out to see the guard, and did not appear by any means too bashful. She evidently wished for a closer acquaintance, and I asked my friend to request her to go back to her companions; but this she declined to do, and wanted particularly to know why we were dressed in petticoats, and if we were not part of the Queen of England's regiment of eunuchs, and chaffed me a good deal about my fair hair and youthful appearance. I was twenty-four hours on that guard before the begums were removed by Major Bruce to a house somewhere near the Martinière, and during that twenty-four hours I learned more, through the assistance of the English-speaking eunuch, about the virtues of polygamy and the domestic slavery, intrigues, and crimes of the harem than I have learned in all my other thirty-five years in India. If I dared, I could write a few pages that would give the Government of India and the public of England ten times more light on those cherished institutions than they now possess. The authorities professed to take charge of those caged begums for their own safety, but I don't think many of them were over-thankful for the protection. Major Bruce, with an escort, removed the ladies the next day, and I took leave of my communicative friend and the begums without reluctance, and rejoined my company, glad to be rid of such a dangerous charge.

Except the company which stormed the Doorgâh, the rest of the Ninety-Third were employed more as guards on our return to the city; but about the 23rd of the month Captain Burroughs and his company were detailed, with some of Brazier's Sikhs, to drive a lot of rebels from some mosques and large buildings which were the last positions held by the enemy. If I remember rightly, Burroughs was then fourth on the list of captains, and he got command of the regiment five years after, through deaths by cholera, in Peshâwar in 1862. The Ninety-Third had three commanding officers in one day! Lieutenant-Colonel MacDonald and Major Middleton both died within a few hours of each other, and Burroughs at once became senior major and succeeded to the command, the senior colonel, Sir H. Stisted, being in command of a brigade in Bengal. Burroughs was born in India and was sent to France early for his education, at least for the military part of it, and was a cadet of the *Ecole Polytechnique* of Paris. This accounted for his excellent swordsmanship, his thorough knowledge of French, and his foreign accent. Burroughs was an accomplished *maître d'armes.* When he joined the Ninety-Third as an ensign in 1850 he was known as "Wee Frenchie." I don't exactly remember his height, I think it was under five feet; but what he wanted in size he made up in pluck and endurance. He served throughout the Crimean war, and was never a day absent. It was he who volunteered to lead the forlorn hope when it was thought the Highland Brigade were to storm the Redan, before it was known that the Russians had evacuated the position. At the relief of Lucknow he was not the first man through the hole in the Secundrabâgh; that was Lance-Corporal Dunley of Burroughs' company; Sergeant-Major Murray was the second, and was killed inside; the third was a Sikh *sirdâr*, Gokul Sing, of the Fourth Punjâb Infantry, and Burroughs was either the fourth or fifth. He was certainly the first *officer* of the regiment inside, and was immediately attacked by an Oude Irregular *sowâr* armed with *tulwâr* and shield, who nearly slashed Burroughs' right ear off before he got properly on his feet. It was the wire frame of his feather bonnet that saved him; the *sowâr* got a straight cut at his head, but the sword glanced off the feather bonnet and nearly cut off his right ear. However, Burroughs soon gathered himself together (there was so little of him!) and showed his tall opponent that he had for once met his match in the art of fencing; before many seconds Burroughs' sword had passed through his opponent's throat and out at the back of his neck. Notwithstanding his severe wound, Burroughs fought throughout the capture of the Secundrabâgh, with his right ear nearly severed from his head, and the blood running down over his shoulder to his gaiters; nor did he go to have his wound dressed till after he had mustered his company, and reported to the colonel how many of No. 6 had fallen that morning. Although his men disliked many of his ways, they were proud of their little captain for his pluck and good heart. I will relate two instances of this:—When promoted,

Captain Burroughs had the misfortune to succeed the most popular officer in the regiment in the command of his company, namely, Captain Ewart (now Lieutenant-General Sir John Alexander Ewart, K.C.B., etc.), and, among other innovations, Burroughs tried to introduce certain *Polytechnique* ideas new to the Ninety-Third. At the first morning parade after assuming command of the company, he wished to satisfy himself that the ears of the men were clean inside, but being so short, he could not, even on tiptoe, raise himself high enough to see; he therefore made them come to the kneeling position, and went along the front rank from left to right, minutely inspecting the inside of every man's ears! The Ninety-Third were all tall men in those days, none being under five feet six inches even in the centre of the rear rank of the battalion companies; and the right hand man of Burroughs' company was a stalwart Highlander named Donald MacLean, who could scarcely speak English and stood about six feet three inches. When Burroughs examined Donald's ears he considered them dirty, and told the colour-sergeant to put Donald down for three days' extra drill. Donald, hearing this, at once sprang to his feet from the kneeling position and, looking down on the little captain with a look of withering scorn, deliberately said, "She will take three days' drill from a man, but not from a monkey!" Of course Donald was at once marched to the rear-guard a prisoner, and a charge lodged against him for "insubordination and insolence to Captain Burroughs at the time of inspection on morning parade." When the prisoner was brought before the colonel he read over the charge, and, turning to Captain Burroughs, said: "This is a most serious charge, Captain Burroughs, and against an old soldier like Donald MacLean who has never been brought up for punishment before. How did it happen?" Burroughs was ashamed to state the exact words, but beat about the bush, saying that he had ordered MacLean three days' drill, and that he refused to submit to the sentence, making use of most insolent and insubordinate language; but the colonel could not get him to state the exact words used, and the colour-sergeant was called as second witness. The colour-sergeant gave a plain, straightforward account of the ear-inspection; and when he stated how MacLean had sprung to his feet on hearing the sentence of three days' drill, and had told the captain, "She will take three days' drill from a man, but not from a monkey," the whole of the officers present burst into fits of laughter, and even the colonel had to hold his hand to his mouth. As soon as he could speak he turned on MacLean, and told him that he deserved to be tried by a court-martial and so forth, but ended by sentencing him to "three days' grog stopped." The orderly-room hut was then cleared of all except the colonel, Captain Burroughs, and the adjutant, and no one ever knew exactly what passed; but there was no repetition of the kneeling position for ear-inspection on morning parade. I have already said that Burroughs had a most kindly heart, and for the next three days after this incident, when the grog bugle sounded, Donald

MacLean was as regularly called to the captain's tent, and always returned smacking his lips, and emphatically stating that "The captain was a Highland gentleman after all, and not a French monkey." From that day forward, the little captain and the tall grenadier became the best of friends, and years after, on the evening of the 11th of March, 1858, when the killed and wounded were collected after the capture of the Begum's Kothee in Lucknow, I saw Captain Burroughs crying like a tender-hearted woman by the side of a *dooly* in which was stretched the dead body of Donald MacLean, who, it was said, received his death-wound defending his captain. I have the authority of the late colour-sergeant of No. 6 company for the statement that from the date of the death of MacLean, Captain Burroughs regularly remitted thirty shillings a month, through the minister of her parish, to Donald's widowed mother, till the day of her death seven years after. When an action of this kind became generally known in the regiment, it caused many to look with kindly feelings on most of the peculiarities of Burroughs.

The other anecdote goes back to Camp Kamara and the spring of 1856, when the Highland Brigade were lying there half-way between Balaclava and Sebastopol. As before noticed, Burroughs was more like a Frenchman than a Highlander; there were many of his old *Polytechnique* chums in the French army in the Crimea, and almost every day he had some visitors from the French camp, especially after the armistice was proclaimed.

Some time in the spring of 1856 Burroughs had picked up a Tartar pony and had got a saddle, etc., for it, but he could get no regular groom. Not being a field-officer he was not entitled to a regulation groom, and not being well liked, none of his company would volunteer for the billet, especially as it formed no excuse for getting off other duties. One of the company had accordingly to be detailed on fatigue duty every day to groom the captain's pony. On a particular day this duty had fallen to a young recruit who had lately joined by draft, a man named Patrick Doolan, a real Paddy of the true Handy Andy type, who had made his way somehow to Glasgow and had there enlisted into the Ninety-Third. This day, as usual, Burroughs had visitors from the French camp, and it was proposed that all should go for a ride, so Patrick Doolan was called to saddle the captain's pony. Doolan had never saddled a pony in his life before, and he put the saddle on with the pommel to the tail and the crupper to the front, and brought the pony thus accoutred to the captain's hut. Every one commenced to laugh, and Burroughs, getting into a white heat, turned on Patrick, saying, "You fool, you have put the saddle on with the back to the front!" Patrick at once saluted, and, without the least hesitation, replied, "Shure, sir, you never told me whether you were to ride to Balaclava or the front." Burroughs was so tickled with the ready wit of the reply that from that day he took Doolan into his service as soldier-servant, taught him his work, and retained him till March, 1858, when

Burroughs had to go on sick leave on account of wounds. Burroughs was one of the last men wounded in the taking of Lucknow. Some days after the Begum's Kothee was stormed, he and his company were sent to drive a lot of rebels out of a house near the Kaiserbâgh, and, as usual, Burroughs was well in advance of his men. Just as they were entering the place the enemy fired a mine, and the captain was sent about a hundred feet in the air; but being like a cat (in the matter of being difficult to kill, I mean), he fell on his feet on the roof of a thatched hut, and escaped, with his life indeed, but with one of his legs broken in two places below the knee. It was only the skill of our good doctor Munro that saved his leg; but he was sent to England on sick leave, and before he returned I had left the regiment and joined the Commissariat Department. This ends my reminiscences of Captain Burroughs. May he long enjoy the rank he has attained in the peace of his island home in Orkney! Notwithstanding his peculiarities, he was a brave and plucky soldier and a most kind-hearted gentleman.

By the end of March the Ninety-Third returned to camp at the Dilkooshá, glad to get out of the city, where we were suffocated by the stench of rotting corpses, and almost devoured with flies by day and mosquitoes by night. The weather was now very hot and altogether uncomfortable, more especially since we were without any means of bathing and could obtain no regular changes of clothing.

By this time numbers of the townspeople had returned to the city and were putting their houses in order, while thousands of *coolies* and low-caste natives were employed clearing dead bodies out of houses and hidden corners, and generally cleaning up the city.

When we repassed the scene of our hard-contested struggle, the Begum's palace,—which, I may here remark, was actually a much stronger position than the famous Redan at Sebastopol,—we found the inner ditch, that had given us so much trouble to get across, converted into a vast grave, in which the dead had been collected in thousands and then covered by the earth which the enemy had piled up as ramparts. All round Lucknow for miles the country was covered with dead carcases of every kind,—human beings, horses, camels, bullocks, and donkeys,—and for miles the atmosphere was tainted and the swarms of flies were horrible, a positive torment and a nuisance. The only comfort was that they roosted at night; but at meal-times they were indescribable, and it was impossible to keep them out of our food; our plates of rice would be perfectly black with flies, and it was surprising how we kept such good health, for we had little or no sickness during the siege of Lucknow.

During the few days we remained in camp at the Dilkooshá the army was broken up into movable columns, to take the field after the different parties of rebels and to restore order throughout Oude; for although Lucknow had fallen, the rebellion was not by any means over; the whole of Oude was still against us, and had to be reconquered. The Forty-Second, Seventy-Ninth, and Ninety-Third (the regiments which composed the famous old Highland Brigade of the Crimea) were once more formed into one brigade, and with a regiment of Punjâb Infantry and a strong force of engineers, the Ninth Lancers, a regiment of native cavalry, a strong force of artillery, both light and heavy,—in brief, as fine a little army as ever took the field, under the command of General Walpole, with Adrian Hope as brigadier,—was detailed for the advance into Rohilcund for the recapture of Bareilly, where a large army still held together under Khân Bahâdoor Khân. Every one in the camp expressed surprise that Sir Colin should entrust his favourite Highlanders to Walpole.

On the morning of the 7th of April, 1858, the time had at last arrived when we were to leave Lucknow, and the change was hailed by us with delight. We were glad to get away from the captured city, with its horrible smells and still more horrible sights, and looked forward with positive pleasure to a hot-weather campaign in Rohilcund. We were to advance on Bareilly by a route parallel with the course of the Ganges, so striking our tents at 2 A.M. we marched through the city along the right bank of the Goomtee, past the Moosabâgh, where our first halt was made, about five miles out of Lucknow, in the midst of fresh fields, away from all the offensive odours and the myriads of flies. One instance will suffice to give my readers some idea of the torment we suffered from these pests. When we struck tents all the flies were roosting in the roofs; when the tents were rolled up the flies got crushed and killed by bushels, and no one who has not seen such a sight would credit the state of the inside of our tents when opened out to be repitched on the new ground. After the tents were pitched and the roofs swept down, the sweepers of each company were called to collect the dead flies and carry them out of the camp. I noted down the quantity of flies carried out of my own tent. The ordinary kitchen-baskets served out to the regimental cooks by the commissariat for carrying bread, rice, etc., will hold about an imperial bushel, and from one tent there were carried out five basketfuls of dead flies. The sight gave one a practical idea of one of the ten plagues of Egypt! Being now rid of the flies we could lie down during the heat of the day, and have a sleep without being tormented.

The defeated army of Lucknow had flocked into Rohilcund, and a large force was reported to be collected in Bareilly under Khân Bahâdoor Khân and Prince Feroze Shâh. The following is a copy of one of Khân Bahâdoor Khân's proclamations for the harassment of our advance: "Do not attempt to meet the regular columns of the infidels, because they are superior to you in discipline and have more guns; but watch their movements; guard all the *ghâts* on the rivers; intercept their communications; stop their supplies; cut up their piquets and *dâks;* keep constantly hanging about their camps; give them no rest!"

These were, no doubt, the correct tactics; it was the old Mahratta policy revived. However, nothing came of it, and our advance was unopposed till we reached the jungle fort of Nirput Singh, the Rajpoot chief of Rooyah, near the village of Rhodamow. I remember the morning well. I was in the advance-guard under command of a young officer who had just come out from home as a cadet in the H. E. I. Company's service, and there being no Company's regiments for him, he was attached to the Ninety-Third before we left Lucknow. His name was Wace, a tall young lad of, I suppose, sixteen or seventeen years of age. I don't remember him before that morning, but he was most anxious for a fight, and I recollect that before we marched off our camping-ground, Brigadier Hope called up young Mr. Wace, and gave him instructions about moving along with great caution with about a dozen picked men for the leading section of the advance-guard.

We advanced without opposition till sunrise, and then we came in sight of an outpost of the enemy about three miles from the fort; but as soon as they saw us they retired, and word was passed back to the column. Shortly afterwards instructions came for the advance-guard to wait for the main column, and I remember young Mr. Wace going up to the brigadier, and asking to be permitted to lead the assault on the fort, should it come to a fight. At this time a summons to surrender had been sent to the Râja, but he vouchsafed no reply, and, as we advanced, a 9-pounder shot was fired at the head of the column, killing a drummer of the Forty-Second. The attack on the fort then commenced, without any attempt being made to reconnoitre the position, and ended in a most severe loss, Brigadier Hope being among the killed. Lieutenant Willoughby, who commanded the Sikhs,—a brother of the officer who blew up the powder-magazine at Delhi, rather than let it fall into the hands of the enemy,—was also killed; as were Lieutenants Douglas and Bramley of the Forty-Second, with nearly one hundred men, Highlanders and Sikhs. Hope was shot from a high tree inside the fort, and, at the time, it was believed that the man who shot him was a European.[1] After we retired from the fort the excitement was so great among the men of the Forty-Second and Ninety-Third, owing to the sacrifice of so many officers and men through sheer mismanagement, that if the officers had given the men the least encouragement, I am convinced they would have turned out in a body and hanged General Walpole. The officers who were killed were all most popular men; but the great loss sustained by the death of Adrian Hope positively excited the men to fury. So heated was the feeling on the night the dead were buried, that if any non-commissioned officer had dared to take the lead, the life of General Walpole would not have been worth half an hour's purchase.

After the force retired,—for we actually retired!—from Rooyah on the evening of the 15th of April, we

[1] See Appendix B.

encamped about two miles from the place, and a number of our dead were left in the ditch, mostly Forty-Second and Sikhs; and, so far as I am aware, no attempt was made to invest the fort or to keep the enemy in. They took advantage of this to retreat during the night; but this they did leisurely, burning their own dead, and stripping and mutilating those of our force that were abandoned in the ditch. It was reported in the camp that Colonel Haggard of the Ninth Lancers, commanding the cavalry brigade, had proposed to invest the place, but was not allowed to do so by General Walpole, who was said to have acted in such a pig-headed manner that the officers considered him insane. Rumour added that when Colonel Haggard and a squadron of the Lancers went to reconnoitre the place on the morning of the 16th, it was found empty; and that when Colonel Haggard sent an aide-de-camp to report this fact to the general, he had replied, "Thank God!" appearing glad that Râja Nirput Singh and his force had slipped through his fingers after beating back the best-equipped movable column in India. These reports gaining currency in the camp made the general still more unpopular, because, in addition to his incapability as an officer, the men put him down as a coward.

During the day the mutilated bodies of our men were recovered from the ditch. The Sikhs burnt theirs, while a large fatigue party of the Forty-Second and Ninety-Third was employed digging one long grave in a *tope* of trees not far from the camp. About four o'clock in the afternoon the funeral took place, Brigadier Hope and the officers on the right, wrapped in their tartan plaids, the non-commissioned officers and the privates on their left, each sewn up in a blanket. The Rev. Mr. Cowie, whom we of the Ninety-Third had nicknamed "the Fighting Padre," afterwards Bishop of Auckland, New Zealand, and the Rev. Mr. Ross, chaplain of the Forty-Second, conducted the service, Mr. Ross reading the ninetieth Psalm and Mr. Cowie the rest of the service. The pipers of the Forty-Second and Ninety-Third, with muffled drums, played *The Flowers of the Forest* as a dead march. In all my experience in the army or out of it I never witnessed such intense grief, both among officers and men, as was expressed at this funeral. Many of all ranks sobbed like tender-hearted women. I especially remember our surgeon, "kind-hearted Billy Munro" as the men called him; also Lieutenants Archie Butter and Dick Cunningham, who were aides-de-camp to Adrian Hope. Cunningham had rejoined the regiment after recovery from his wounds at Kudjwa in October, 1857, but they had left him too lame to march, and he was a supernumerary aide-de-camp to Brigadier Hope; he and Butter were both alongside the brigadier, I believe, when he was struck down by the renegade ruffian.

We halted during the 17th, and strong fatigue-parties were employed with the engineers destroying the fort by blowing up the gateways. The place was ever after known in the Ninety-Third as "Walpole's Castle.' On the 18th we marched, and on the 22nd we came upon the retreating rebels at a place called Sirsa, on the Râmgunga. The Ninth Lancers and Horse-Artillery and two companies of the Ninety-Third (I forget their numbers) crossed the Râmgunga by a ford and intercepted the retreat of a large number of the enemy, who were escaping by a bridge of boats, the material for which the country people had collected for them. But their retreat was now completely cut off, and about three hundred of them were reported either killed or drowned in the Râmgunga.

About 3 P.M. a tremendous sandstorm, with thunder, and rain in torrents, came on. The Râmgunga became so swollen that it was impossible for the detachment of the Ninety-Third to recross, and they bivouacked in a deserted village on the opposite side, without tents, the officers hailing across that they could make themselves very comfortable for the night if they could only get some tea and sugar, as the men had biscuits, and they had secured a quantity of flour and some goats in the village. But the boats which the enemy had collected had all broken adrift, and there was apparently no possibility of sending anything across to our comrades. This dilemma evoked an act of real cool pluck on the part of our commissariat *gomâshta*,[1] *bâboo* Hera Lâll Chatterjee, whom I have before mentioned in my seventh chapter in reference to the plunder of a cartload of biscuits at Bunnee bridge on the retreat from Lucknow. By this time Hera Lâll had become better acquainted with the "wild Highlanders," and was even ready to

[1] Native assistant in charge of stores.

risk his life to carry a ration of tea and sugar to them. This he made into a bundle, which he tied on the crown of his head, and although several of the officers tried to dissuade him from the attempt, he tightened his *chudder*[1] round his waist, and declaring that he had often swum the Hooghly, and that the Râmgunga should not deprive the officers and men of a detachment of his regiment of their tea, he plunged into the river, and safely reached the other side with his precious freight on his head! This little incident was never forgotten in the regiment so long as Hera Lâll remained the commissariat *gomáshta* of the Ninety-Third. He was then a young man, certainly not more than twenty. Although thirty-five more years of rough-and-tumble life have now considerably grizzled his appearance, he must often look back with pride to that stormy April evening in 1858, when he risked his life in the Râmgunga to carry a tin-pot of tea to the British soldiers.

Among the enemy killed that day were several wearing the uniforms stripped from the dead of the Forty-Second in the ditch of Rooyah; so, of course, we concluded that this was Nirput Singh's force, and the defeat and capture of its guns in some measure, I have no doubt, re-established General Walpole in the good opinion of the authorities, but not much in that of the force under his command.

Nothing else of consequence occurred till about the 27th of April, when our force rejoined the Commander-in-Chief's column, which had advanced *via* Futtehghur,

[1] A wrapper worn by Bengalee men and up-country women.

and we heard that Sir William Peel had died of small-pox at Cawnpore on his way to Calcutta. The news went through the camp from regiment to regiment, and caused almost as much sorrow in the Ninety-Third as the death of poor Adrian Hope.

CHAPTER XV

BATTLE OF BAREILLY—GHÂZIS—A TERRIBLE ACCIDENT—HALT AT BAREILLY—ACTIONS OF POSGAON, RUSSOOLPORE, AND NOWRUNGABAD—REST AT LAST!

THE heat was now very oppressive, and we had many men struck down by the sun every day. We reached Shâhjehânpore on the 30th of April, and found that every building in the cantonments fit for sheltering European troops had been destroyed by order of the Nânâ Sâhib, who, however, did not himself wait for our arrival. Strange to say, the bridge of boats across the Râmgunga was not destroyed, and some of the buildings in the jail, and the wall round it, were still standing. Colonel Hale and a wing of the Eighty-Second were left here with some guns, to make the best of their position in the jail, which partly dominated the city. The Shâhjehânpore distillery was mostly destroyed, but the native distillers had been working it, and there was a large quantity of rum still in the vats, which was found to be good and was consequently annexed by the commissariat.

On the 2nd of May we left Shâhjehânpore *en route* for Bareilly, and on the next day reached Futtehgunge.

Every village was totally deserted, but no plundering was allowed, and any camp-followers found marauding were soon tied up by the provost-marshal's staff. Proclamations were sent everywhere for the people to remain in their villages, but without any effect. Two days later we reached Furreedpore, which we also found deserted, but with evident signs that the enemy were near; and our bazaars were full of reports of the great strength of the army of Khân Bahâdoor Khân and Feroze Shâh. The usual estimate was thirty thousand infantry, twenty-five thousand cavalry, and about three hundred guns, among which was said to be a famous black battery that had beaten the European artillery at ball-practice a few months before they mutinied at Meerut. The left wing of the Ninety-Third was thrown out, with a squadron of the Lancers and Tombs' battery, as the advance piquet. As darkness set in we could see the fires of the enemy's outposts, their patrol advancing quite close to our sentries during the night, but making no attack.

About 2 A.M. on the 5th of May, according to Sir Colin's usual plan, three days' rations were served out, and the whole force was under arms and slowly advancing before daylight. By sunrise we could see the enemy drawn up on the plain some five miles from Bareilly, in front of what had been the native lines; but as we advanced, they retired. By noon we had crossed the nullah in front of the old cantonments, and, except by sending round-shot among us at long distances, which did not do much harm, the enemy did not dispute our advance. We were halted in the middle of a bare, sandy plain, and we of the rank and file then got to understand why the enemy were apparently in some confusion; we could hear the guns of Brigadier Jones ("Jones the Avenger" as he was called) hammering at them on the other side. The Ninety-Third formed the extreme right of the front line of infantry with a squadron of the Lancers and Tombs' battery of horse-artillery. The heat was intense, and when about two o'clock a movement in the mango *topes* in our front caused the order to stand to our arms, it attained such a pitch that the barrels of our rifles could not be touched by our bare hands!

The Sikhs and our light company advanced in skirmishing order, when some seven to eight hundred matchlock-men opened fire on them, and all at once a most furious charge was made by a body of about three hundred and sixty Rohilla Ghâzis, who rushed out, shouting "*Bismillâh! Allâh! Allâh! Deen! Deen!*" Sir Colin was close by, and called out, "Ghâzis, Ghâzis! Close up the ranks! Bayonet them as they come on." However, they inclined to our left, and only a few came on to the Ninety-Third, and these were mostly bayoneted by the light company which was extended in front of the line. The main body rushed on the centre of the Forty-Second; but as soon as he saw them change their direction Sir Colin galloped on, shouting out, "Close up, Forty-Second! Bayonet them as they come on!" But that was not so easily done; the Ghâzis charged in blind fury, with their round shields on their left arms, their bodies bent low, waving their *tulwârs* over their heads, throwing themselves under the bayonets, and cutting at the men's legs. Colonel Cameron, of the Forty-Second, was pulled from his horse by a Ghâzi, who leaped up and seized him by the collar while he was engaged with another on the opposite side; but his life was saved by Colour-Sergeant Gardener, who seized one of the enemy's *tulwârs*, and rushing to the colonel's assistance cut off the Ghâzi's head. General Walpole was also pulled off his horse and received two sword-cuts, but was rescued by the bayonets of the Forty-Second. The struggle was short, but every one of the Ghâzis was killed. None attempted to escape; they had evidently come on to kill or be killed, and a hundred and thirty-three lay in one circle right in front of the colours of the Forty-Second.

The Commander-in-Chief himself saw one of the Ghâzis, who had broken through the line, lying down, shamming dead. Sir Colin caught the glance of his eye, saw through the ruse, and called to one of the Forty-Second, "Bayonet that man!" But the Ghâzi was enveloped in a thick quilted tunic of green silk, through which the blunt Enfield bayonet would not pass, and the Highlander was in danger of being cut down, when a Sikh *sirdâr*[1] of the Fourth Punjâbis rushed to his assistance, and took the Ghâzi's head clean off with one sweep of his keen *tulwâr*. These Ghâzis, with a very few exceptions, were gray-bearded men of the Rohilla race, clad in green, with green

[1] Native officer.

turbans and *kummerbunds*,[1] round shields on the left arm, and curved *tulwârs* that would split a hair. They only succeeded in wounding about twenty men—they threw themselves so wildly on the bayonets of the Forty-Second! One of them, an exception to the majority, was quite a youth, and having got separated from the rest challenged the whole of the line to come out and fight him. He then rushed at Mr. Joiner, the quartermaster of the Ninety-Third, firing his carbine, but missing. Mr. Joiner returned the fire with his revolver, and the Ghâzi then threw away his carbine and rushed at Joiner with his *tulwâr*. Some of the light company tried to take the youngster prisoner, but it was no use; he cut at every one so madly, that they had to bayonet him.

The commotion caused by this attack was barely over, when word was passed that the enemy were concentrating in front for another rush, and the order was given for the spare ammunition to be brought to the front. I was detached with about a dozen men of No. 7 company to find the ammunition-guard, and bring our ammunition in rear of the line. Just as I reached the ammunition-camels, a large force of the rebel cavalry, led by Feroze Shâh in person, swept round the flank and among the baggage, cutting down camels, camel-drivers, and camp-followers in all directions. My detachment united with the ammunition-guard and defended ourselves, shooting down a number of the enemy's *sowârs*. I remember the Rev. Mr. Ross,

[1] Sashes.

chaplain of the Forty-Second, running for his life, dodging round camels and bullocks with a rebel *sowâr* after him, till, seeing our detachment, he rushed to us for protection, calling out, "Ninety-Third, shoot that impertinent fellow!" Bob Johnston, of my company, shot the *sowâr* down. Mr. Ross had no sword nor revolver, and not even a stick with which to defend himself. Moral—When in the field, *padres*, carry a good revolver! About the same time as Mr. Ross gained our protection, we saw Mr. Russell, of *The Times*, who was ill and unable to walk from the kick of a horse, trying to escape on horseback. He had got out of his *dooly*, undressed and bareheaded as he was, and leaped into the saddle, as the *syce* had been leading his horse near him. Several of the enemy's *sowârs* were dodging through the camels to get at him. We turned our rifles on them, and I shot down the one nearest to Mr. Russell, just as he had cut down an intervening camel-driver and was making for "Our Special"; in fact, his *tulwâr* was actually lifted to swoop down on Mr. Russell's bare head when my bullet put a stop to his proceedings. I saw Mr. Russell tumble from his saddle at the same instant as the *sowâr* fell, and I got a rare fright, for I thought my bullet must have struck both. However, I rushed to where Mr. Russell had fallen, and I then saw from the position of the slain *sowâr* that my bullet had found its proper billet, and that Mr. Russell was down with sunstroke, the blood flowing freely from his nose. There was no time to lose. Our Mooltânee Irregulars were after the enemy, and I had to hasten to the line with the spare ammunition; but before I left Mr. Russell to his fate, I called some of the Forty-Second baggage-guards to put him into his *dooly* and take him to their doctor, while I hastened back to the line and reported the occurrence to Captain Dawson. Next morning I was glad to hear that Mr. Russell was still alive, and likely to get over his stroke.

After this charge of the rebel cavalry we were advanced; but the thunder of Jones' attack on the other side of the city evidently disconcerted the enemy, and they made off to the right of our line, while large numbers of Ghâzis concentrated themselves in the main buildings of the city. We suffered more from the sun than from the enemy: and after we advanced into the shelter of a large mango *tope* we were nearly eaten alive by swarms of small green insects, which invaded our bare legs in thousands, till we were glad to leave the shelter of the mango trees and take to the open plain again. As night drew on the cantonments were secured, the baggage was collected, and we bivouacked on the plain, strong piquets being thrown out. My company was posted in a small field of onions near a *pucca*[1] well with a Persian wheel for lifting the water. We supped off the biscuits in our haversacks, raw onions, and the cool water drawn from well, and then went off to sleep. I wish I might always sleep as soundly as I did that night after my supper of raw onions and dry biscuits!

[1] In this instance this word of many meanings implies "masonry."

On the 6th of May the troops were under arms, and advanced on the city of Bareilly. But little opposition was offered, except from one large house on the outskirts of the town, in which a body of about fifty Rohilla Ghâzis had barricaded themselves, and a company (I think it was No. 6 of the Ninety-Third) was sent to storm the house, after several shells had been pitched into it. This was done without much loss, except that of one man; I now forget his name, but think it was William MacDonald. He rushed into a room full of Ghâzis, who, before his comrades could get to his assistance, had cut him into sixteen pieces with their sharp *tulwârs!* As the natives said, he was cut into annas.[1] But the house was taken, and the whole of the Ghâzis slain, with only the loss of this one man killed and about half a dozen wounded.

While this house was being stormed the townspeople sent a deputation of submission to the Commander-in-Chief, and by ten o'clock we had pitched our camp near the ruins of the church which had been destroyed twelve months before. Khân Bahâdoor Khân and the Nânâ Sâhib were reported to have fled in the direction of the Nepâl Terâi, while Feroze Shâh, with a force of cavalry and guns, had gone back to attack Shâhjehânpore.

About mid-day on the 6th a frightful accident happened, by which a large number of camp-followers and cattle belonging to the ordnance-park were killed. Whether for concealment or by design (it was never known which) the enemy had left a very large quantity

[1] Is it necessary to explain that sixteen annas go to the rupee?

of gunpowder and loaded shells in a dry well under a huge tree in the centre of the old cantonment. The well had been filled to the very mouth with powder and shells, and then covered with a thin layer of dry sand. A large number of ordnance *khalásies*,[1] bullock-drivers, and *dooly*-bearers had congregated under the tree to cook their mid-day meal, lighting their fires right on the top of this powder-magazine, when it suddenly exploded with a most terrific report, shaking the ground for miles, making the tent-pegs fly out of the hard earth, and throwing down tents more than a mile from the spot. I was lying down in a tent at the time, and the concussion was so great that I felt as if lifted clear off the ground. The tent-pegs flew out all round, and down came the tents, before the men, many of whom were asleep, had time to get clear of the canvas. By the time we got our arms free of the tents, bugles were sounding the assembly in all directions, and staff-officers galloping over the plain to ascertain what had happened. The spot where the accident had occurred was easily found. The powder having been in a deep well, it acted like a huge mortar, fired perpendicularly; an immense cloud of black smoke was sent up in a vertical column at least a thousand yards high, and thousands of shells were bursting in it, the fragments flying all round in a circle of several hundred yards. As the place was not far from the ammunition-park, the first idea was that the enemy had succeeded in blowing up the ammunition; but those who had

[1] Tent-pitchers.

ever witnessed a similar accident could see that, whatever had happened, the concussion was too great to be caused by only one or two waggon-loads of powder. From the appearance of the column of smoke and the shells bursting in it, as if shot out of a huge mortar, it was evident that the accident was confined to one small spot, and the belief became general that the enemy had exploded an enormous mine. But after some time the truth became known, the troops were dispersed, and the tents repitched. This explosion was followed in the afternoon by a most terrific thunder-storm and heavy rain, which nearly washed away the camp. The storm came on as the non-commissioned officers of the Ninety-Third and No. 2 company were falling in to bury Colour-Sergeant Mackie, who had been knocked down by the sun the day before and had died that forenoon. Just when we were lowering the body into the grave, there was a crash of thunder almost as loud as the explosion of the powder-mine. The ground becoming soaked with rain, the tent-pegs and many tents were again thrown down by the force of the hurricane; and as everything we had became soaked, we passed a most uncomfortable night.

On the morning of the 7th of May we heard that Colonel Hale and the wing of the Eighty-Second left in the jail at Shâhjehânpore had been attacked by Feroze Shâh and the Nânâ Sâhib, and were sore pushed to defend themselves. A brigade, consisting of the Sixtieth Rifles, Seventy-Ninth Highlanders, several native regiments, the Ninth Lancers, and some batteries of artillery, under Brigadier John Jones ("the Avenger") was at once started back for the relief of Shâhjehânpore—rather a gloomy outlook for the hot weather of 1858! While this brigade was starting, the remainder of the force which was to hold Bareilly for the hot season, consisting of the Forty-Second, Seventy-Eighth, and Ninety-Third, shifted camp to the sandy plain near where Bareilly railway station now stands, hard by the little fort in the centre of the plain. There we remained in tents during the whole of May, large working parties being formed every morning to assist the engineers to get what shelter was possible ready for the hottest months. The district jail was arranged as barracks for the Ninety-Third, and we moved into them on the 1st of June. The Forty-Second got the old *cutchery*[1] buildings with a new thatch roof; and the Seventy-Eighth had the Bareilly College. There we remained till October, 1858.

I omitted to mention in its proper place that on the death of Adrian Hope, Colonel A. S. Leith-Hay, of the Ninety-Third, succeeded to the command of the brigade, and Major W. G. A. Middleton got command of the regiment till we rejoined the Commander-in-Chief, when it was found that Lieutenant-Colonel Ross, who had exchanged with Lieutenant-Colonel C. Gordon, had arrived from England and taken command before we retook Bareilly.

We remained in Bareilly from May till October in comparative peace. We had one or two false alarms,

[1] Court-house.

and a wing of the Forty-Second, with some cavalry and artillery, went out about the beginning of June to disperse a body of rebels who were threatening an attack on Morâdabâd.

These reminiscences do not, as I have before remarked, profess to be a history of the Mutiny except in so far as I saw it from the ranks of the Ninety-Third. But I may correct historical mistakes when I find them, and in vol. ii., p. 500, of *The Indian Empire*, by R. Montgomery Martin, the following statement occurs: "Khân Bahâdoor Khân, of Bareilly, held out in the Terâi until the close of 1859; and then, hemmed in by the Goorkhas on one side and the British forces on the other, was captured by Jung Bahâdoor. The Khân is described as an old man, with a long white beard, bent almost double with rheumatic fever. His life is considered forfeited by his alleged complicity in the Bareilly murders, but his sentence is not yet pronounced." This is not historically correct. Khân Bahâdoor Khân was captured by the Bareilly police-levy early in July, 1858, and was hanged in my presence in front of the *kotwâlee* in Bareilly a few days after his capture. He was an old man with a long white beard, but not at all bent with age, and there was certainly no want of proof of his complicity in the Bareilly murders. Next to the Nânâ Sâhib he was one of the most active instigators of murder in the rebel ranks. He was a retired judge of the Company's service, claiming descent from the ancient rulers of Rohilcund, whom the English, in the time of Warren Hastings, had assisted the Nawâb of Lucknow to put down in the Rohilla war. His capture was effected in the following manner:—Colonel W. C. M'Donald, of the Ninety-Third, was on the staff in the Crimea, and he had in his employ a man named Tâhir Beg who was a sort of confidential interpreter. Whether this man was Turkish, Armenian, or Bulgarian I don't know, but this much I do know; among Mahommedans Tâhir Beg was a strict Mussulman, among Bulgarians he was a Roman Catholic, and in the Ninety-Third he had no objections to be a Presbyterian. He was a good linguist, speaking English, French, and Turkish, as well as most of the vernaculars of Asia Minor; and when the Crimean war was over, he accompanied Major M'Donald to England in the capacity of an ordinary servant. In 1857, when the expedition under Lord Elgin was being got ready for China, Colonel M'Donald was appointed quarter-master-general, and started for Canton taking Tâhir Beg with him as a servant; but, the expedition to China having been diverted for the suppression of the Mutiny, M'Donald rejoined the regiment with Tâhir Beg still with him in the same capacity. From his knowledge of Turkish and Persian Tâhir Beg soon made himself master of Hindoostanee, and he lived in the regimental bazaar with the Mahommedan shop-keepers, among whom he professed himself a strict follower of the Prophet. After he became pretty well conversant with the language, it was reported that he gained much valuable information for the authorities. When Bareilly was recaptured arrangements were made for the enlistment of a police-levy, and Tâhir Beg got the appointment of city *kotwâl*[1] and did valuable service by hunting out a great number of leading rebels. It was Tâhir Beg who heard that Khân Bahâdoor Khân had returned to the vicinity of Bareilly with only a small body of followers; and he arranged for his capture, and brought him in a prisoner to the guard-room of the Ninety-Third. Khân Bahâdoor Khân was put through a brief form of trial by the civil power, and was found guilty of rebellion and murder upon both native and European evidence. By that time several Europeans who had managed to escape to Naini Tâl on the outbreak of the Mutiny through the favour of the late Râja of Râmpore, had returned; so there was no doubt of the prisoner's guilt.

I must mention another incident that happened in Bareilly. Among the gentlemen who returned from Naini Tâl, was one whose brother had been shot by his bearer, his most trusted servant. This ruffian turned out to be no other than the very man who had denounced Jamie Green as a spy. It was either early in August or at the end of July that a strange European gentleman, while passing through the regimental bazaar of the Ninety-Third, noticed an officer's servant, who was a most devout Christian, could speak English, and was a regular attendant at all soldiers' evening services with the regimental chaplain. The gentleman (I now forget his name) laid hold of our devout Christian brother in the bazaar, and made him over to the nearest European guard, when he was tried and found guilty of the

[1] Magistrate.

murder of a whole family of Europeans—husband, wife, and children—in May, 1857. There was no want of evidence, both European and native, against him. Thus was the death of the unfortunate Jamie Green avenged. I may add a rather amusing incident about this man. His master evidently believed that this was a case of mistaken identity, and went to see the brigadier, Colonel A. S. Leith-Hay, on behalf of his servant. But it turned out that the man had joined the British camp at Futtehghur in the preceding January, and Colonel Leith-Hay was the first with whom he had taken service and consequently knew the fellow. However, the brigadier listened to what the accused's master had to urge until he mentioned that the man was a most devout Christian, and read the Bible morning and evening. On this Colonel Leith-Hay could listen to the argument no longer, but shouted out:—"He a Christian! that be d—d for a statement! He's no more a Christian than I am! He served me for one month, and robbed me of more than ten times his pay. Let him be hanged." So he was made over to the civil commissioner, tried, found guilty, and hanged.

We rested in Bareilly till October. About the end of September the weather was comparatively cool. Many people had returned from Naini Tâl to look after their wrecked property. General Colin Troup with the Sixty-Sixth Regiment of Goorkhas had come down from Kumâon, and soldiers' sports were got up for the amusement of the troops and visitors. Among the latter was the loyal Râja of Râmpore, who presented a thousand rupees for prizes for the games and five thousand for a dinner to all the troops in the garrison. At these games the Ninety-Third carried off all the first prizes for putting the shot, throwing the hammer, and tossing the caber. Our best athlete was a man named George Bell, of the grenadier company, the most powerful man in the British army. Before the regiment left England Bell had beaten all comers at all the athletic games throughout Scotland. He stood about six feet four inches, and was built in proportion, most remarkably active for his size both in running and leaping, and also renowned for feats of strength. There was a young lad of the band named Murdoch MacKay, the smallest boy in the regiment, but a splendid dancer; and the two, "the giant and the pigmy," as they were called, attended all the athletic games throughout Scotland from Edinburgh to Inverness, always returning covered with medals. I mention all this because the Bareilly sports proved the last to poor George Bell. An enormous caber having been cut, and all the leading men (among them some very powerful artillerymen) of the brigade had tried to toss it and failed. The brigadier then ordered three feet to be cut from it, expressing his opinion that there was not a man in the British army who could toss it. On this George Bell stepped into the arena, and said he would take a turn at it before it was cut; he put the huge caber on his shoulders, balanced it, and tossed it clean over. While the caber was being cut for the others, Bell ran in a hundred yards' race, which he also won; but he came in with his mouth full of blood. He had, through over-exertion, burst a blood-vessel in his lungs. He slowly bled to death and died about a fortnight after we left Bareilly, and lies buried under a large tree in the jungles of Oude between Fort Mithowlie and the banks of the Gogra. Bell was considered an ornament to, and the pride of, the regiment, and his death was mourned by every officer and man in it, and by none more than by our popular doctor, Billy Munro, who did everything that a physician could do to try and stop the bleeding; but without success. Bell gradually sank till he died.

We left Bareilly on the 10th of October, and marched to Shâhjehânpore, where we were joined by a battalion of the Sixtieth Rifles, the Sixty-Sixth Goorkhas, some of the Sixth Carabineers, Tomb's troop of horse-artillery, and a small train of heavy guns and mortars. On the 17th of October we had our first brush with the enemy at the village of Posgaon, about twenty miles from Shâhjehânpore. Here they were strong in cavalry, and tried the Bareilly game of getting round the flanks and cutting up our camp-followers. But a number of them got hemmed in between the ammunition-guard and the main line, and Cureton's Mooltânee cavalry, coming round on them from both flanks, cut down about fifty of them, capturing their horses. In the midst of this scrimmage two of the enemy, getting among the baggage-guard, were taken for two of our native cavalry, till at length they separated from the main body and got alongside of a man who was some distance away. One of them called to the poor fellow to look in another direction, when the second one cut his head clean off, leaped from his horse, and, lifting the head, sprang into his saddle and was off like the wind! Many rifle-bullets were sent after him, but he got clear away, carrying the head with him.

The next encounter we had was at Russoolpore, and then at Nowrungabad, where the Queen's proclamation, transferring the government from the Company to the Crown, was read. After this all our tents were sent into Mahomdee, and we took to the jungles without tents or baggage, merely a great-coat and a blanket; and thus we remained till after the taking of Mithowlie. We then returned to Sitapore, where we got our tents again the day before Christmas, 1858; and by the new year we were on the banks of the Gogra, miles from any village. The river swarmed with alligators of enormous size, and the jungles with wild pig and every variety of game, and scarcely a day passed without our seeing tigers, wolves, and hyænas. But by this time fighting was over. We remained in those jungles across the Gogra, in sight of the Nepaul hills, till about the end of February, by which time thousands of the rebels had tendered their submission and returned to their homes. The Ninety-Third then got the route for Subâthoo, in the Himalayas near Simla. Leaving the jungles of Oude, we marched *via* Shâhjehânpore, Bareilly, Morâdabad, and thence by the foot of the hills till we came into civilised regions at Sahârunpore; thence to Umballa, reaching Subâthoo about the middle of April with our clothes completely in rags. We had received no new clothing since we had arrived in India, and our kilts were torn into ribbons. But the men were in splendid condition, and could have marched thirty miles a day without feeling fatigued, if our baggage-animals could have kept up with us. On our march out from Kalka, the Commander-in-Chief passed us on his way to Simla.

This ended the work of the old Ninety-Third Sutherland Highlanders in the Mutiny, and here, for the present, I will end my reminiscences.

APPENDIX A

THE HISTORY OF THE MURDER OF MAJOR NEILL AT AUGUR IN 1887

I WILL relate an incident of an unusual kind, told to me by a man whom I met in Jhânsi, which has reference to the executions ordered by General Neill at Cawnpore in July and August, 1857. But before I do so I may mention that in Cawnpore, Jhânsi, and Lucknow I found the natives very unwilling to enter into conversation or to give any information about the events of that year. In this statement I don't include the natives of the class who acted as guides, etc., or those who were in the service of Government at the time. *They* were ready enough to talk; but as a rule I knew as much myself as they could tell me. Those whom I found suspicious of my motives and unwilling to talk, were men who must have been on the side of the rebels against us. I looked out for such, and met many who had evidently served as soldiers, and who admitted that they had been in the army before 1857; but when I tried to get them to speak about the Mutiny, as a rule they pretended to have been so young that they had forgotten all about it,—generally a palpable falsehood, judging from their personal appearance,—or they professed to have been absent in their villages and to know nothing about the events happening in the great centres of the rebellion. The impression left on my mind was that they were either afraid or ashamed to talk about the Mutiny.

In the second chapter of these reminiscences it may be

remembered I asked if any reader could let me know whether Major A. H. S. Neill, commanding the Second Regiment Central India Horse, who was shot on parade by Sowar Mazar Ali at Augur, Central India, on the 14th March, 1887, was a son of General Neill of Cawnpore fame. The information has not been forthcoming[1]; and for want of it I cannot corroborate the following statement in a very strange story.

In 1892 I passed two days at Jhânsi, having been obliged to wait because the gentleman whom I had gone to see on business was absent from the station; and I went all over the city to try and pick up information regarding the Mutiny. I eventually came across a man who, by his military salute, I could see had served in the army, and I entered into conversation with him.

At first he pretended that his connection with the army had merely been that of an armourer-*mistree*[2] of several European regiments; and he told me that he had served in the armourer's shop of the Ninety-Third when they were in Jhânsi twenty-four years ago, in 1868 and 1869. After I had informed him that the Ninety-Third was my regiment, he appeared to be less reticent; and at length he admitted that he had been an armourer in the service of Scindia before the Mutiny, and that he was in Cawnpore when the Mutiny broke out, and also when the city was retaken by Generals Havelock and Neill.

After a long conversation he appeared to be convinced that I had no evil intentions, but was merely anxious to collect reliable evidence regarding events which, even now, are but slightly known. Amongst other matters he told me that the (late) Mâharâja Scindia was not by any means so loyal as the Government believed him to be; that he himself (my informant) had formed one of a deputation that was sent to Cawnpore from Gwalior to the Nânâ Sâhib before the outbreak; and that although keeping in

[1] Major Neill *was* a son of Brigadier-General Neill commanding at Cawnpore during the first relief of Lucknow. General Neill went to the front as colonel commanding the First Madras Fusiliers.

[2] Workman; in this case a blacksmith.

the background, the Mâharâja Scindia incited his army to rebellion and to murder their officers, and himself fled as a pretended fugitive to Agra to devise means to betray the fort of Agra, should the Gwalior army, as he anticipated would be the case, prove victorious over the British. He also told me that the farce played by Scindia about 1874, viz. the giving up a spurious Nânâ Sâhib, was a pre-arranged affair between Scindia and the *fakeer* who represented the Nânâ. But, as I expressed my doubts about the truth of all this, my friend came down to more recent times, and asked me if I remembered about the murder of Major Neill at Augur in Central India in 1887, thirty years after the Mutiny? I told him that I very well remembered reading of the case in the newspapers of the time. He then asked me if I knew why Major Neill was murdered? I replied that the published accounts of the murder and trial were so brief that I had formed the conclusion that something was concealed from the public, and that I myself was of opinion that a woman must have been the cause of the murder,—that Major Neill possibly had been found in some intrigue with one of Mazar Ali's womenkind. To which he replied that I was quite wrong. He then told me that Major Neill was a son of General Neill of Cawnpore fame, and that Sowâr Mazar Ali, who shot him, was a son of Suffur Ali, *duffadâr* of the Second Regiment Light Cavalry, who was unjustly accused of having murdered Sir Hugh Wheeler at the Suttee Chowrah *ghât*, and was hanged for the murder by order of General Neill, after having been flogged by sweepers and made to lick clean a portion of the blood-stained floor of the slaughter-house.

After the recapture of Cawnpore, Suffur Ali was arrested in the city, and accused of having cut off General Wheeler's head as he alighted from his palkee at the Suttee Chowrah *ghât* on the 27th of June, 1857. This he stoutly denied, pleading that he was a loyal servant of the Company who had been compelled to join in the Mutiny against his will. General Neill, however, would not believe him, so he was taken to the slaughter-house and flogged by Major Bruce's sweeper-police till he cleaned up his spot of blood from the floor of the house where the women and children were murdered. When about to be hanged Suffur Ali adjured every Mahommedan in the crowd to have a message sent to Rohtuck, to his infant son, by name Mazar Ali, to inform him that his father had been unjustly defiled and flogged by sweepers by order of General Neill before being hanged, and that his dying message to him was that he prayed God and the Prophet to spare him and strengthen his arm to avenge the death of his father on General Neill or any of his descendants.

My informant went on to tell me that Mazar Ali had served under Major Neill for years, and had been treated by him with special kindness before he came to know that the Major was the son of the man who had ordered his father's execution; that while he was lying ill in hospital a *fakeer* one day arrived in the station from some remote quarter of India, and told him of his father's dying imprecation, and that Major Neill being the son of General Neill, it was the decree of fate that Mazar Ali should shoot Major Neill on parade the following day; which he did, without any apparent motive whatever.

I expressed my doubts about the truth of all this, when my informant told me he could give me a copy of a circular, printed in Oordoo and English, given to the descendants of Suffur Ali, directing them, as a message from the other world, to avenge the death and defilement of their father. The man eventually brought the leaflet to me in the *dâk* bungalow in Jhânsi. The circular is in both Oordoo and English, and printed in clean, clear type; but so far as I can read it, the English translation, which is printed on the leaflet beneath the Oordoo, and a copy of which I reproduce below, does not strike me as a literal translation of the Oordoo. The latter seems to me to be couched in language calculated to prove a much stronger incitement to murder than the English version would imply. However, the following is the English version *verbatim*, as it appears on the leaflet, word for word and point for point, italics and all.

The imprecation, vociferated by SUFFUR ALI, *Duffadâr 2nd Regiment Light Cavalry, who was executed at the Slaughter-house, on the 25th July, 1857, for killing* SIR HUGH WHEELER, *at the Suttechoura Ghât.*

Oh Mahomed Prophet! be pleased to receive into Paradise the soul of your humble servant, whose body Major Bruce's Mehtur police are now defiling by lashes, forced to lick a space of the blood-stained floor of the Slaughter-house, and hereafter to be hanged, by the order of General Neill. And, oh Prophet! in due time inspire my infant son Mazar Ali of Rohtuck, that he may revenge this desecration on the General and his descendants.

Take notice!—Mazar Ali, Sowar, 2nd Regiment, Central India Horse, who under divine mission, shot Major A. H. S. Neill, Commanding the Corps, at Augur, Central India, on the 14th March 1887, was sentenced to death by Sir Lepel Griffin, Governor-General's Agent.

The Oordoo in the circular is printed in the Persian character without the vowel-points, and as I have not read much Oordoo since I passed my Hindoostanee examination thirty-three years ago, I have had some difficulty in translating the leaflet, especially as it is without the vowel-points. The man who gave it to me asked if I knew anything about the family of General Neill, and I replied that I did not, which was the truth. When I asked why he wanted to know, he said that if any more of his sons were still in India, their lives would soon be taken by the descendants of men who were defiled and hanged at Cawnpore under the brigade-order of General Neill, dated Cawnpore, 25th of July, 1857. This is the order to which I have alluded in the second chapter of my reminiscences, and which remained in force till the arrival of Sir Colin Campbell at Cawnpore in the following November. As I had never seen a copy of it, having only heard of it, I asked my informant how he knew about it. He told me that thousands of copies, in English, Oordoo, and Hindee, were in circulation in the bazaars of Upper India. I told my friend that I should very much like to see a copy, and he promised to bring me one. Shortly after he left me in the *dâk* bungalow, undertaking to return with a copy of the order, as also numerous proclamations from the English Government, and the counter-proclamations on the part of the leaders of the rebellion. I thought that here I had struck a rich historical mine; but my friend did not turn up again! I sat up waiting for him till long after midnight, and as he did not return I went into the city again the following day to the place where I had met him; but all the people around pretended to know nothing whatever about the man, and I saw no more of him. However, I was glad to have got the leaflet *re* the assassination of Major Neill, because several gentlemen have remarked, since I commenced my reminiscences, that I mention so many incidents not generally known, that many are inclined to believe that I am inventing history rather than relating facts. But that is not so; and, besides what I have related, I could give hundreds of most interesting incidents that are not generally known nor ever will be known.[1]

Now, in my humble opinion, is the time that a history of the real facts and causes of the Mutiny should be written, if a competent man could devote the time to do so, and to visit the centres of the rebellion and get those

[1] "Some of the incidents related by Mr. Forbes-Mitchell, and now for the first time brought to light in his most interesting series of Reminiscences, are of so sensational an order that we are not surprised that many persons to whom the narrator is a stranger should regard them with a certain incredulity. We may take this opportunity therefore of stating that, so far as it is possible at this date to corroborate incidents that occurred thirty-five years ago, Mr. Forbes-Mitchell has afforded us ample proof of the accuracy of his memory and the general correctness of his facts. In the case under notice, we have been shown the leaflet in which Mazar Ali's cold-blooded murder of his commanding officer is vindicated, and of which the English translation above given is an exact reproduction. The leaflet bears no evidence whatever to disclose its origin, but we see no reason to doubt that, as Mr. Forbes-Mitchell's informant declared, it was widely circulated in the bazaars of Upper India shortly after Mazar Ali paid the penalty of his crime with his own life."—ED. *Calcutta Statesman*.

who took part in the great uprising against the rule of the Feringhee to come forward, with full confidence of safety, and relate all they know about the affair. Thousands of facts would come to light which would be of immense historical importance, as also of great political value to Government, facts that in a few years will become lost to the world, or be remembered only as traditions of 1857. But the man who is to undertake the work must be one with a thorough knowledge of the native character and languages, a man of broad views, and, above all, one who would, to a certain extent, sympathise with the natives, and inspire them with confidence and enlist their assistance. As a rule, the Englishman, the Government official, the *Sâhib Bahâdoor*, although respected, is at the same time too much feared, and the truth would be more or less concealed from him. I formed this opinion when I heard of the circumstances which are supposed to have led to the assassination of Major Neill. If true, we have here secret incitement to murder handed down for generations, and our Government, with its extensive police and its Thuggee Department, knowing nothing about it![1]

[1] The *vendetta* is such a well-known institution among the Pathâns, that no further explanation of Major Neill's murder by the son of a man who was executed by the Major's father's orders is necessary.

APPENDIX B

EUROPEANS AMONG THE REBELS

ALTHOUGH recollections of the Mutiny are fast being obliterated by the kindly hand of time, there must still be many readers who will remember the reports current in the newspapers of the time, and elsewhere in 1857 and 1858, of Europeans being seen in the ranks of the rebels. In a history of *The Siege of Delhi, by an Officer who served there* (name not given), published by Adam and Charles Black, Edinburgh, 1861, the following passages occur. After describing the battle of Budlee-ke-Serai, the writer goes on to say: "The brave old Afghân chief, Jân Fishân Khân,[1] who with some horsemen had followed our star from Meerut, was heard crying out, his stout heart big with the enthusiasm of the moment: 'Another such day, and I shall become a Christian!'" And in his comments on this the writer says: "And sad to tell, a European deserter from Meerut had been struck down fighting in the sepoy ranks, and was recognised by his former comrades." After describing the opening of the siege and the general contempt which the Europeans had for the enemy's artillery, the writer states that the tone of conversation in the camp was soon changed, and "From being an object of contempt, their skill became one of wonder and admiration, perhaps too great. Some artillery officers protested that their practice was better than our

[1] Two of his sons joined Hodson's Horse, and one of them, Atâoollah Khân, was our representative at Caubul after the last Afghân war.

own. Many believed that their fire was under the superintendence of Europeans. Two men with solar helmets could be seen, by the help of our best glasses, in their batteries, but no one who knew how much of the work in India was really done by natives, wondered at the practical skill they now showed." Turning from Delhi to Lucknow, many will remember the account of the disastrous action at Chinhut by Mr. Rees. He says: "The masses of the rebel cavalry by which the British were outflanked near the Kookrail bridge, were apparently commanded by some European who was seen waving his sword and attempting to make his men follow him and dash at ours. He was a handsome-looking man, well-built, fair, about twenty-five years of age, with light moustaches, wearing the undress uniform of a European cavalry officer, with a blue, gold-laced cap on his head." Mr. Rees suggests the possibility of this person having been either a Russian or a renegade Christian.

The only other case to which I will allude came under my own observation. I have told in my fourteenth chapter how Brigadier Adrian Hope was killed in the abortive attack on the fort of Rooyah, by a shot fired from a high tree inside the fort, and how it was commonly believed that the man who fired the shot was a European. I myself thought at the time that such was the case, and now I am convinced of it. I was the non-commissioned officer of a party of the Ninety-Third sent to cover an engineer-officer who had either volunteered or been ordered to take a sketch of one of the fort gates and its approaches, in the hope of being able to blow it in, and thus gain an entrance to the fort, which was surrounded by a deep ditch, and inside the ditch an almost impenetrable belt of prickly bamboos about ten yards in breadth, so interwoven and full of thorns that a cat could scarcely have passed through it. Under the guidance of a native of the Intelligence Department we managed to advance unseen, and got under cover of a thick clump of bamboos near the gate. Strict orders had been given that no one on any account whatever was to speak, much less to fire a shot, unless we should be attacked, for fear of drawing attention to our proceedings, till the engineer had had time to make a rough sketch of the position of the gate and its approaches. During this time we were so close to the fort that we could hear the enemy talking inside; and the man who was on the tree could be seen and heard by us quite plainly, calling to the stormers on the other face in unmistakable barrack-room English: "Come on, you —— Highlanders! Come on, Scotty! you have a harder nut to crack than eating oatmeal porridge. If you can come through these bamboos we'll warm your —— for you, if you come in here!" etc., etc. In short, the person talking showed such a command of English slang and barrack-room abuse that it was clear he was no native. Every one of my party was convinced that the speaker was a European, and if we had been aware at the time that this man had just killed Brigadier Hope he would certainly have paid the penalty with his own life; but we knew nothing of this till we retired, and found that the stormers had been recalled, with the butcher's bill already given.

The events above related had almost passed from my recollection, till they were recalled by the following circumstance. A vacancy having occurred among the *durwâns*[1] in the factory under my charge, among several candidates brought by the *jemadâr*[2] for the vacant post was a fine-looking old man, who gave me an unmistakable military salute in the old style, square from the shoulder —quite different from the present mongrel German salute, which the English army has taken to imitating since the Germans beat their old conquerors, the French; I mean the present mode of saluting with the palm of the hand turned to the front. As soon as I saw this old man I knew he had been a soldier; my heart warmed to him at once, and I determined to give him the vacant appointment. So turning to him I said: "You have served in the army; are you one of the sepoys of 1857?" He at once admitted that he had formerly belonged to the Ninth

[1] Doorkeepers. [2] Head-man.

Native Infantry, and that he was present with the regiment when it mutinied at Allyghur on the 20th of May, 1857. He had accompanied the regiment to Delhi, and had fought against the English throughout the siege, and afterwards at Lucknow and throughout the Oude campaigns. "But, *Sâhib*," said he, "the Ninth Regiment were almost the only regiment which did not murder their officers. We gave each of them three months' pay in advance from the treasury, and escorted them and their families within a safe distance of Agra before we went to Delhi, and all of us who lived to come through the Mutiny were pardoned by the Government." I knew this to be the truth, and ordered the *jemadâr* to enrol the applicant, by name Doorga, or Doorga Sing, late sepoy of the Ninth Native Infantry, as one of the factory *durwâns*, determining to have many a talk with him on his experiences of the Mutiny.

Many of my readers may recollect that, after escorting their European officers to the vicinity of Agra, the Ninth Regiment went to Delhi, and throughout the siege the men of this regiment proved the most daring opponents of the British Army. According to Mead's *Sepoy Revolt*, "The dead bodies of men bearing the regimental number of the Ninth Regiment were found in the front line of every severe engagement around Delhi and at the deadly Cashmere Gate when it was finally stormed." After engaging Doorga Sing it was not long before I made him relate his experiences of the siege of Delhi, and afterwards at Lucknow and in Oude, and one day I happened to ask him if it was true that there were several Europeans in the rebel army. He told me that he had heard of several, but that he personally knew of two only, one of whom accompanied the mutineers from Meerut and was killed at the battle of Budlee-ke-Serai,—evidently the deserter alluded to above. The other European was a man of superior stamp, who came to Delhi from Rohilcund with the Bareilly Brigade, and the King gave him rank in the rebel army next to General Bukht Khân, the titular Commander-in-Chief. This European commanded the artillery throughout the siege of Delhi, as he had formerly been in the Company's artillery and knew the drill better than any man in the rebel army. I asked Doorga Sing if he had ever heard his name or what rank he held before the Mutiny, and he said he had heard his name at the time, but had forgotten it, and that before the Mutiny he had held the rank of sergeant-major, but whether in the native artillery or in one of the native infantry regiments at Bareilly he did not now recollect. But the Bâdshâh promoted him to be general of artillery immediately on the arrival of the Bareilly Brigade, and he was by far the bravest and most energetic commander that the rebels had, and the most esteemed by the revolted sepoys, whose respect he retained to the last. Even after they had ceased saluting their native officers they continued to turn out guards and present arms to the European *sâhib.* Throughout the siege of Delhi there was never a day passed that this man did not visit every battery, and personally correct the elevation of the guns. He fixed the sites and superintended the erection of all new batteries to counteract the fire of the English as the siege advanced. On the day of the assault, the 14th of September, he fought like *shâitân*,[1] fighting himself and riding from post to post, trying to rally defeated sepoys, and bringing up fresh troops to the support of assailed points. Doorga Sing's company had formed the guard at the Cashmere Gate, and he vividly described the attack and defence of that post, and how completely the sepoys were surprised and the powder-bags fixed to the gate before the sentries of the guard were aware of the advance of the English.

After the assault Doorga Sing did not see the European till the beaten army reached Muttra, when he again found him superintending the arrangements for crossing the Jumna. About thirty thousand sepoys had collected there in their retreat from Delhi, a common danger holding them together, under the command of Bukht Khân and Feroze Shâh. But they paid more respect to the

[1] Satan.

European, and obeyed his orders with far more alacrity than they did those of Bukht Khân or any other of their nominal leaders. After crossing the Jumna the European remained with the rebels till they reached a safe retreat on the Oude side of the Ganges, when he left the force in company with the Râja of Surâjpore, a petty state on the Oude side about twenty or twenty-five miles above Cawnpore. About this time my informant, Doorga Sing, having been wounded at Delhi, left the rebel army *en route* to Lucknow, and returned to his village near Onâo in Oude; but hearing of the advance of the English, and expecting no mercy, he and several others repaired to Lucknow, and rejoined their old comrades.

He did not again see the European till after the fall of Lucknow, when he met him at Fort Rooyah, where he commanded the sepoys, and was the principal adviser of the Râja Nirput Singh, whom he prevented from accepting the terms offered by the English through General Walpole. I am fully convinced that this was the man whom we saw in the tree, and who was reported to have killed Brigadier Hope.

After their retreat from Rooyah the sepoys, under this European, remained in the jungles till the English army had passed on to Bareilly, when they reattacked Shâhjehânpore, and would have retaken it, if a brigade had not arrived from Bareilly to its relief. After being driven back from Shâhjehânpore the sepoys held together in Mahomdee, Sitapore, and elsewhere, throughout the hot season of 1858, mostly under the guidance of the European and Bukht Khân. The last time Doorga Sing saw the renegade was after the battle of Nawâbgunge in Oude, where Bukht Khân was killed and a large number of the sepoys were driven across the Raptee into Nepaul territory, upon which they held a council among themselves and determined to follow their leaders no longer, but to give themselves up to the nearest English post under the terms of the Queen's proclamation. The European tried to dissuade them from doing this, telling them that if they gave themselves up they would all be hanged like dogs or sent in chains across the *Kâlâ Pâni.*[1] But they had already suffered too much to be further imposed upon, and one of their number, who had gone to get information about other parties who were known to have given themselves up to the English, returned at this time with information that all sepoys who had not taken part in murdering their officers were, after giving up their arms, provided with a pass and paid two rupees each, and allowed to return to their villages. On this the greater part of the sepoys, including all left alive of the Ninth Regiment, told the European that they had resolved to listen to him no longer, but to return to their villages and their families, after giving themselves up at the nearest English post. Thereupon the *sâhib* sat down and commenced to shed tears, saying *he* had neither home nor country to return to. There he was left, with a few more whose crimes had placed them beyond the hope of pardon; and that was the last which Doorga Sing saw or heard of the European general of the mutineer artillery.

Before writing this, I have often cross-questioned Doorga Sing about this European, and his statements never vary. He says that the time is now so long past that he could not be sure of the *sâhib's* name even if he heard it; but he is positive he came from Bareilly, and that his rank before the Mutiny was sergeant-major, and that he had formerly been in the Company's artillery. He thinks, however, that at the time of the Mutiny this sergeant was serving with one of the native infantry regiments in Bareilly; and he further recollects that it was commonly reported in the sepoy ranks that when the Mutiny broke out this sergeant-major had advised the murder of all the European officers, himself shooting the adjutant of the regiment with his own hand to prove his loyalty to the rebel cause.

The whole narrative is so extraordinary that I publish it with a view to discovering if there are any still living who can give facts bearing on this strange, but, I am con-

[1] "The Black Water," *i.e.* the sea, which no orthodox Hindoo can cross without loss of caste.

vinced, true story. Doorga Sing promised to find for me one or two other mutineer sepoys who knew more about this European and his antecedents than he himself did. I have no detailed statement of the Mutiny at Bareilly, and the short account which I possess merely says that, "As soon as the artillery fired the signal gun in their lines, Brigadier Sibbald mounted his horse and galloped off to the cavalry lines, but was met on the way by a party of infantry, who fired on him. He received a bullet in his chest, and then turned his horse and galloped to the appointed rendezvous for the Europeans, and, on arriving there, dropped dead from his horse." The account then goes on to say: "The European sergeant-major had remained in the lines, and Adjutant Tucker perished while endeavouring to save the life of the sergeant-major." The question arises—Is it possible that this sergeant-major can have been the same man whom Doorga Sing afterwards met in command of the rebel ranks in Delhi, and who was said to have killed his adjutant?

APPENDIX C

A FEW WORDS ON SWORD-BLADES

A SHORT time back I read an article on sword-blades, reprinted I believe from some English paper. Now, in a war like the Mutiny sword-blades are of the utmost importance to men who depend on them either for taking or preserving life; I will therefore state my own experience, and give opinions on the swords which came under my observation, and I may at once say that I think there is great room for improvement in our blades of Birmingham manufacture. I consider that the swords supplied to our officers, cavalry and artillery, are far inferior as weapons of offence to a really good Oriental *tulwâr.* Although an infantry man I saw a good deal of sword-practice, because all the men who held the Secundrabâgh and the Begum's Kothee were armed with native *tulwârs* from the King of Oude's armoury, in addition to their muskets and bayonets, and a large proportion of our men were killed and wounded by sword-cuts.

In the first place, then, for cutting our English regulation swords are too straight; the Eastern curved blade is far more effective as a cutting weapon. Secondly, our English swords are far too blunt, whereas the native swords are as keen in edge as a well-stropped razor. Our steel scabbards again are a mistake for carrying sharp blades; and, in addition to this, I don't think our mounted branches who are armed with swords have proper appliances given to them for sharpening their edges. Even in time of peace, but especially in time of war, more attention ought to be given to this point, and every soldier armed with a sword ought to be supplied with the means of sharpening it, and made to keep it with an edge like a razor. I may mention that this fact was noticed in the wars of the Punjâb, notably at Râmnugger, where our English cavalry with their blunt swords were most unequally matched against the Sikhs with *tulwârs* so keen of edge that they would split a hair.

I remember reading of a regiment of British cavalry charging a regiment of Sikh cavalry. The latter wore voluminous thick *puggries* round their heads, which our blunt swords were powerless to cut through, and each horseman had also a buffalo-hide shield slung on his back. They evidently knew that the British swords were blunt and useless, so they kept their horses still and met the British charge by lying flat on their horses' necks,[1] with their heads protected by the thick turban and their backs by the shields; and immediately the British soldiers passed through their ranks the Sikhs swooped round on them and struck them back-handed with their sharp, curved swords, in several instances cutting our cavalry men in two. In one case a British officer, who was killed in the charge I describe, was hewn in two by a back-handed stroke which cut right through an ammunition-pouch, cleaving the pistol-bullets right through the pouch and belt, severing the officer's backbone and cutting his heart in two from behind. It was the same in the Balaclava charge, both with the Heavy and the Light Brigade. Their swords were too straight, and so blunt that they would not cut through the thick coats and sheep-skin caps of the Russians; so that many of our men struck with the hilts at the faces of the enemy, as more effective than attempting to cut with their blunt blades.

In the article on English sword-blades to which I have referred, stress is laid on the superiority of

[1] In which case they would have been simply ridden over.

blades of spring steel, tempered so that the tip can be bent round to the hilt without breaking or preventing the blade assuming the straight immediately it is released. Now my observations lead me to consider spring steel to be totally unfitted for a sword-blade. The real Damascus blade that we have all read about, but so few have seen, is as rigid as cast-iron, without any spring whatever,—as rigid as the blade of a razor. The sword-blade which bends is neither good for cut nor thrust, even in the hands of the most expert and powerful swordsman. A blade of spring steel will not cut through the bone; directly it encounters a hard substance, it quivers in the hand and will not cut through. Let any sword-maker in Birmingham try different blades in the hands of an expert swordsman on a green tree of soft wood, and the rigid blade of well-tempered steel will cut four times as deep as the blade of highly tempered spring steel which you can bend into a circle, tip to hilt. My opinion is that the motto of a sword-blade ought to be the same as the Duke of Sutherland's—"*Frangas non flectes*, Thou mayest break but not bend"; and if blades could be made that would neither break nor bend, so much the better.

I believe that the manufacture of real Damascus steel blades is a lost art. When serving in the Punjâb about thirty years ago, I was well acquainted with an old man in Lahore who had been chief armourer to Runjeet Sing, and he has often told me that the real Damascus blades contained a large percentage of arsenic amalgamated with the steel while the blades were being forged, which greatly added to their hardness, toughness, and strength, preserved the steel from rust, and enabled the blades to be sharpened to a very fine edge. This old man's test for a sword-blade was to get a good-sized fish, newly caught from the river, lay it on a soft, yielding bed,—cotton quilt folded up, or any soft yielding substance,—and the blade that did not cut the fish in two across the thickest part behind the gills, cutting against the scales, at one stroke, was considered of no account whatever. From what I have seen no sword-blade that bends, however sharp it may be, will do that, because the spring in the steel causes the blade to glance off the fish, and the impetus of the cut is lost by the blade quivering in the hand. Nor will any of our straight sword-blades cut a large fish through in this manner; whereas the curved Oriental blade, with a drawing cut, severs it at once, because the curved blade presents much more cutting surface. One revolution of a circular saw cuts much deeper into wood than one stroke of a straight saw, although the length of the straight saw may be equal to the circumference of the circular one. So it is with sword-blades. A stroke from a curved blade, drawn through, cuts far deeper than the stroke from a straight blade.[1]

I will mention one instance at Lucknow that came under my own notice of the force of a sword-cut from a curved sword of rigid steel. There were three brothers of the name of Ready in the Ninety-Third called David, James, and John. They were all powerful, tall men, in the prime of life, and all three had served through the Crimea. David was a sergeant, and his two brothers were privates. When falling in for the assault on the Begum's palace, John Ready took off his Crimean medal and gave it to his brother David, telling him that he felt a presentiment that he would be killed in that attack, and that David had better keep his medal, and send it home to their mother. David tried to reason him out of his fears, but to no purpose. John Ready replied that he had no fear, and his mother might know that he had died doing his duty. Well, the assault took place, and in the inner courts of the palace there was one division held by a regiment of dismounted cavalry, armed with swords as keen as razors, and circular shields, and the party of the Ninety-Third who got into that court were far out-

[1] These remarks of Mr. Mitchell's are quite true as regards curved swords; but he forgets that the *point* is the most effective attack against Eastern swordsmen.

numbered on this occasion, as in fact we were everywhere else. On entering James Ready was attacked by a *sowâr* armed with sword and shield. Ready's feather bonnet was knocked off, and the *sowâr* got one cut at him, right over his head, which severed his skull clean in two, the sword cutting right through his neck and half-way down through the breast-bone. John Ready sprang to the assistance of his brother, but too late; and although his bayonet reached the side of his opponent and was driven home with a fatal thrust, in doing so he came within the swoop of the same terrible sword, wielded by the powerful arm of a tall man, and he also was cut right through the left shoulder diagonally across the chest, and his head and right arm were clean severed from the body. The *sowâr* delivered his stroke of the sword at the same moment that he received the bayonet of John Ready through his heart, and both men fell dead together. David Ready, the sergeant, seized the *tulwâr* that had killed both his brothers, and used it with terrible effect, cutting off heads of men as if they had been mere heads of cabbage. When the fight was over I examined that sword. It was of ordinary weight, well-balanced, curved about a quarter-circle, as sharp as the sharpest razor, and the blade as rigid as cast-iron. Now, my experience is that none of our very best English swords could have cut like this one. A sword of that quality would cut through a man's skull or thigh-bone without the least quiver, as easily as an ordinary Birmingham blade would cut through a willow.

I may also mention the case of a young officer named Banks, of the Seventh Hussars, who was terribly cut up in charging through a band of Ghâzis. One leg was clean lopped off above the knee, the right arm cut off, the left thigh and left arm both cut through the bone, each wound produced by a single cut from a sharp, curved *tulwâr*. I don't know if the young fellow got over it;[1] but he was reported to be still alive, and even cheerful when we marched from Lucknow.

[1] He did not.

In this matter of sword-blades, I have no wish to dogmatise or to pose as an authority; I merely state my observations and opinion, in the hopes that they may lead to experiments being made. But on one point I am positive. The sharpening of our cavalry swords, if still the same as in 1857, receives far too little attention.

APPENDIX D

THE OPIUM QUESTION

ON the afternoon of the 19th August, 1892, I left Lucknow. As I was a few minutes before time, I walked along the railway-platform to see the engine, and, strange to relate, the engine attached to the train which was to take me into Lucknow (under circumstances very different from those of 1857) was No. 93! In 1857 I had crossed the Ganges in the ranks of the Ninety-Third Highlanders, with the figures 93 on the front of my cap, and here I was, under very different circumstances, revisiting Lucknow for the first time thirty-five years after, and the engine to the train was No. 93! I need not say that I lifted my hat to that engine. As a matter of fact, I never do pass the old number without giving it a salute; but in this instance I looked upon it as a happy omen for the success of my journey.

I took my seat in the carriage, and shortly after was joined by a gentleman whom I took to be a Mahommedan; but to my surprise he told me that he was a Christian employed in the Educational Department, and that he was going to Lucknow for a month's holiday. He appeared to be a man of over sixty years of age, but said he was only fifty-four, and that he would retire from Government service next year. Of course I introduced the subject of the Mutiny, and asked him where he had been at the time. He stated that when the Mutiny broke out he was at school in Bareilly, and that he was then a Mahommedan, but did not join in the rebellion; that on the outbreak of the Mutiny, when all the Europeans were either killed or fled from Bareilly, he had retired to his village near Shâhjehânpore, and remained there till order was re-established on the advance of the English into Rohilcund in May, 1858, after Khân Bahâdoor Khân had reigned in Bareilly twelve months.

In course of conversation I asked my companion if he could give any reason why it was that the whole rural population of Oude had joined the urban population against the British in 1857, whereas on the south side of the Ganges the villagers were in favour of the British, where they were not overawed by the mutineers? He told me a strange thing, and that was that he was fully convinced that the main reason why the village population of Oude joined the city population of Lucknow was owing to the oppression caused by our introduction of the opium-tax among the people.

At first I misunderstood him, and thought I had come across an agent of the Anti-Opium Society. "So you are against Government control of the opium-cultivation and sale of the drug," I said. "By no means," he answered. "I consider the tax on opium a most legitimate source of revenue. What I mean is that although a just tax, it was a highly obnoxious one to the citizens of Lucknow and the rural population of Oude at the time of the Mutiny." He went on to state that although a Christian convert from Mahommedanism and a strictly temperate man, he had no sympathy with the anti-opium party; that he considered them a most dangerous set of fanatics, who would set the whole country in rebellion again before a twelvemonth if they could get the Government to adopt their narrow-minded views. Regarding 1857, he continued, and I quote his exact words, as I noted them down immediately after I got to the hotel:

"Under the rule of the Nawâbs of Lucknow many taxes were imposed, which were abolished by the British; but in their stead the opium-tax was introduced, which was the most unpopular tax that could have been devised, because it touched every one, from the *coolie* in the bazaar to the noble in his palace. Before the annexation of Oude opium was untaxed, and was largely consumed by all classes of the people, both in the capital and in the villages. Though the mass of the people were well-affected to British rule in general, disloyal agitators had merely to cite the opium-tax as a most obnoxious and oppressive impost, to raise the whole population against the British Government, and the same would be the case again, if ever the British Government were weak enough to be led by the Anti-Opium Society."

"Then," said I, "since you are so much against the Anti-Opium Society, I suppose you are also against Christian missionaries." "That by no means follows," was the answer. "Many of our most Christian and able missionaries have as little sympathy with the anti-opium propagandists as I have. The true missionary aims at reforming the people through the people, not by compelling moral reformation through the Government, which would be merely a return to the Inquisition of Rome in another form. I would encourage missionaries by every possible means; but they must be broad-minded, earnest, pious men, who mind their own business, and on no pretence whatever attempt to dictate to Government, or to control its action either in the matter of taxation or in any other way. I would never encourage men who go about the country railing against the Government for collecting revenue from one of the most just sources that can be named. Missionaries of experience know that the mass of the population are miserably poor, and a pill of opium is almost the only stimulant in which they indulge. Then, why attempt to deprive them of it, merely to please a score or so of sentimental faddists? Let the missionaries mind their own business, and render to Cæsar the the things which are Cæsar's, and unto God the things which are God's. Let them confine themselves to proclaiming the Gospel to the heathen, and teach the Bible in their schools; but don't allow them to mix in politics, or in any way interfere with the government or taxation of the country. I would throw the English education of the people more into the hands of the missionaries. Our Government schools are antichristian, and are making infidels of the people."

THE END